FROM HERE TO MATURITY

From Here to Maturity

Overcoming the Juvenilization
of American Christianity

Thomas E. Bergler

WILLIAM B. EERDMANS PUBLISHING COMPANY
GRAND RAPIDS, MICHIGAN / CAMBRIDGE, U.K.

Published 2014 by

Wm. B. Eerdmans Publishing Co.

2140 Oak Industrial Drive N.E., Grand Rapids, Michigan 49505 /

P.O. Box 163, Cambridge CB3 9PU U.K.

www.eerdmans.com

Library of Congress Cataloging-in-Publication Data

Bergler, Thomas E., 1964-

From here to maturity: overcoming the juvenilization of American Christianity /
Thomas E. Bergler.

pages   cm

Includes bibliographical references and index.

ISBN 978-0-8028-6944-9 (pbk.: alk. paper)

1. Church work with youth — United States.

2. Christian youth — Religious life — United States — History — 20th century.

3. Spiritual formation.   I. Title.

BV4447.B477   2014

277.3′083 — dc23

2014026888

Lyrics to "Draw Me Close" by Kelly Carpenter used by permission of Mercy/Vineyard Publishing (ASCAP) admin. in North America by Music Services o/b/o Vineyard Music USA

The National Study of Youth and Religion, http://youthandreligion.nd.edu, whose data were used by permission in Figure 4.1 and 4.2, was generously funded by Lilly Endowment Inc., under the direction of Christian Smith, of the Department of Sociology at the University of Notre Dame and Lisa Pearce, of the Department of Sociology at the University of North Carolina at Chapel Hill.

Scripture quotations are from the New Revised Standard Version Bible, copyright © 1989 the Division of Christian Education of the National Council of the Churches of Christ in the United States of America. Used by permission. All rights reserved.

To Stephen B. Clark
and Dallas Willard

Contents

List of Figures and Tables   ix

Acknowledgments   x

Introduction   xii

1. We're All Adolescents Now   1

2. Growing up into Christ   26

3. Helping Adults Mature   54

4. Reaching the Tipping Point:
   Youth Ministries That Help the Whole Church Mature   81

5. From Here to Maturity   113

   Appendix A: Thirty-Three Characteristics of Maturing
   Christian Youth That Combine to Form the Seven
   Characteristics of "Vital, Maturing Faith"   143

   Appendix B: Resources for Cultivating Congregational
   Cultures of Spiritual Maturity   147

   Appendix C: Questions for Observing a Congregational Culture   150

   Appendix D: Questions for Interpreting an Element of
   Congregational Culture   152

Contents

Appendix E: Questions for Evaluating an Element of
Congregational Culture in Light of Biblical Spiritual Maturity   154

Notes   156

Index   170

List of Figures and Tables

Figures

2.1 Relationship Between Spiritual Maturity and Holiness   49
3.1 Relationship Between Will, Thoughts, and Feelings   70
4.1 Paths from Strong Teenage Faith to Strong Emerging
     Adult Faith   94
4.2 Paths from Strong Teenage Faith to Weak Emerging
     Adult Faith   95
5.1 Cyclical Process of Ministry Discernment   124

Tables

2.1 Biblical Spiritual Maturity vs. Contemporary
     American Spirituality   53
3.1 Traits of Spiritual Maturity with Corresponding
     Vision and Means   62
3.2 Emotional Patterns and Spiritual Maturity   79
4.1 "Vital, Maturing Faith" Compared with Biblical Traits
     of Spiritual Maturity   86

Acknowledgments

Every book builds on the work of others, but this book especially draws on the research, insights, and life's work of many different people. First, I want to acknowledge Stephen B. Clark, who both taught me how to think about Christian culture and, more importantly, has devoted his life to cultivating "communities of disciples on mission." He and the other leaders and members of the Sword of the Spirit have done more to build spiritually mature communities than this book can ever do.

I owe a debt to the late Dallas Willard, who has deeply influenced how I think about spiritual growth and maturity. I have not added much to his profound insights on these matters. Rather, I have tried to explain how his ideas could be put into practice in a congregation.

I am grateful to my colleagues in the Association of Youth Ministry Educators. A good many of their writings are cited here. And conversations with many more of them at our annual conferences have challenged me to think ever more deeply about youth ministry and the church.

Special thanks go to several groups of people who provided specific feedback that strengthened this book. My colleagues in the Division of Philosophy and Religious Studies at Huntington University, David Alexander, Kent Eilers, Mark Fairchild, Luke Fetters, Paul Fetters, Bo Helmich, Karen Jones, Jonathan Krull, and John Noble, gave helpful feedback on two different occasions. Dan Keating and the Servants of the Word theologian's group offered their insights as well. I also want to thank the people who read *The Juvenilization of American Christianity* or listened to one of my presentations on spiritual maturity. I have tried to make good use of their questions and comments to make this book as useful as possible to pastors, youth ministers, and other church leaders.

Acknowledgments

In addition, I want to thank the many students I have had the privilege of teaching over the years at Huntington University. Through them I have learned a lot about what churches are building into the lives of young people. Much of the material found here has been tested on my students and refined in response to their feedback. Their zeal for God and burning desire to help people know him more has inspired me. And seeing God work in their lives has given me great joy. I especially want to thank several Ministry and Missions Department student workers who over the past several years provided research assistance and other practical help that made this book possible: Ashley Haynes, Holly Lutton, Jessica Redhage, Jessica (Palmer) Burris, Jenna (Rodgers) Strick, and Anna Stampfl.

I also want to thank the many people who provided other kinds of support and encouragement for this project. I thank David Bratt and the other staff at Eerdmans for offering me this opportunity and for guiding this book into print. Academic Dean Del Doughty, the members of the Faculty Appointments and Tenure Committee, and the Board of Trustees at Huntington University generously granted me a sabbatical to complete this project. My friends in the Ministry and Missions Department at Huntington University, Luke Fetters, Bo Helmich, Karen Jones, and RuthAnn Price, cheerfully shouldered the extra work that came their way because of my sabbatical. Their friendship has been an important source of joy and encouragement for many years now. The staff of the Richlyn Library at Huntington University, Anita Gray, Pat Jones, Jean Michelson, Randy Neuman, and Deb Springer, generously provided me an office to complete the last month of writing. Finally, I wish to thank the many family members and friends who encourage me in my work and who inspire me with their love for Christ. I especially want to thank my wife Sarah for sharing life with me and for loving me and our children so well.

Introduction

In *The Juvenilization of American Christianity,* I argued that beginning in the 1930s and 1940s, youth ministries contributed to a process by which the spiritual traits of adolescents become accepted or even celebrated by Christians of all ages. Youth ministries did not cause the juvenilization of American culture. But it was in youth groups that adults and teenagers first responded to the cultural forces that now make spiritual maturity harder to attain. Youth ministries have been good at getting adolescents to like Jesus and Christianity. But neither youth ministries nor juvenilized churches have been as good at helping people grow out of an adolescent faith into a spiritually mature one.

The process of juvenilization has been uneven, with some individuals, congregations, and even whole streams of Christianity in America being more affected than others. For example, white evangelical Protestants have been the leaders in creating youth ministries and churches that cater to both the positive and negative traits of adolescent Christians. Roman Catholics, Mainline Protestants, and African American Christians have been less affected by juvenilization, but their churches have also struggled more to sustain the long-term loyalty of young people. In some cases, Christians in these other streams of American Christianity have had the worst of both worlds: they have juvenilized some aspects of their faith without winning much loyalty among young people.

Many readers agreed that juvenilization and spiritual immaturity are real problems in contemporary American Christianity. But those who agreed with my argument often were not satisfied to stop there: they expressed a desire for more information about what to do to foster spiritual maturity. Other readers raised objections to my claims about juvenilization. Some thought I was just being a grumpy old man, the kind of person who thinks that drums and electric guitars are of the devil and shouldn't be used in church. Others thought I was against any kind of age-specific ministry with youth. Some thought that youth ministries did not really play much of a role in creating the spiritual immaturity we see in churches today. Still others thought that my way of describing spiritual maturity was moralistic or even legalistic and not in keeping with the Christian gospel.

Although this book will not spend much time directly addressing these objections, I think the careful reader will see that many of them are answered by what I have to say here. Even those who are not convinced by my argument about juvenilization can still benefit from this book. My goal is to provide some help to church leaders who care about fostering spiritual maturity in their congregations but wonder how to overcome the many obstacles they face.

This book is intended to be an accessible and practical guide to fostering maturity in local congregations. There may be any number of details that I have not gotten quite right, but the general approach found here is biblically sound and can guide us to church practices that make a difference. If I am right about spiritual maturity, it should be relatively straightforward, if not necessarily easy, to pursue it together as Christians. Spiritual maturity is not complicated or mysterious; it is simply neglected.

I also intend this book to be an ecumenical guide that can be of benefit to Christians from many different churches and theological traditions. Christians have important theological differences that bear on how they think about the process of spiritual growth, and I will note some of those differences throughout the book. The approach taken here is to stick closely to what we can learn about spiritual maturity from the New Testament passages that explicitly talk about it. These passages teach that mature Christians achieve a set of core competencies that can be affirmed by a broad spectrum of Christians. So the process for thinking about and pursuing maturity that I suggest here can still be of benefit even if the reader does not agree with every point I make theologically. Indeed, I hope every reader will take the basic process I describe here and strengthen it with the riches of his or her own theological tradition. Along the way I will note dimensions of spiritual growth or spiritual maturity that especially require readers to bring their own theology to bear.

There are two theological views that I do want to challenge. Some Christians regard spiritual maturity as equivalent to an unattainable perfection.

Others view spiritual growth as a kind of magical process that is inaccessible to human effort or intentionality. Not surprisingly, these views often go together. I hope that as a result of reading this book, those Christians will reconsider their beliefs about spiritual growth to maturity. Of course, no one grows to maturity without God's grace. But in this process, as in any other, if we don't have directions and don't think we can make it, we are unlikely to reach our destination.

I am convinced that just thinking and writing about spiritual maturity over the past couple of years has helped me grow in Christ. I am more likely to ask myself, "What is the spiritually mature thing for me to do in this situation?" And I am also more likely than before to joyfully choose a mature response. Such experiences have convinced me that much progress can be made just by thinking and talking more about spiritual maturity. I hope that you will find the same to be true for you.

CHAPTER 1

We're All Adolescents Now

Americans of all ages are not sure they want to grow up. If you listen carefully, you can sometimes hear thirty- or forty-year-olds say things like "I guess I have to start thinking of myself as an adult now." Greeting cards bear messages like "Growing old is inevitable. Growing up is optional." A recent national study of the sexual lives of eighteen- to twenty-three-year-olds found that most want to get married and have children — eventually. But they think of settling down as the end of the good part of their lives. One young woman spoke for many in the study when she said that having children will be "what makes your life, like, full, after like, you are done with your life, I guess."[1]

Try this experiment. Ask a group of college students to raise their hands if they think they are adults. They won't know what to do. You can be sure they won't all raise their hands.

The problem goes deeper than just a fear of growing old. Early in my teaching career, I asked a group of undergraduate students, "What does a mature Christian look like? Let's list some traits of spiritual maturity." The question made my students uncomfortable, so they pushed back with responses like these: "I don't think we ever arrive in our spiritual growth"; "We're not supposed to judge one another"; "No one is perfect"; and "We can't be holy in this life." Sadly, these students who had been raised in church and were attending a Christian college did not think of spiritual maturity as attainable or perhaps even desirable. They wrongly equated it with an unattainable perfection.

Where did this problem of low expectations originate? Beginning in the 1930s and 1940s, three factors combined to create the juvenilization of

American Christianity. First, new and more powerful youth cultures created distance between adults and adolescents. Second, in an attempt to convert, mobilize, or just hang on to their teenage children, Christian adults adapted the faith to adolescent tastes. As a result of these first two factors, the stereotypical youth group that combines fun and games with a brief, entertaining religious message was born. In the years since, this model of youth ministry has become a taken-for-granted part of church life. Finally, the journey to adulthood became longer and more confusing, with maturity now just one among many options. The result was juvenilization: the process by which the religious beliefs, practices, and developmental characteristics of adolescents become accepted — or even celebrated — as appropriate for Christians of all ages.

This dynamic of juvenilization leaped out at me when I realized that there was nothing happening in the seeker-friendly ministry of Willow Creek Community Church in the 1990s that had not already been done in the Youth for Christ rallies of the 1950s. The only difference was that the pioneers of Youth for Christ believed that what they were doing was not suitable for Sunday morning worship, but should only be done in an evangelistic rally outside the four walls of the church.[2]

Other branches of American Christianity — I examined Mainline Protestants, Roman Catholics, and African Americans — either were latecomers to juvenilization or picked the wrong elements of youth culture to imitate. As a result, the white Evangelical model of youth ministry came to dominate not just the church basement, but increasingly, the adult worship service as well.[3] To be sure, not all churches look like white Evangelical ones in their worship practices or other activities. But all churches compete for customer loyalty in a religious marketplace in which many people of all ages share similar adolescent preferences for an emotionally comforting, self-focused, and intellectually shallow faith.

It is important to realize that many benefits have come from injecting more youthfulness into American Christianity. Church growth, mission trips, and racial reconciliation all received a big boost from the youth ministries of the past seventy-five years. Churches that made compromises with youth culture sometimes managed to inspire long-term loyalty in their young people and even make church more attractive to adults. In contrast, churches that ignored the preferences of young people tended to decline in numbers and in effectiveness. For example, conservative Protestant churches have grown relative to liberal Protestant ones over the past forty years because conservative church members have had more children and conservative churches have done better at retaining those children through juvenilized youth ministries.[4] Big churches are not necessarily more faithful to Christ than small churches, but churches without members have a hard time fulfilling their missions.

Youth ministries are laboratories of innovation that at their best keep churches vibrant and help them adapt to the unique challenges of each generation. One of the few studies we have that asked the same questions about religion in the same town over a long period of time showed that between the 1920s and the 1970s the top reason people reported for going to church changed from "habit" to "enjoyment." Because youth culture put teenagers especially at risk for abandoning their faith, youth ministers were the first to learn how to make church more enjoyable. And what they learned along the way has kept people of all ages coming to church.[5]

But this attempt to make Christianity as pleasurable as youth culture had some dangers. In the 1950s, one teenage girl who was a member of Youth for Christ had this to say about Elvis Presley: "The fact of the matter is, I've found something else that has given me more of a thrill than a hundred Presley's ever could! It's a new friendship with the most wonderful Person I've ever met, a Man who has given me happiness and thrills and something worth living for."[6] In other words, Jesus is just like a teen idol, only better. Juvenilization kept Christianity popular, but did little to promote spiritual maturity.

It is important to realize that because of juvenilization, the problem of immaturity is no longer just a youth problem to be solved by adolescents, parents, or youth ministers. One pastor told me that the concept of juvenilization helped him understand some of the struggles he is having with congregants in their sixties. These Baby Boomers raised in the founding era of juvenilization want church to revolve around their preferences. But the problem is not just the old oppressing the young. The young leaders of a church that targets twenty-somethings asked a middle-aged woman to leave the music team because she did not "project the right image." That is, she looked too old. Not only is it easy to find people of all ages who are immature, it is now the whole life course — the normal pattern of moving from childhood to adulthood — that has been compromised as a path to spiritual maturity.

Growing Up Isn't What It Used to Be

There have always been immature people, and there always will be. When I was young, if someone pulled a selfish prank, a classmate or sibling might yell "Grow up!" or "That's really mature!" To be sure, growing up was typically something that other irritating kids should do, rather than something to which we all aspired. Yet this admittedly immature form of exhortation implied a shared notion that growing up included something called "maturity." Today, there is less shared understanding of what "growing up" should include. In recent decades important changes in the patterns of human development have made immaturity easier and maturity harder. Both the journey to adulthood and the destination have changed.

A Troubled Journey: Adolescence and Emerging Adulthood

Adolescence starts early and lasts a long time. The total time between the onset of puberty and a clearly embraced adult identity can now be as much as twenty years. If we still think of youth or adolescence as a relatively short period of transition in a person's life, our perception is out of step with reality. Over the past 100 years, the average age of at first menstrual period has dropped for girls from about 14 to 12.5. Secondary sexual characteristics are coming even earlier for some, with 47 percent of African American girls and 7 percent of Caucasian girls beginning to develop breasts by age 7. Some studies suggest that more and more boys are developing earlier as well. Studies show a correlation between precocious puberty, especially early menarche, and numerous health and psychological problems, including mood disorders, substance abuse, adolescent pregnancy and reproductive cancers. There is an ongoing debate in the medical community about the nature and extent of the problem of early puberty. But the overall pattern is clear: a significant number of children are entering puberty at very young ages. These children must cope with inherently difficult sexual changes with even less emotional readiness than they would have later. At least some experts believe that we as a society are not doing very well at developing medical and social supports for these children.[7]

But biology is not the only factor that encourages precocious adolescence. Common cultural beliefs and powerful economic interests are driving adolescence downward into childhood. Clothing, cosmetic, and entertainment companies market products with teenage appeal to younger children. This marketing strategy works because many eight- to twelve-year-olds aspire to look and behave like teenagers. Fourth-grade girls who don't wear thong underwear have been teased by those who do.[8] Thankfully, many adults and children are resisting the disappearance of childhood, but they are increasingly on their own. Pressures to start adolescence early are many; social supports for protecting children are few.[9] And as childhood contracts, adolescence expands downward.

In theory, entering puberty earlier could lead to growing up sooner. But that does not happen, because the institutions that structure adolescence are better at keeping people immature than pushing them to grow up. Two key institutions that drive youth culture are schools and businesses that target teenage customers. Ever since the mid-twentieth century, almost all adolescents have spent significant time in high schools. But lumped together in large numbers, young people create their own beliefs and behaviors, some of which diverge from what adults would prefer. Thus the irony is that institutions adults created to move young people toward maturity also teach them to revel in immaturity.

But simply eliminating age-segregated environments would not eliminate youth culture or juvenilization; there's simply too much money to be made from young people. Starting in the 1940s and getting better at it ever since, the "merchants of cool" have studied teenagers and tried to discern their tastes. They have also worked hard to influence those tastes, especially through various forms of electronic media and advertising. Teenagers can be a fickle audience and often respond better to products that feel authentic because they have bubbled up from their peers. So media companies and other businesses turn to "cool hunting": searching for new music, clothing, slang, and other styles that are emerging among trendsetting teenagers. Enterprising business leaders then repackage, mass produce, and sell those products to as many teenagers as they can. But when millions of teenagers buy the latest style, it drives the teenage trendsetters even further into deviance or even immorality in order to find something uniquely "theirs" that shocks adults. Meanwhile, fierce competition among the merchants of cool over a long period of time has a way of lowering moral standards. The merchants of cool usually excuse themselves by saying that they are just giving teenagers what they want. They also claim that media content does not influence the behavior of teenagers.[10] But that's not what they tell the companies paying them millions of dollars for advertisements.

At the other end of the process, the transition to adulthood has receded into the distant future not just for twelve-year-olds, but even for twenty-year-olds. Developmental psychologists have identified a new life stage they call *emerging adulthood*. After extensive, nationally representative research into the lives of eighteen- to twenty-three-year-old Americans, Christian Smith and his team concluded that emerging adulthood means

. . . not making commitments, not putting down roots, not setting a definite course for the long term. It is about experimenting, exploring, experiencing, preparing, anticipating, having fun, and hopefully not screwing things up too badly in the meantime. Emerging adulthood entails few significant obligations, relatively little accountability to others, and (for those with the means) plenty of interesting detours and escape hatches. It is a time of limbo, of transition, of being neither a teen nor a real adult.[11]

Emerging adults are consumed with navigating many difficult transitions: from living at home to living on their own, from being single to being heavily involved in romantic relationships and sexual activity, from tagging along with their parents to church to deciding if faith is something they will continue to pursue on their own, from being in school to finding a job or career — the list goes on and on. They navigate these many transitions detached from significant relationships with older adults.[12]

The result is a life stage that is beset with problems, losses, and even tragic outcomes, but populated by people who put a bold face on matters and insist they have "no regrets." In particular, Smith and his research team found that American society is not preparing young people to become healthy, productive adults in five important areas of life: moral reasoning, higher life purpose, substance use, sexuality, and civic engagement. First, they are unable to think clearly about moral matters. They can't say what makes some things right and others wrong. About all they can say is that they "just know" or "just feel" when something is wrong. They're pretty sure that each person needs to make up his or her own mind about morality. Second, they unquestioningly accept consumerism and the American Dream and do not have any higher aspirations in life. Third, many abuse alcohol, and a significant minority abuse drugs. Fourth, they do not hold a high view of sex as something powerful that should be treated with care. Most follow a pattern of serial monogamy, and most romantic relationships involve sexual intercourse. Fifth, they do not participate in politics, community service, or charitable giving. They hope to be more civically minded "someday," just as they hope to achieve the American Dream with a happy family and lots of stuff.[13]

In an adaptation of a slogan promoting Las Vegas tourism, emerging adults believe that what happens in emerging adulthood stays in emerging adulthood. But both common sense and sociological research suggest that the ways many of them are behaving with regard to sex and substance use, to name but two common problems, are likely to have some lingering bad effects on their lives and character.[14] But for now, all that "growing up" stuff can be relegated to some indeterminate future. A good many plan to be back in church when they turn thirty, but no one knows for sure what the effects of a ten-year hiatus will be. Indeed, some evidence suggests that over time, fewer people in each birth cohort are returning to church after their young adult period of wandering.[15]

If there is something about which all those who study emerging adulthood seem to agree, it is that emerging adults are not primarily to blame for the negative outcomes we observe in their lives. Numerous factors have combined to create a lengthy and difficult transition to adulthood. Global economic changes have reduced job security, lowered wages, and made it more important than ever to get as much education as possible. Because of rising costs and the need to work to earn their way through school, more young people are taking longer than the traditional four years to get a degree. Many parents are willing to support their children financially and even give them a place to live as they take a few years to get established in life. The average age at first marriage has been rising for various reasons. Many are waiting longer to get married in order to complete their education or explore life options. The relatively easy availability of sex and the protection from pregnancy that birth control promises combine with the social acceptance of cohabitation to remove many of the factors that used to push people toward marriage. Many young people have experienced divorce in their families and want to "make sure" that they find the right person before marrying. What these and other factors mean is that the five key transitions that used to mark the beginning of full adulthood — finishing school, moving away from home, getting a job, getting married, and having children — are happening later in life for more and more people.[16]

It is certainly possible to imagine a society in which people tried desperately to escape their imprisonment in an unnaturally long life stage between childhood and adulthood. In fact, many of the deviant behaviors of adolescence can probably be traced in part to the fact that a long adolescence, particularly one with inadequate support and help from caring adults, is difficult to bear. Indeed, the subtitle of the book *Generation Me* describes today's younger Americans as "more miserable than ever before." But surprisingly, most Americans have not rebelled significantly against extended adolescence. Although powerful influences like media, consumerism, and friends encourage a prolonged adolescence, Americans also choose it because it seems pleasurable. Even in the early stages of commercialized youth culture it was clear that teenagers were not simply puppets being manipulated by marketers. In fact, when the term "teenager" was first coined, most adults still wanted young people to grow up as soon as possible. For example, in the 1940s, the articles in *Seventeen* taught teenage girls to aspire to adulthood and advertised household goods they might purchase when they graduated from high school and got married. But already then, a girl in the newsreel *Teenage Girls* claimed, "We just want to live our own lives. We're not in a hurry to grow up and get all serious and morbid like older people."[17]

A Dubious Destination: The New Adulthood

Over time, this adolescent desire to stay young and avoid the perceived liabilities of adulthood has permeated society. In the 1960s, advertising experts discovered that adults would buy products that promised to make them feel young and hip.[18] But as more and more media products praised youth as a time of freedom and self-expression, adulthood seemed boring, restrictive, and inauthentic by comparison.

By now, the assumption that youth is better than adulthood is widely accepted. This cultural belief is visible whenever adults tell teenagers that "this is the best time of your life" or when college students say "this is my time to have fun." Christian youth leaders have often contributed to the worship of youth by praising young people as model Christians and looking to them to save the world.[19]

It would be understandable if people simply wanted to retain the strength and physical beauty of youth. But what makes other adolescent attributes attractive? For one thing, immaturity boosts sales. In the early twentieth century, advertisements still explained the features of products and invited the customer to make a rational choice based on how well the product would meet a need. Of course many of those "needs" were created by the advertisers, but at least it was assumed that the customer would be making a rational choice about whether to buy the product. Today, advertisers use images, music, and a minimal amount of the spoken or written word. These techniques aim to bypass conscious reasoning and inflame desires for identity, belonging, sensual gratification or even spiritual transcendence. The most innovative advertisers sometimes dispense with describing the product at all, or even showing an image of it. The product is much less important than the intangible benefits it will supposedly impart.[20]

People who know who they are, who think carefully about purchases, and who exercise self control are harder to persuade to buy products they don't really need. In contrast, impulsive people who are searching for a sense of identity, who are looking to salve their emotional pain, who desperately crave the approval of others, and who have lots of discretionary income (or are willing to spend as if they do) make ideal consumers. In other words, encouraging people to settle into some of the worst traits of adolescence is good for business. Not all businesses and advertisers operate on this basis, but enough do to encourage the cult of youth and discourage people from growing up. Considerable evidence suggests that consumers can see through these techniques and resist them to some extent.[21] But immersed as we all are in the culture of adolescence, it becomes increasingly hard to embrace the self-denial and character formation necessary to achieve what used to be called mature adulthood.

Yet it will not work simply to tell people to "grow up" or to stop being so driven by their emotional needs. Deep processes are at work in society that cause people to be especially starved for meaning, identity, belonging, and emotional comfort. In a society that teaches educated, middle-class adults to put much of their identity in work, many end up in jobs that are high on frustration and low on meaning. Economic insecurity plagues the middle class, with costs of housing, education, child care, and health care all rising faster than wages. Divorce, remarriage, and single parenthood have become commonplace. In addition to the well-documented negative financial impact of divorce on mothers and children, there is also the emotional impact on parents who must rebuild their lives and who therefore have less to give to their children. Although it is hard to say why, happiness seems to have decreased in western industrialized nations as economic prosperity has increased. Scores on standardized psychological tests show that younger Americans are more narcissistic on average than the young people of previous generations, yet feel less empowered to change the world. Geographic mobility, which has always been high in the United States relative to other societies, has only increased. People of all ages have more information and more choices than ever before. Very few people assume that their children will follow in their footsteps by choosing the same career and living in the same community. Clubs, political organizations, neighborhoods, and families that used to help people gain a sense of belonging and identity are either no longer functioning effectively or simply not available.[22]

The result of all these changing life patterns is that young people grow up knowing that they need to figure out for themselves who to be, what to do, and what to believe. Indeed, most contemporary Americans of all ages *want* to define themselves and chart their own course. Believing that you should invent yourself by yourself can be exhilarating, but it can also be burdensome and terrifying. The pressure causes some to take the path of least resistance and settle for the quasi-adulthood offered by the entertainment industries and consumerism.[23] In extreme cases, adolescents, emerging adults, and adults who can't take the pressure or "stand on their own" fall into serious problems like depression, suicide, addictions, or crime.[24] The fact that such problems are widespread even among the advantaged in American society suggests that the process of growing to healthy, mature adulthood may be more than just difficult. It might be broken altogether.

As a result of these and other factors, the very nature of adulthood has changed in at least two fundamental ways. First, in the past, the transition to adulthood came early and suddenly. Second, when that adulthood came, it was generally understood that its most important element was taking responsibility for others. Responsibility, self-denial, and service to others were considered valuable adult traits. Sometimes people even talked as if "settling down" through marriage and parenthood would automatically produce the character needed to succeed in those endeavors. Of course many people did not cope very well with a sudden and early transition to adulthood, but it was harder to put it off and there were more social supports (and sometimes sanctions) to encourage people to grow up.[25]

Although many still believe that one key marker of adulthood is caring for others, especially one's children, the importance of subjective, emotional criteria has increased. One woman in her early thirties described how adulthood works for her: "You don't see yourself as an adult all the time. You just think of yourself as yourself, and every once in a while, you'll have an adult moment when you have to make an adult decision . . . doing things that adults do." The process of becoming an adult can be lengthy, it can backtrack, and it may be unending. One twenty-something female thought she would finally feel like an adult "when I accomplish everything I want to in life . . . I'll have my own place, have a family, have my kids . . . It's never ending. It's like a job, you know, there's always more to it."[26]

At least among younger Americans, taking responsibility for oneself may have even edged out taking responsibility for others as the most important trait of adulthood. Twenty-eight-year-old Lisa Caldwell was living at home with her parents and paying down debt she acquired during a few years of trying to live on her own when researchers caught up with her. She described adulthood this way: "I guess [an adult] would be someone who takes responsibility and ownership of their life. I'm not an adult yet though I'm becoming it. For the past six years I've just been living a life without any real responsibilities other than to myself and my dog."[27] This new way of understanding adulthood that one theorist called "psychological adulthood" is ambiguous and self-defined.[28] It becomes increasingly hard to know when one has really become an adult — or even if adulthood is desirable. There are potentially as many definitions of adulthood as there are people, with few shared standards and little social accountability.

Most significantly for our discussion of juvenilization and its impact on the church, the connection between adulthood and maturity has been severed. As a middle-aged Christian woman I met on a plane recently told me, "I'm never going to grow up." Adults are free to define themselves in almost any way they choose, whether or not their personalized vision of adulthood is beneficial to themselves, to their communities, or to their children. For example, most contemporary Americans take it for granted that it was bad, and maybe even counterproductive, for adults of previous generations to stay married "for the sake of the children." Yet much research suggests that the older wisdom remains true: divorce is bad for children. In particular, children of divorce are much less likely to be religious and to be members of a faith community. Meanwhile, phrases like "be yourself," "respect yourself," "stand up for yourself," and "you have to love yourself before you can love someone else" have become unquestioned guidelines for how to behave in relationships. Yet in practice, such slogans promote an unhealthy self-absorption and may even be harmful to relationships.[29]

In the classic modern theories of human development, such as the extremely influential theory of Erik Erikson, adolescence was the time to search for one's identity, and it was assumed that this task required a certain amount of self-absorption. That search was supposed to produce an "autonomous" adult who could make his own decisions with integrity based on a clear and stable sense of personal identity and who would achieve "generativity" — the ability to give back to the young and to society. But as we have seen, adults today face as many transitions and disruptions as adolescents and emerging adults. Just think of the number of people who will not be married to the same person for their entire adult lives. Not surprisingly, a stable sense of identity seems increasingly elusive even for adults. Much like adolescents, adults find themselves in an unending state of becoming.[30]

Adults caught in the many transitions of life who are trying to figure out who to become sometimes have little left to give to others, even their own children. An ethnographic study of a large high school in southern California revealed that most teenagers there felt abandoned by adults. These teenagers believed that there was not a single adult in their lives who truly knew them and truly cared about them. Although some of this was probably adolescent misperception and even self-absorption, there were plenty of adults who were sending the wrong messages. Coaches cared only about winning, teachers paid attention only to the top students and labeled the others as hopeless, and parents were "out of control," so their children felt unsafe telling them what was really happening in their lives. A few parents who got divorced even demanded that their children keep the divorce secret from the rest of the family. The author of the study theorized that many adolescent problems, including cynicism, mistrust of adults, casual sex, cheating, and alcohol abuse, could be traced to this systemic abandonment.[31] To the extent that adults are too busy with their own self-construction (or reconstruction) projects to care for the young, our juvenilized society has ironically become harmful to adolescents. Of course, many people still aspire to maturity and achieve it. But in this adolescent society, there are fewer supports for those wanting to grow up and many tempting detours or just plain dead ends along the way.

"It's All about You": Spirituality on the Path to the New Adulthood

The popular Evangelical Christian worship song "The Heart of Worship" is about returning to a focus on God, yet ironically there is still an awful lot of talk about "me" in it. Lines like "I'm coming back to the heart of worship" and "I'm sorry, Lord, for the thing I've made it" seem to compete with the intended core message of the song: "It's all about you, Jesus." The song serves as a metaphor for just how hard it is to escape the relentless self-focus of American culture. Even our efforts to dethrone our therapeutic god of self are often done in therapeutic ways. I am not singling out this song for blame; it merely illustrates the powerful gravitational pull exerted by the new patterns of human development and notions of the "self" in contemporary America. That pull distorts Christian discipleship in different ways in each stage of life, although as we shall see, some common themes emerge.

Adolescent Faith: "If I'm Having a Hard Time, It Makes Me Feel Better"

In their landmark National Study of Youth and Religion, Christian Smith and his team of researchers found that the majority of American teenagers are not alienated from religion or the church. On the contrary, even teenagers not personally involved in religious activities think that religion is basically a good thing. Many of them have learned this favorable view of religion through contact with church youth groups. An astonishing 69 percent of all teenagers in America have attended a religious youth group at one time or another.[32]

There is a spectrum of religious belief and devotion: Mormons, Black Protestants, and Conservative Protestants score higher on most measures of religious practice and fervor than Mainline Protestants or Roman Catholics. But when it comes to influencing life outcomes, the researchers found that it was not so much the church tradition, but rather the intensity of devotion, that made the difference. Teenagers who go to church regularly and say their faith is important to them are less likely to smoke, drink alcohol, do drugs, engage in sexual activities of various kinds, lie to their parents, or cheat in school, and they are more likely to care about those in need and volunteer. The most highly devoted teenagers, who attend church weekly, say faith is very or extremely important to them, feel very or extremely close to God, attend a church youth group, pray a few times a week, and read the Bible twice a month or more show the most positive life outcomes. Even after controlling for many other possible factors, it seems that religion still exerts some independent influence on the positive activities and healthy choices that these religiously devoted teens make.[33]

Unfortunately, Christianity seems to be helping teenagers without passing through their brains or across their lips. Smith's research team found that American teenagers are surprisingly inarticulate about their faith. When asked what they believed, even some young people who attend church and youth group regularly said things like "Um, Jesus and God and all them guys . . . that they are up there watching out for us." The biblical language of faith is a foreign language to American teenagers. They seldom used words like "faith," "salvation," "sin," or even "Jesus" to describe their beliefs. Instead, they returned again and again to the language of personal fulfillment. The phrase "feel happy" appeared over 2,000 times in the 267 interviews in which teenagers tried to describe their religious beliefs. As one teenage boy put it, the thing that is so good about faith is that "If I'm having a hard time, it makes me feel better."[34]

Smith and his research team came up with the label "Moralistic, Therapeutic Deism" to summarize the religious beliefs that emerged in their in-depth interviews with teenagers. Teenagers are "moralistic" in that they believe that God wants us to be good, and the main purpose of religion is to help people be good. But many think that it is possible to be good without being religious, which means religion is an optional tool for being good that may be chosen by those who find it helpful. Further, they believe most people are good and will go to heaven. American Christianity is "therapeutic" in that, like the teenagers in the study, we believe that God and religion are valuable because they help us feel better about our problems. Finally, American teenagers show their "deism" in that they believe in a God who remains in the background of their lives. He is always there watching over them, ready to help them with their problems. But he is not at the center of their lives.[35]

There may be any number of reasons that so many teenagers hold such a superficial set of religious beliefs. One reason is certainly that they have not learned the vocabulary of faith. Perhaps adults have *talked to* teenagers a lot about faith but seldom helped teens to *talk about* their own beliefs. In many cases, the interviewer got the feeling that she was the first person to ever ask this teenager what she believed about God and religion. American teenagers have little practice with, and seem to place little importance on, talking about faith matters. But if something is truly important to a person, it doesn't tend to stay in the background the way the god of moralistic, therapeutic deism does. These same teenagers who floundered awkwardly as they tried to say *anything* meaningful about their religious beliefs could talk easily about other subjects that were either more exciting to them (like their extracurricular activities) or in which they had been better instructed (such as the dangers of drug abuse). And it is important to note that it was not just nominal Christian teenagers who seemed to espouse moralistic, therapeutic deism. Quite a few who attended church regularly and claimed that faith was very or extremely important to them could not articulate anything deeper when asked.[36]

Most importantly, teenagers absorb these religious beliefs from the adults in their lives. It is the American culture religion. One of the clearest findings in the study was the strong correlation between the religious beliefs and practices of parents and those of their teenage children. As Smith and his team put it, when it comes to forming their children's faith, parents will "get what they are."[37] This way of being religious is not something that can be easily overcome. It is the default position in American society, the magnetic north with which young people tend to align unless they are actively and persistently formed in a more countercultural way of following Jesus Christ.

Sociologists of religion often measure what some call the "3 Bs" of religion: Believing, Belonging, and Behaving. The National Study of Youth and Religion revealed that churches at their best seem to help adolescents achieve a warm sense of belonging that helps them to avoid harmful behaviors. But even a good many churchgoing adolescents fail to internalize a strong set of religious beliefs or form internally motivated, godly patterns of behavior. As a result, our children do not do so well when they leave the nest after high school graduation.

Emerging Adult Faith: "My Faith Is What's Best for Me"

To keep things in perspective, it is important to note that it is quite amazing that *any* emerging adults are seriously religious. Their life stage is almost perfectly suited to reducing religious interest and involvement. The lives of emerging adults are full of transitions, distractions, and disruptions. They switch residences, cities, jobs, schools, relationships, and everything else, and these changes wreak havoc with church attendance and personal religious practices. Emerging adults strive to keep their options open and are careful to affirm that everyone is entitled to his or her opinion on all important matters. Their driving goal is to become self-sufficient, so they see churches as "elementary schools of morals" that they are ready to leave behind. They put off marriage and childbearing, two life events that have traditionally driven young adults back to church. They feel the need to differentiate themselves from their parents, and religious beliefs seem like an especially safe — that is, unimportant — arena in which to depart from how they were raised. Although they tend to choose friends who are similar to them religiously, they typically don't talk much with those friends about matters of faith. Many of their peers tell them by word and example that "they are supposed to devote themselves to hanging out, partying, and perhaps drinking, doing drugs, and hooking up." None of these typical elements of emerging adult lives tends to promote stronger religious belief and involvement. The only exception would be that their many life transitions sometimes include personal tragedies or hardships that push them to revisit their childhood faith or explore a new branch of Christianity.[38] The good news is that despite all these built-in obstacles, some emerging adults are serious about their faith. The bad news is that even many of the serious ones may not be well grounded or prepared to mature in it.

In Waves II and III of the National Study of Youth and Religion, researchers followed the same teenagers into their young adult years. Moralistic, Therapeutic Deism seems alive and well among these eighteen- to twenty-three-year-olds, but diversity of religious belief and practice did increase. A few emerging adults became stronger in their faith and more

15

articulate about their beliefs. Some questioned the beliefs with which they were raised. Many stopped going to church or putting much effort of any kind into their faith.[39]

Emerging adults still think of religion as a good thing, especially for children, even if they are personally indifferent to it right now. They think most religions share the same key principles and that religious particularities are unimportant. A few believe that their religion is uniquely true, but they are unable to explain why. Most think that it is impossible to choose between truth claims in any definitive way; each person just decides for himself or herself. As a typical emerging adult put it, "I think that what you believe depends on you."[40]

Emerging adults can be sorted into six religious types: Committed Traditionalists (15 percent), Selective Adherents (30 percent), Spiritually Open (15 percent), Religiously Indifferent (25 percent), Religiously Disconnected (5 percent), and Irreligious (10 percent). Of these types, only the first three are likely to put any effort whatsoever into their spiritual life. Committed Traditionalists can articulate some Christian beliefs, attend church reasonably regularly, and see faith as an important part of their lives and identities. But even they "focus more on inner piety and personal moral integrity than, say, social justice or political witness, and can keep their faith quite privatized." And like all emerging adults, they tend to think that religious beliefs and practices are matters of personal choice and should be based on what works or feels right to the individual. As one young Catholic put it, "my faith is what's best for me." A subgroup of the Committed Traditionalists (about 5 percent of all emerging adults) are the most devoted to their faith and attend religious services at least weekly, say faith is very or extremely important to them, feel very or extremely close to God, pray at least a few times a week, and read Scripture at least once or twice a month. This group does better than their peers at avoiding harmful behaviors like alcohol and drug abuse and engaging in positive ones like charitable giving and volunteering. But these differences are not as dramatic as they were among adolescents.[41]

Selective Adherents typically come from reasonably strong religious upbringings but are now in the process of picking and choosing what to keep. They are especially likely to disregard what their church and parents taught them about the need for regular church attendance, belief in hell, drinking alcohol, taking drugs, and use of birth control (for Catholics). Some feel conflicted or guilty about discarding elements of their religious upbringing; many do not. They compartmentalize their faith more than Committed Traditionalists and are likely to say things like "I still have the same *ideas* now; I just don't go to church." Selective adherents show little difference from the general population of emerging adults in terms of religious beliefs and positive life outcomes. Finally, the Spiritually Open are not personally committed to any one faith, but show varying degrees of interest in exploring Christianity or other types of spirituality. They most often come from non-religious backgrounds or from a Christian background that they have abandoned.[42] Clearly the life stage of emerging adulthood does not encourage people to grow toward spiritual maturity. A few do so anyway, but they have to swim upstream.

Adult Faith: "Religious Doctrines Get in the Way of Truly Relating to God"

Many Christian adults and even Protestant pastors do not have a very clear understanding of spiritual maturity. In a national survey conducted in 2009, the Barna Research group found that 81 percent of self-identified Christian adults agreed or strongly agreed that "trying hard to follow the rules in the Bible" was a key element of spiritual maturity. When asked an open-ended question about how their church defines "a healthy, spiritually mature" Christian, about half were unable to answer. Of those who ventured a guess, responses varied and tended to be generic: "having a relationship with Jesus" (16 percent), "practicing spiritual disciplines like prayer and Bible study" (9 percent), "living according to the Bible" (8 percent), "being obedient" (8 percent), "being involved in church" (7 percent), and "having concern for others" (6 percent). When asked to describe their personal beliefs about the content of spiritual maturity, respondents as a group produced a similar list of answers. Significantly, most respondents offered only one measure or trait of spiritual maturity, even though interviewers probed repeatedly for more ideas.[43] Evidently religiously inarticulate teenagers grow up to be religiously inarticulate adults, at least when it comes to describing spiritual maturity.

The same survey also found that a majority of self-identified Christian adults rated themselves as "completely" (14 percent) or "mostly" (40 percent) spiritually healthy. Not surprisingly, most were also "completely" (22 percent) or "mostly" (43 percent) satisfied with their spirituality. It is possible that at least some who were "mostly satisfied" still desired to grow. And even if that group was spiritually complacent, there was still a large group, as much as one-third of all respondents, who recognized that they were not spiritually healthy and did not like it.[44] But if an accurate working knowledge of spiritual maturity is necessary in order to grow toward it, then a good many American Christians may be in trouble. Even those who want to grow may not be able to do so.

Pastors did not do much better. Nine out of ten pastors surveyed believed that spiritual maturity was a significant problem in the American church, but most did not think it was a problem in *their* congregation. Pastors listed the following measures of spiritual maturity: "the practice of spiritual disciplines" (19 percent), "involvement in church activities" (15 percent), "witnessing to others" (15 percent), "having a relationship with Jesus" (14 percent), "having concern for others" (14 percent), "applying the Bible to life" (12 percent), "being willing to grow spiritually" (12 percent), and "having knowledge of Scripture" (9 percent). Only a small minority of churches had a written statement of their spiritual maturity goals for members. Pastors seemed ill-prepared to describe which specific Scripture passages shaped their understanding of spiritual maturity. When asked to do so, three quarters of all pastors offered generic answers like "the whole Bible" or "the life of Christ" or "the letters of Paul."[45]

In contrast to their uncertainty about the meaning of spiritual maturity, most American Christians and their pastors are quite familiar with the idea of "spiritual growth" and view it as an important part of life and a significant part of what churches have to offer. When asked in a national survey, "how important has it been to you as an adult to grow in your spiritual life?" the general population was evenly divided across the spectrum of motivation, with 26 percent saying it was extremely important, 28 percent saying it was very important, 23 percent saying it was fairly important, and 21 percent saying it has not been very important.[46]

But what did these people mean by "spiritual growth"? For those who responded to the survey and follow-up interviews, "spiritual" generally meant the inner, experiential dimension of religion especially in contrast with the rules, doctrines, and structures of organized religion. A majority believed that "personal experience is the best way to understand God" (61 percent) while only 33 percent agreed that "church doctrines and teachings are the best way to understand God." Even among those most highly interested in spiritual growth, about half agreed that "religious doctrines get in the way of truly relating to God." Thus the participants in the study perceived themselves to be growing spiritually if they had feelings of closeness, assurance, forgiveness, or comfort from God, especially if they believed that the frequency of such feelings was increasing in their lives.[47]

The same study revealed that American adults generally believe that church attendance can be helpful to spiritual growth, but is not necessary. About 70 percent agreed that "My spirituality does not depend upon being involved in a religious organization." Yet among those who say that spiritual growth is "extremely important" to them, 80 percent attend church "almost weekly" and 74 percent reported that attending church has been very important to their spiritual growth. On the other hand, among the next lower group, those who still claimed that spiritual growth is "very important" to them, only 53 percent attend church "almost weekly" and only 56 percent say attending church services has been very important to their spiritual growth.[48]

The evidence regarding adults' engagement with particular faith traditions and doctrines is mixed. Those who say that spiritual growth is "very" or "extremely important" to them tend to agree with general Christian beliefs such as "God is fully revealed in Jesus" (79 percent) or "Christianity is the best way to understand God" (74 percent). On the other hand, these same believers do not differ from the general population in their general agreement (70 percent range) that "All religions contain some truth about God." And even those extremely interested in spiritual growth have not typically put much effort into learning the theology or heritage of their church.[49]

Church shopping is quite common; 47 percent of Americans have searched for a new church at least once and one-third have done so a "few times." About half of all church shoppers had to look for a new church because they moved. That means that one-quarter of all American adults have shopped for a church for some other reason. When asked to rate reasons they chose their current congregation, theology, worship, and family members were most often cited as "very important," closely followed by clergy.[50] What a church teaches and how it worships are clearly the most important things that draw people to it.

No matter what kind of church people choose and for what reasons, the act of choosing itself may shape them and their understanding of what Christianity is. Bill Monson is enthusiastic about Saddleback Church because "Pastor Rick really emphasizes the relationship with God" rather than "religion," which is "all about rules." In contrast, June Henderson left Saddleback Church because she was "looking for something with a little more meat" when it came to theology and preaching.[51] Steve and Julie joined a large Pentecostal church because "we liked the music" and "they had lots of good programs for the kids" but then left that church because "it was too impersonal. You felt lost in the shuffle." After experimenting with Buddhism, Tara started reading about Catholicism but found the typical American Catholic liturgy and music uninspiring. She eventually found her home in a parish that celebrated the Latin Mass. "The music, the art, the liturgy, everything comes together in the Latin Mass," she said. "Something sacred is taking place."[52] Each of these people took for granted the importance of choosing a church based on their personal needs or aesthetic preferences. But choosing church this way may turn the believer into a consumer and church into a business selling spiritual experiences. At the very least, the unavoidable need to make a personal choice may incline believers to see religious beliefs and practices as *nothing more than* personal preferences exercised toward the goal of self-development.

There is a significant minority of American adults who are highly motivated toward spiritual growth and who are putting effort into that growth. These highly motivated believers tend to agree with their pastors that spiritual growth is closely associated with spiritual disciplines like prayer, meditation, or Bible reading. Among those who say that spiritual growth is "extremely important" to them, 61 percent report having devoted "a great deal of effort" to their spiritual lives in the past year, 84 percent pray every day, and 75 percent report that their interest in spirituality has increased in the past year. On the other hand, of those who say spiritual growth is "very important," only 21 percent have devoted a great deal of effort in the past year, and only 52 percent say their interest has increased. About half of those who say spiritual growth is "extremely important" to them are involved in charitable giving, social service activities, or volunteering, compared to about one-third of the general population.[53] While these figures are encouraging, it should be noted that many people who say spiritual growth is "very important" to them but who fall short of saying it is "extremely important" are not putting much effort into spiritual growth and so probably aren't growing.

American Protestants who go to church at least once a month score reasonably well when asked how strongly they believe basic Christian doctrines, although they are somewhat selective in their beliefs. In a 2007 study of 2,500 Protestant church attenders, 72 percent agreed strongly that Jesus was physically resurrected, 70 percent believed strongly in the Trinity, and 74 percent believed strongly in an "all-knowing, all-powerful, perfect deity who created the universe and still rules it today." By comparison, 58 percent agreed strongly that "The Bible is the written word of God and is totally accurate in all that it teaches" and that "Eternal salvation is only possible through God's grace." Half or less of the respondents agreed strongly that all people are sinners, Jesus was sinless, Jesus will return, that Christianity is the only path to salvation, or that hell or Satan really exists. Perhaps most revealing was the fact that only 52 percent of Evangelicals gave the ideally Evangelical responses to all twelve theological statements even though the survey was designed by Evangelicals with Evangelical theological priorities in mind. Among "born again" Christians who in some ways might have been expected to do even better, only 44 percent gave the ideal responses.[54] Of course even those able to give the "right" answers on a survey may not deeply understand and embrace those beliefs. One wonders how many of the respondents could have provided this list of beliefs if asked to describe their own religious faith in an open-ended interview.

However clear or convinced they may be in their theological beliefs, this group of American Protestants was not particularly teachable. About one-half to two-thirds were only moderately interested or active in learning from other Christians: 46 percent attended Christian education classes at their church at least once a month, 46 percent said they had been mentored by another Christian, 36 percent agreed strongly that they are "open and responsive to those in my church who teach the Bible," 32 percent agreed strongly that Christians should consider themselves accountable to other Christians, and only 17 percent agreed strongly that they "tend to accept the constructive criticism and correction of other Christians."[55] These responses show that many of these Christians were not actively learning about their faith.

Even if these Christians were open to spiritual input from others, too few had the kinds of spiritual friendships that could help them grow. A mere 27 percent strongly agreed that they had "significant relationships" with people at their church and an additional 33 percent agreed somewhat. Only 18 percent made it a high priority to spend time with other Christians, with 29 percent doing so "somewhat." On the other hand, about half had shared personal "feelings, joys, struggles or needs" with fellow Christians at least sometimes, and 43 percent indicated that spiritual matters were a normal part of their daily conversations with other Christians. Relationships with other Christians had a definite service component: 50 percent said they were currently serving in some ministry in their church, and 38 percent said that at least once in their lives they had mentored a less spiritually mature person by meeting with them at least once a month. But only 22 percent strongly agreed that "it is necessary for a Christian's spiritual well being to give time on a regular basis to some specific ministry within his/her church" with 32 percent agreeing somewhat.[56] So although many were currently serving others, they saw such service as but one option among many for pursuing spiritual growth.

And even if this group is learning about God, going to church, spending time with other Christians, and volunteering, those experiences may not be resulting in spiritual transformation. Although 48 percent read the Bible at least once a week, only 37 percent strongly believed that doing so had made significant changes in the way they live their lives. Only 23 percent agreed strongly that when they realize something in their life is not right in God's eyes, they make the necessary changes. Just 19 percent strongly disagreed with the statement "When I realize that I have a choice between 'my way' and 'God's way' I usually choose my way" with an additional 31 percent disagreeing "somewhat."[57]

Perhaps one reason that this group of believers found it hard to obey God is that they had not fully understood or accepted the call to follow Christ. Only 28 percent agreed strongly that "A Christian must learn to deny himself/herself in order to serve Christ" and another 28 percent agreed "somewhat." Similarly, 36 percent agreed strongly that "with reference to my values and priorities, I can honestly say that I try to put God first in my life" with another 35 percent choosing "agree somewhat." When it came to making difficult choices, 36 percent could not recall a single time in the past six months when they had made a decision to obey God even though they knew it might be costly to them, 20 percent said they could recall making one such tough choice for God, and 44 percent said they had made two or more such choices.[58] Perhaps denying the self seems alien or even wrong to people whose lives are dominated by self-construction projects.

A significant minority of these Christians were able to have spiritually positive experiences of suffering. When facing difficult circumstances, 44 percent said they experienced little or no doubt that God loves them and would provide for them and 40 percent strongly agreed that they "express praise and gratitude to God even in difficult circumstances." On the other hand, only 17 percent could strongly affirm that their lives were not filled with anxiety or worry.[59]

Following up with the same group a year later, the researchers found that 3.5 percent of the respondents showed a net increase in their overall scores on the spiritual formation inventory, while 3 percent showed a net decrease. One interesting finding was that even in one year this group of Christians experienced considerable volatility in terms of beliefs and religious experiences, with 17 percent changing into or out of the category "born again" and 13 percent changing into or out of the category "Evangelical." These changes were measured not by how the participants labeled themselves, but by how they answered the questions in the survey about their personal religious beliefs, practices, and experiences. As we would expect from what we have seen so far, this religious volatility was especially pronounced among people under the age of 30.[60]

When asked to evaluate how their spiritual life had changed over the past year, 22 percent said they had grown "a lot," 33 percent said they had grown "a little," 31 percent said no change, 9 percent thought they had declined a little, and 4 percent thought they had declined a lot. A full 13 percent of the sample had stopped going to church altogether. As evidence of their personal spiritual growth, participants offered statements like these:

"I'm much calmer."
"I'm a better friend."
"I'm a better person and more caring."
"My marriage is better."
"I am better at running my household to care for my family; I made some changes to facilitate hospitality in our home."
"I am more tolerant of people."
"There aren't many outward signs. The growth I experienced is manifested more on a personal level."[61]

At least some people recognized that getting better at loving others was a sign of spiritual growth. But invisible, inward changes related to emotional states also seemed to be a significant theme. And there was little that was explicitly Christian or theological in these comments.

What factors contributed to spiritual growth or decline over the course of the year? Not surprisingly, those who attended church less than weekly, were not involved as lay leaders in a church, did not participate in Sunday school or other Christian education, or did not participate in a small group were all statistically more likely to decline spiritually over the year of the study. The researchers also interviewed 100 of those whose overall scores on the spiritual assessment had improved over the past year and asked them to describe their experiences. Many credited their growth to church involvement or more engagement with God's Word. But the most frequently mentioned factor was difficult life events like divorce, death of loved ones, or serious illnesses. Without trivializing anyone's suffering or denying the deep experiences of comfort they received from God, I am nonetheless struck by some of the language used to describe these experiences. One woman whose husband of eighteen years left her said she learned that "You can make it through anything. But you have to fall in love with God in order to be able to do that."[62] "Falling in love with Jesus," a metaphor first popularized by youth workers trying to appeal to teenagers, has now become unquestioningly accepted by many adults.[63] And it is not just tolerated as a beginner approach to God, but is often celebrated as the highest form of authentic spirituality.

These patterns of adult religious life are not unique to Protestants. Robert Wuthnow's study found that Catholics were about as likely as Protestants to be extremely interested in spiritual growth, but only 56 percent of Catholics thought that attending religious services was very important compared to 64 percent of Mainline Protestants and 83 percent of Evangelical and Fundamentalist Protestants. Catholics were less likely than Protestants to believe that "God's nature is fully revealed in Jesus." On most other questions in Wuthnow's survey, Catholics answered about the same as Evangelical and Mainline Protestants.[64] Like their Protestant counterparts, many Catholics feel free to decide for themselves which parts of their faith are most important and even which ones they will accept. For example, while most think a "good Catholic" should believe that the Eucharist is really the body and blood of Christ and that Christ really rose from the dead, they don't think a "good Catholic" needs to obey the Church's teachings about birth control, giving to the poor, or attending Mass weekly.[65] As these examples suggest, Catholics are especially likely to ignore church teachings that impose lifestyle demands. And like Protestants, at least some Catholics feel empowered to choose which local church is right for them; about one-third of all Catholics have shopped for a parish.[66]

There is one bit of evidence that suggests that the average level of spiritual health among Roman Catholic adults may be even worse than it is among Protestants: Catholic teenagers. The National Study of Youth and Religion found that Catholic teenagers scored 5 to 25 percentage points below their Black Protestant, Conservative Protestant, and Mainline Protestant counterparts on all measures of religious devotion and practice. Why? Catholic parents of teenagers are less likely than their Protestant counterparts to say faith is "very important" to them, to attend church regularly, and to be involved in other church activities. All of these parental religious factors are significantly correlated with lower religious fervor in teenage children. Simply stated, religious faith is less important to Catholic teenagers than to Protestant teenagers because it is less important to their parents.[67]

The Challenge of Juvenilized Faith

Of course not every Christian in America is spiritually immature. A significant minority cares deeply about spiritual growth and is actively pursuing it. Nevertheless, many American Christians display the symptoms of juvenilization. They value a "relationship with God" above all and like the idea of "falling in love with Jesus." They don't see much value in the rules, strict beliefs, or structures of "religion," although they like going to church if it helps them feel closer to God. They are largely uninformed about the teachings of their churches and may even see doctrine or theology as enemies of authentic spirituality. They like the sense of belonging and acceptance that they find in their congregations but are not very open to being corrected by fellow believers. Their God is always there to help them feel better about their problems, and this is one of the chief benefits they see in their faith. They like the idea of spiritual growth, but they may not know much about how to grow and may rate themselves more highly than they should. They are drawn to religious experiences that produce emotional highs and sometimes assume that experiencing strong feelings is the same thing as spiritual authenticity. They see themselves as in charge of their own search for a satisfying sense of religious identity. In short, American Christianity looks a lot like we would expect it to look if many Americans were stuck in a Christianized version of adolescent narcissism. It could be that most American churches have been fighting a heroic but failing battle against these trends toward a self-focused, immature faith. But the fact that so few American churchgoers know much about spiritual maturity and so few pastors have a plan to foster it suggests otherwise.

Yet churches did not create the new immature adults and their religious preferences, at least not by themselves. Americans display these patterns of believing and behaving because the path from adolescence to adulthood is beset with many gorges, switchbacks, washed-out bridges, and wrong turns. It is a wilderness trail that is poorly marked, poorly maintained, and in some cases actively sabotaged by those who stand to profit from keeping people away from the summit. Although some adults along the way try to help, the young people who are walking this trail must primarily rely on one another for guidance and support. The trail is so poorly marked that many never make it. Indeed, even some of the people who are Christian "success stories" because they take faith seriously and attend church regularly may not be growing toward spiritual maturity. Thus if we would like to see Christians reach a mature faith that involves more than good feelings, vague beliefs, and a sovereign self, we must overcome the challenge of juvenilization.

CHAPTER 2

Growing up into Christ

*Just another moralist Christian telling us to live up to "his" stan-
dards. . . . I have no standards, only Jesus. Get a life.*

Response to a blog about
The Juvenilization of American Christianity

*It is ludicrous to suppose that any sensible God can wish adult men
and women to crawl about in spiritual rompers in order to preserve
a rather sentimental Father-child relationship.*

J. B. Phillips, *Your God Is Too Small,* 1961

Many American Christians are confused about spiritual maturity. What
is it? How do we get there? Is it even possible? Many are also not making much progress toward it. While there are many reasons people may be
slow to grow up into Christ, it seems doubtful that someone who is largely
ignorant of the whole idea will get very far. So if we want to overcome juvenilization and the immature Christians it produces, we must learn what
the Bible says about spiritual maturity. The concept of "maturity" and the
related metaphor of growing from infancy to adulthood are not the only
tools the New Testament writers used to describe how Christ transforms
human beings. But contemporary American Christians especially need to
learn and experience these biblical truths.

In particular, Christians who are tempted to stay stuck in immaturity
need a better understanding of the beginning, end, and process of spiritual

growth to maturity in Christ. First, they need to embrace the gospel of Jesus Christ as good news of spiritual transformation. Second, they need to be captured by a vision of spiritual maturity that is desirable, attainable, and has clear content. Third, they need to understand the process of growth to maturity so they can actively participate in it.

Not all readers will agree with the biblical theology of spiritual maturity presented here. That is to be expected given our different theological traditions. But hopefully the approach taken here will challenge each reader to do his or her own theological reflection on what the Bible says about spiritual growth. At the very least, all those with a teaching role in their family or church need to ask themselves, "Is the theology of spiritual growth that I teach likely to overcome the challenge of juvenilization?" In some cases, Christian teachers are communicating the right things about spiritual growth, but people are refusing to listen. But it may also be that some parents and church leaders are not teaching the right truths, or not teaching them clearly or compellingly. Teaching includes more than telling, and later chapters will address how to help people experience the spiritual transformation described here. Still, good teaching does need to begin with good content.

Beginning Well: The Good News of Transformation

Although it is a bit embarrassing to have to discuss it, we must begin by facing the fact that a significant number of Christians do not regard growing up in Christ to be an intrinsic part of what it means to be a follower of Jesus. As we have seen, most American Christians like the idea of spiritual growth. But when asked "What is your faith all about?" or even "What is the gospel?" many will not think to mention spiritual transformation into Christlikeness. They may have a theoretical expectation of growth, but practically speaking, it is not central to their lived theology. They think a lot about God making them happy; they rarely think about God making them holy. We should not be surprised if people do not grow after accepting a gospel that is silent about spiritual transformation. They did not sign up for that.

Many ordinary Christians in America describe the gospel as something like this: "Jesus died for your sins so you can go to heaven when you die." This gospel is what most of the college students I teach have learned growing up in their churches. If we look closely, we notice that this way of describing the gospel leaves a big blank spot where most of our life in this world should be. It is all about past sins and future reward. Is the rest of life just waiting until heaven? Is there no spiritual growth or participation in Christ's mission in the meantime?

It would be bad enough if Christians just forgot about spiritual growth, but the problem is worse than that. A good many Christians seem committed to the idea that we can expect little spiritual progress in this life. Remember the things my students in Understanding the Christian Faith class said when asked to describe spiritual maturity: "We never arrive in our spiritual growth." "No one is perfect in this life." "We can't be holy in this life." Another common slogan among American Christians is "We're all just sinners, saved by grace." Others like to remind us, "The only difference between Christians and unbelievers is that Christians are forgiven."[1]

These popular theological slogans emphasize that salvation is a gift from God, and not something we earn. That part of the gospel is crucially important. Much of the New Testament was written to remind people who were already following Jesus that being a good, observant religious person does not earn one's salvation. But this truth needs to be connected with other equally important truths about the gospel. Otherwise, the default understanding can become "miserable sinner" Christianity — the idea that we're all just miserable sinners saved by grace and that very little progress is possible in this life.[2] But do we truly believe that Jesus Christ, the Son of God, died on the cross, rose from the dead and sent the Holy Spirit to live in us so we can be the same "miserable sinners" on the day we die as on the day we received the free gift of salvation? Is that what the New Testament presents as the Good News about Jesus Christ? If not, then we need to think more carefully about how we present the gospel.

The Good News that Jesus himself preached clearly included spiritual transformation. Here is Mark's brief summary of Jesus' message: "Now after John was arrested, Jesus came to Galilee, proclaiming the good news of God and saying, 'The time is fulfilled, and the kingdom of God has come near; repent and believe in the good news'" (Mark 1:14-15). In saying "the time is fulfilled and the kingdom of God has come near" Jesus was alluding to the many Old Testament prophecies about a coming golden age when God would perfectly rule the world and restore the fortunes of Israel. Many of these prophecies included promises that God would transform his people by doing things like writing his law "on their hearts" (Jeremiah 31:31-34) and exchanging their "heart of stone" for a "heart of flesh" (Ezekiel 36:26-27). The result would be a renewed people who could finally renounce their idols and obey the life-giving commands of God. Even if Jesus' first hearers did not think about these prophecies when they heard him preaching, they certainly would have understood that a call to "repent" was a call to spiritual transformation.

The proper response to the good news of the Kingdom of God was to become a follower of Jesus. When Jesus called disciples (followers, students, apprentices), he called them to spiritual transformation. "Follow me, and I will make you fish for people" (Mark 1:17). To change from being a fisherman to being a rabbi was not just a change of occupation. Each of those who dropped everything to follow Jesus knew that he was entering into a process of being trained to be just like his rabbi. "A student is not above his teacher, but everyone who is fully trained will be like his teacher," Jesus would later tell them (Luke 6:40, NIV). This saying would not have been a surprise to those who first heard it. Everyone knew that is how the rabbi-disciple relationship worked. A disciple might not achieve the full greatness of his rabbi, but if he did not eventually become a rabbi himself, the process of discipleship had failed. No one signs up for a course of study or intensive training with the expectation of failure. Imagine the medical school or electrician's apprenticeship that advertised itself by saying, "Come work hard to learn about an occupation for which you will never be qualified."[3]

If anything, Jesus promised his followers a more radical experience of transformation than the typical rabbi's apprentice might expect. "If any want to become my followers, let them deny themselves and take up their cross daily and follow me. For those who want to save their life will lose it, and those who lose their life for my sake will save it" (Luke 9:23-24). Those who hoped to add Jesus to their lives while leaving everything else undisturbed did not really understand the good news. This "my life plus Jesus" approach was what sunk the rich young ruler (Mark 10:17-22, Matthew 19:16-22, Luke 18:18-23). The Good News of the Kingdom of God is not a self-help message that provides three easy steps to a better life. Self-help techniques keep the self firmly in charge. Rather, to accept the gospel is to submit to a death and resurrection process accomplished by God the Father, Son, and Holy Spirit. Jesus offered a stark choice: hang onto your life and lose it or lose your life and find true life in him.

Toward the end of his time on earth, Jesus instructed his followers to continue his work of spiritual transformation: "Go therefore and make disciples of all nations, baptizing them in the name of the Father and of the Son and of the Holy Spirit, and teaching them to obey everything that I have commanded you" (Matthew 28:19-20). People who are baptized into the name of the Triune God and are living according to the teachings of Jesus are people who have been spiritually transformed.

If the Good News that Jesus preached included the promise that his followers would become like him, where do Christians get a truncated, "miserable sinner" gospel? Most likely the problem is a misunderstanding of Paul's teachings. Paul fought hard against an influential faction among the first Christians who insisted that Gentiles who decided to become followers of Jesus needed to also become fully observant Jews. It was not enough to obey the Great Commandments and the Ten Commandments; these Gentile converts also had to get circumcised and obey all the dietary and ceremonial laws found in the books of Moses. Paul rightly saw the dangerous direction of this teaching: It would become a false gospel of "works" in which people would see themselves as accepted by God because of their correct behavior or their observation of the stipulations of the Old Covenant, rather than by the grace of God given through the work of Jesus Christ. In response, Paul fervently preached that no one could be saved by observing the law, but only by putting faith in Christ: "For by grace you have been saved through faith, and this is not your own doing; it is the gift of God — not the result of works, so that no one may boast" (Ephesians 2:8-9). This fight against a false gospel of works permeates Paul's writings, especially Romans, Galatians, and Ephesians. And it must be noted that there is a persistent temptation to credit ourselves with somehow earning God's favor or even salvation itself. This spiritual danger is real, and we must fight against it, as Paul did so well.

But unfortunately, this gospel of salvation by grace received through faith can be misused to justify low expectations for spiritual transformation. That is not what Paul had in mind. We see this especially well in a passage in which Paul starts by attacking the false gospel of works and ends by talking about maturity. In Philippians 3, Paul warns his readers to beware those Christian teachers who insist on circumcision and other requirements of the Law (v. 2). He then describes his own impeccable Jewish credentials: "circumcised on the eighth day, a member of the people of Israel, of the tribe of Benjamin, a Hebrew born of Hebrews; as to the law, a Pharisee; as to zeal, a persecutor of the church; as to righteousness under the law, blameless" (vv. 3-6). Even though he had the best possible resume for earning a good standing with God, "whatever gains I had, these I have come to regard as loss because of Christ. . . . I have suffered the loss of all things and I regard them as rubbish" (vv. 7-8). Paul counted these supposed spiritual "strengths" as no more valuable than the inedible food scraps one would throw out into the street for the dogs to eat.[4]

Paul eagerly and joyfully renounced his greatest religious attainments because of the "surpassing worth of knowing Christ Jesus my Lord" and to "gain Christ and be found in him, not having a righteousness of my own that comes from the law, but one that comes through faith in Christ" (Philippians 3:8-9). Clearly Paul had no interest in anything that could be interpreted as his own, humanly manufactured righteousness. But neither did Paul's spirituality bear much resemblance to "miserable sinner" Christianity. He writes, "I want to know Christ and the power of his resurrection and the sharing of his sufferings by becoming like him in his death, if somehow I may attain the resurrection from the dead" (vv. 10-11). His devoted pursuit of Christ pushed him to invoke athletic imagery: "forgetting what lies behind and straining forward to what lies ahead, I press on toward the goal for the prize of the heavenly call of God in Christ Jesus" (vv. 13-14). Paul was running hard to be ever more closely united to Christ and conformed to the pattern of his death and resurrection. He confessed that he had "not already obtained this" or "already reached the goal." Some people distort this idea of not reaching the goal of perfect union with Christ in this life into a kind of "treadmill theology": we try and try to become more like Jesus but never get anywhere.[5] Certainly many American Christians are especially eager to agree with Paul that we "never arrive" or are "never perfect" in this life. But it is at just this point in his argument that Paul invokes the word "mature": "Let those of us then who are mature be of the same mind" (v. 15).

Several important conclusions can be drawn from the somewhat surprising appearance of the word "mature" in this context. First, Paul assumed that at least some of his readers were already "mature" and so would agree with what he had been saying. Second, whatever "mature" means, it can't mean "perfect" or "already having reached the goal" of fully knowing Christ and becoming fully like him. Third, a mature follower of Christ understands the gospel well enough to avoid *both* "works righteousness" *and* low expectations for spiritual transformation in Christ. "Miserable sinner" Christianity is a misinterpretation of the gospel that Paul preached.

All Christians, especially those with a responsibility to teach others, must carefully examine the gospel we preach. Does the story we tell of Jesus and the salvation he brings include spiritual transformation? Or are we telling a story in which becoming like Christ becomes an optional afterthought? Here's a simple way to state the gospel that doesn't leave out transformation:

The Good News is that Jesus died and rose from the dead in order to transform everything in the world to become more and more the way God wants it to be — and that includes all parts of you.

31

And here is a slightly longer version:

> *The Good News is that Jesus is God breaking into the world in a new way. He lived a perfect life, taught us the truth about God, died and rose again, and sent the Holy Spirit to live inside and among his followers. By doing these things Jesus created a community of people who are being transformed to be like him and who are sharing in his mission of transforming the world to be more and more the way God wants it to be.*

The expanded version emphasizes that the gospel creates a community of disciples on mission,[6] which is an important corrective to the self-focus of much American spirituality.

The point of offering these examples is not for everyone to adopt my particular way of describing the gospel. But it is important for all Christians, especially those charged with teaching others, to articulate a clear, memorable, and effective way to explain the connection between the Christian gospel and each believer's transformation into Christlikeness. Christians from different theological traditions will favor different ways of explaining this crucial connection. Even Paul and James had different ways of explaining it. But every Christian teacher has a sacred responsibility to explain the connection between the gospel and spiritual transformation publicly and often.

If we do this right, we can raise expectations for what God wants to do in each of our lives and in our churches without falling into either self-flagellation or pride in our religious accomplishments. It is indeed good news that Jesus has done what we could not do so that we can become more like him and share in the work he is doing in the world. As Paul noted in Galatians, the true gospel is truly freeing, "For freedom Christ has set you free" (Galatians 5:1).

Excluding transformation from the gospel detracts from the glory of God in Christ because it implies that God the Father, Son, and Holy Spirit could not figure out a way to actually fix us to any significant degree. In that theological scenario it is sin, rather than Christ, that is victorious in this world. Although the kingdom of God will not be fully realized in this age, it is not absent either. In the lives of believers and the communal life of the church we should be able to see living signs of the inbreaking Kingdom of God. One of the glories of the gospel is that God graciously accepts us and forgives us even though we are unworthy sinners. But another glory of the gospel is that God does not leave us mired in our sinfulness. Both Romans 8:1, "there is now no condemnation for those who are in Christ Jesus," and

Romans 6:22, "now that you have been freed from sin and enslaved to God, the advantage you get is sanctification," can and should be true of the redeemed followers of Jesus.

A Vision for Maturity: Basic Competence in the Christian Life

As we have seen, the way some people understand the gospel might cause them to neglect spiritual maturity. But most Christians probably agree that *some* kind of spiritual growth is at least implied in the basic Christian message. So other parts of their thinking may be deficient too. One possibility that seems to be confirmed by social science research is that many Christians are confused about what spiritual maturity is. As we have seen, even to talk about "signs" or "traits" of spiritual maturity strikes many contemporary American Christians as a bad idea that will inevitably lead to pride or spiritual stagnation. In fact, the idea of growing up into something called "maturity" is a consistent and fairly clear theme in the New Testament. It is only one among several ways that the New Testament writers talk about spiritual growth, and that may be part of the problem. It can be easy to overlook the theme of growing to maturity because even those New Testament writers who use it tend to assume that the reader will know what they mean and do not expound on it at length. Added to that is the confusion caused by some translations of the relevant words in the Bible. To have a hope of overcoming juvenilization, we need to rediscover what the New Testament writers meant when they talked about growing from spiritual infancy to spiritual maturity.

In some passages modern translators choose "mature" to translate various forms of the Greek word *teleios,* and in other passages they choose "perfect." Although the focus in what follows will be on passages where "mature" is clearly the best translation, it is important to discuss passages where "perfect" is used. When *teleios* in its various forms is translated "perfect" the passages are sometimes describing something pertaining to God (Romans 12:2; James 1:17, 25; Hebrews 2:10; 5:9; 7:19) or to Christians in heaven (Hebrews 11:40; 12:23). Here the meaning is clearly "flawless" or "not able to be improved upon" and the English word "perfect" conveys the Greek meaning well. But in some cases, the word "perfect" is used to translate *teleios* when the word is somehow describing Christians in this world. Typically these passages have been understood as exhortations to pursue an ideal that cannot be fully reached in this life, and that is certainly the case. But as we shall see, even in such passages, the biblical writers assume that Christians can make genuine progress toward what they are calling "perfection."

Jesus' exhortation in the Sermon on the Mount "be perfect *(teleios)* therefore, as your Father in Heaven is perfect *(teleios)*" (Matthew 5:48) does refer to a high ideal, a righteousness that "exceeds" (5:20) the righteousness of the Pharisees. Such a call would have been shocking and intimidating to Jesus' original audience, since they assumed that the Pharisees were as close to being "perfect" in following the Law as anyone could be. But Jesus saw that the Pharisees were good at being strict rule-keepers while at the same time neglecting God's deeper intentions behind the commandments. Jesus wants his disciples to "exceed" the Pharisees not in mere conformity to a list of rules — the rich man who appears later in Matthew thought he had done that (Matthew 19:20). Rather, he wants them to change their whole approach to righteousness and the place of the commandments in it. Jesus is teaching his followers that they can and should become the kind of people who want to live the way God originally intended, to become as much like their Father in Heaven as possible. Such disciples pursue peace with their brothers, sexual purity, and genuine love even of their enemies rather than congratulating themselves that they are "good" because they have not killed anyone lately (Matthew 5:21-47).[7]

Needless to say, a righteousness that includes things like loving enemies requires the transforming power of God. But God does have that kind of power — and dispenses it in the lives of God's children. Stephen, for example, demonstrated that kind of love, as did the many rank-and-file Christians who accepted Paul as a brother after his conversion (Acts 7:58-60; Acts 9).

Even in Matthew 5 there is some debate about whether *teleios* should be translated "perfect" or "complete" or "whole," since the word seems to be used in at least two senses. First, the word here is used to suggest that one can become "complete" or "whole," even in this life, by entering into a new way of being righteous and making progress in it. Second, the end point of this new path of righteousness is not merely checking off a list of rules, but becoming like God, who is truly perfect, a standard that clearly cannot be reached in this life. Yet the whole tenor of Jesus' teaching assumes that his followers can and should make progress on this new path of righteousness. The choice of the word *teleios* here may even emphasize that this new righteousness "is demanded not only from an upper echelon of spiritual elites but from all who belong to the kingdom of God."[8] Disciples of Jesus should at least be in the process of being transformed by God into the kinds of people who can love their enemies.

When the rich man comes to Jesus and asks for something more than just a conventional keeping of the commandments as a way to eternal life, Jesus answers him, "If you wish to be perfect *(teleios)*, go, sell your possessions, and give the money to the poor, and you will have treasure in heaven; then come, follow me" (Matthew 19:20). Here is a concrete example of the principles Jesus taught in the Sermon on the Mount. This man thought he was a "good person" because he was living a life that was free from serious violations of the commandments. But to his credit, he sensed there must be more to true life in God. Even here, where translators typically choose "perfect," the word *teleios* does not mean one who is already morally flawless, but rather one who is "mature" or "complete" and therefore on the right path. Imagine if the man had obeyed Jesus' command. Would he have then suddenly become sinless or flawless? No, but he would have been completely transformed in his mode of relating to God and in the general orientation of his life. Interestingly, such a change could not be accomplished merely by an inward assent to Jesus' teachings or a feeling of commitment to him. It required a concrete, visible, and consequential action in the real world — selling all his possessions and following Jesus in his travels. As in Jesus' earlier saying in Matthew 5:48, the ideal is both high and to be pursued by all of his followers: give yourself completely to me and my kingdom — and do so in actions, not just internally.[9]

In James, *teleios* means completeness in virtue, not sinlessness. James first uses *teleios* in a discussion of the role of suffering in spiritual transformation: "My brothers and sisters, whenever you face trials of any kind, consider it nothing but joy, because you know that the testing of your faith produces endurance; and let endurance have its full *(teleios)* effect, so that you may be mature *(teleios)* and complete, lacking in nothing" (James 1:4). The word used for "testing" here implies a refinement that both reveals and produces a pure substance — in this case, a pure, genuine faith. The way that the trial and its "testing" produce change is by calling forth endurance in the believer. The trial is a kind of discipline that strengthens the spiritual capacity to endure. It is by persevering through trials with God and allowing him to use those trials to change us that we become mature and whole. In addition, the words used to describe this growth, "mature, complete, lacking in nothing," in Greek indicate a range of meanings both present and future. The believer can become mature, that is, have a godly character of "stable righteousness." Mature believers will continue to grow incrementally toward the state of "lacking in nothing," meaning having all virtues in full measure, an ongoing process that will not be completed in this life. So, for example,

James commends the man who "makes no mistakes in speaking" as "perfect" *(teleios)*.[10] Yet he then exhorts his readers to use their tongues to promote peace, rather than division in the church (3:2-18). He expects that as they "draw near to God" and "humble [them]selves" God will give them grace and they will be able love one another, rather than continue in their "conflicts and disputes" (4:1-10). For James, a follower of Jesus is *teleios* if he or she has made substantial progress toward a complete set of perfected virtues that can only be fully obtained in the age to come.

In the First Letter of John, we read about believers being "perfected" in various ways. One of the recurring themes in the letter is descriptions of various traits that can help the reader distinguish between true and false believers in Christ. The apostle hopes to encourage his readers that they are in fact right with God and warn those who are tempted to follow the ways and teachings of false believers. For example, early in the letter we read that the one who says, "I have come to know him [Jesus]" but does not obey Jesus' commands is a liar, and "the truth is not in him" (2:4). In contrast "whoever obeys his word, truly in this person the love of God has reached perfection *(teleioo)*" and such people can be "sure that [they] are in him" because they "walk just as he walked" (2:5-6). The phrase "reached perfection" is meant to indicate a present reality, a love that is "truly made complete" or "entire and mature."[11] John did not mean that his readers already flawlessly obeyed Jesus' word or experienced a love of God and others that could not be improved, although that was the ultimate goal. After all, he had just exhorted them, "If we say that we have no sin, we deceive ourselves and the truth is not in us" (1:8). Yet at the same time, obeying Jesus' word only works as a sign to distinguish between true and false believers and to reassure believers who were obeying Jesus to some observable degree.

Later in the letter, the apostle returns to the theme of perfection, but he uses it in a surprising way, at least for contemporary American Christians:

> God is love, and those who abide in love abide in God, and God abides in them. Love has been perfected *(teleioo)* among us in this: that we may have boldness on the day of judgment, because as he is, so are we in this world. There is no fear in love, but perfect *(teleios)* love casts out fear; for fear has to do with punishment, and whoever fears has not reached perfection *(teleioo)* in love. We love because he first loved us. Those who say "I love God," and hate their brothers and sisters, are liars; for those who do not love a brother or sister whom they have seen, cannot love God whom they have not seen. (1 John 4:16b-20)

36

To the contemporary American reader, the use of the words "perfect," "perfection," and "perfected" can only mean that the apostle is either exhorting us to do something we can never achieve or warning us about our deficiencies. Certainly there is an element of warning in this passage as there is in similar passages throughout the letter. But here, the apostle is primarily trying to reassure his readers that they are right with God. Two interrelated and reassuring signs are mentioned. First, they experience God's love and acceptance which leads to inner confidence in God rather than fear of judgment. Second, as they experience God's love, that love overflows to their brothers and sisters. And the consistent pattern of loving their fellow Christians that their lives display in turn reassures them that they are indeed right with God. John assumed that his readers had experienced both of these reassuring signs in their lives.[12] But if that interpretation is correct, then it implies that John is using forms of the word *teleios* to refer to things *already present* in his readers' lives. Even if they did not always feel confident in God's love or always love their brothers and sisters, they must have done so at least with some consistency. Otherwise, there is no reassurance in the passage, only warning.

As we have seen, even in passages where "perfect" is a good translation, there is some reason to think that *teleios* can in some measure be realized in this life. In other passages in which modern translators choose "mature" they do so because the biblical writers were using *teleios* to describe something that they definitely expected their readers to experience in this life. In such passages, the background of the word *teleios* is in the realms of human development, education, and philosophy. In antiquity, children were seen as "undeveloped of character, bodily weak, emotionally unstable, and intellectually deficient, and were thus unable to reach the standard of the ideal human being, which was the (male) adult." Children needed a teacher who would form them through a process of moral and intellectual training *(paideia)*. If this training process worked properly, the child would become a "complete," "whole," or "mature" *(teleios)* human being.[13] Some ancient philosophers went further, claiming that only those who had attained true wisdom or correct philosophy were "complete" or "perfect" human beings.[14] But in everyday usage, a person was probably considered *teleios* if they had the physical, emotional, moral, and intellectual capacities to live as a responsible adult. A "mature" or "complete" adult was not perfect, but neither did he suffer from significant deficiencies in any of these areas. In the ancient world, a person was *teleios* if he had achieved basic competency in being human.

The New Testament writers have this background in mind when they use the word *teleios* in conjunction with the metaphor of developing from infancy to adulthood to talk about the process of spiritual growth. In the book of Hebrews, the author pauses in the midst of a lengthy and deep theological discourse on the superiority of Christ to exhort his readers:

> About this we have much to say that is hard to explain, since you have become dull in understanding. For though by this time you ought to be teachers, you need someone to teach you again the basic elements of the oracles of God. You need milk, not solid food; for everyone who lives on milk, being still an infant, is unskilled in the word of righteousness. But solid food is for the mature *(teleios),* for those whose faculties have been trained by practice to distinguish good from evil. Therefore let us go on toward perfection *(teleiotes)*[15] . . . not laying again the foundation. . . . (Hebrews 5:11–6:1)

The author takes for granted that after a reasonable period of time, Christians should move from spiritual infancy to spiritual adulthood, to maturity. In fact, this exhortation makes no sense if "mature" *(teleios)* means an unattainable perfection. The author is actually accusing his readers of having regressed to spiritual infancy — something much worse than being a "baby" Christian for the first time.[16]

Although the primary purpose of the passage is to exhort his readers to stop wavering and instead persevere in their faith in Christ, in the process the author reveals some differences between spiritual "infants" and spiritual "adults." Spiritual infants are still learning the basic teachings about God. And even if they know some of these basics, they are not so good at applying them to life. Mature Christians, in contrast, know foundational Christian teachings well enough to explain them to others. They have begun to eat "solid food" — that is, they are learning deeper theology. They have good discernment: they apply God's word correctly to new situations in order to live a moral life. And they can tell the difference between God's truth and false teachings. The author goes on to say that instead of falling away (Hebrews 6:4-8) his readers need to recall their former days of diligent work and love on behalf of their fellow Christians (Hebrews 6:9-12). The implication is that mature Christians persevere in love, even through hard times. Later, the author goes further to claim that our sufferings are God's loving discipline, which produces righteousness in us. Jesus himself suffered, and as children of God, we should expect the same. We respond to trials by fixing our eyes on Jesus and his mature way of facing trials: with joy and perseverance rather than growing "weary" and "losing heart"

(Hebrews 12:1-11). Americans love the idea of being a child of God and having a relationship with God. But much like the original readers of the book of Hebrews, we have "forgotten" (Hebrews 12:5) that our loving Father disciplines us. In contrast, the writer of Hebrews assumes that trials help us become mature, and that maturity in turn allows us to persevere to the end of life with Christ.[17] As we have already seen, James fully agrees that suffering can produce maturity.

The ways Paul uses words like "mature," "infant," "child," and "adult" to describe the Christian life provide additional information about the content of spiritual maturity. We have already seen that in Philippians 3, Paul teaches that a mature Christian understands the gospel of salvation by grace and is devoted to running hard after Christ. In particular, the mature Christian is being conformed to the death and resurrection of Christ (3:10). Most likely, this means suffering that comes from serving with Christ in his mission on earth. Paul does not make an explicit connection between dying and rising with Christ and his ministry in Philippians 3, but in 2 Corinthians 4:7-12 he talks about his ministry and the sufferings that come from proclaiming the gospel as the way he is "always carrying in the body the death of Jesus." In the context of Philippians, this idea of suffering with Christ also hearkens back to chapter 2, where Paul describes the "mind of Christ" by which Christians are to become humble, loving servants who lay down their lives for one another just as Christ did for us (Philippians 2:1-11). In other words, dying and rising with Christ, while it might apply to any kind of suffering, especially applies to the suffering that comes from serving our fellow Christians and spreading the gospel message.

Mature Christians expend effort to become more and more deeply connected to Christ ("I want to know Christ," "gain Christ," "make it my own," Philippians 3:8, 10, 12), realizing that this can only happen because of the power and grace of God ("the righteousness from God, based on faith," "because Christ Jesus has made me his own," Philippians 3:9, 12). They are actively becoming more and more like Jesus, especially by serving others and proclaiming the gospel just as he did. In so doing, they not only suffer with Christ, they have a personal experience of his resurrection power (Philippians 3:10). Mature Christians are not done growing. In fact, they are the ones who are now truly ready to grow closer to Christ and to become more and more like him. Paul saw this ultimate relational union with Christ *in his sufferings and resurrection* as so valuable he described it as of "surpassing value" and eagerly "suffered the loss of all things" to get it. Paul experienced a kind of closeness to Jesus that can only come through suffering with him in his mission and from serving his people. His state of spiritual maturity allowed him to drink more deeply of this profound reality, and that only fired a deeper thirst for more of Christ. Those who talk glibly of a self-focused "relationship with Jesus" or who see the church as an optional tool for enhancing a privatized "relationship with God" need to reexamine this passage to see what they are missing.

Although he emphasized that proclaiming the gospel was his primary call (1 Corinthians 1:17), Paul saw his work as incomplete if those who accepted his message did not become mature in Christ. Writing to the Colossians he said, "It is he [Jesus] whom we proclaim, warning everyone and teaching everyone in all wisdom, so that we may present everyone mature in Christ" (Colossians 1:28). Just after this passage, Paul mentions he is "struggling" on behalf of his readers with the goal that no one will be able to "deceive you with plausible arguments" (Colossians 2:1, 4). Paul seems to have gotten word that the Christians in Colossae were being disturbed by some false teachings about Jesus and the gospel. So he instructs them in a more accurate understanding of Christ and his work on the cross. Paul hopes his readers will not be swayed by false teaching, but instead, "As you therefore have received Christ Jesus as the Lord, continue to live your lives ('walk') in him, rooted and built up in him and established in the faith, just as you were taught, abounding in thanksgiving" (Colossians 2:6-7). The mature are well grounded not just in the truths about Christ, but in a secure relationship with their Lord which leads to further growth and a godly pattern of life ("walk"). This connection between maturity and spiritual stability is repeated later in the book when Paul mentions that Epaphras "is always wrestling in his prayers on your behalf, so that you may stand mature *(teleios)* and fully assured in everything that God wills" (Colossians 4:12).[18] A person who has lots of good feelings about God but who is easily swayed by false teaching or is stuck in habitual sin is not mature.

In Ephesians, we learn from Paul that the glorious, cosmic plan of God produces communities of believers who are growing together into maturity in Christ. After completing his opening discourse on the amazing plan of God for salvation in Christ, Paul begins a new section of his letter with this exhortation: "I therefore, a prisoner of the Lord, beg you to lead a life worthy of the calling to which you have been called" (Ephesians 4:1). Here he is moving into a section in which he describes how his readers are to live in light of the saving work of God. According to Paul, this worthy life is a life of spiritual maturity that can only be experienced by believers who are connected to the body of Christ:

The gifts he gave were that some would be apostles, some prophets, some evangelists, some pastors and teachers, to equip the saints for the work of ministry, for building up the body of Christ, until all of us come to the unity of the faith and of the knowledge of the Son of God, to maturity *(teleion)*, to the measure of the full stature of Christ. We must no longer be children, tossed to and fro and blown about by every wind of doctrine, by people's trickery, by their craftiness in deceitful scheming. But speaking the truth in love, we must grow up in every way into him who is the head, into Christ, from whom the whole body, joined and knit together by every ligament with which it is equipped, as each part is working properly, promotes the body's growth in building itself up in love. (Ephesians 4:11-16)

This passage has several important things to teach us about spiritual maturity. First, spiritual maturity is central, not incidental, to God's plan. Paul introduces the passage above not just by connecting it to his opening description of God's eternal plan of salvation in chapters 1-3 and by reminding them of the "one Lord, one faith, one baptism" (Ephesians 4:4-5) that unites them, but also by reminding his readers that Christ "ascended on high" so that he could give "gifts to his people" (Ephesians 4:8-9). Connecting spiritual maturity to Christ's ascension connects it to the drama of salvation, to the ultimate purposes of God in Christ. Second, the special gifts and/or roles Christ gives to leaders in the church are for the purpose of equipping all believers to help each other grow up into maturity in Christ. Growth toward spiritual maturity is the job of every Christian, and we need each other's help to get there. Third, maturity includes unity with other believers, knowledge of Christ, and being like Christ. The word "unity" refers back to verse 2, where Paul gave some specific elements of the "life worthy of the calling": "with all humility and gentleness, with patience, bearing with one another in love, making every effort to maintain the unity of the Spirit in the bond of peace." Paul is talking here about more than just feeling emotionally connected to other believers, although that is certainly included. Mature Christians actively love, serve, and maintain peaceful relationships with their brothers and sisters. It is God who has created the unity of the church, but believers must actively maintain it and work to improve it. And given that unity in the body of Christ is the main theme of Ephesians 4:1-16, it is likely that the sort of unloving behaviors that divide the church are especially being singled out as immature. Fourth, Paul insists that we must "no longer be children" who are easily swayed by false doctrines and other deceptions. That must mean that Paul does not envision Christians staying in a state of immaturity.

41

Finally, all of this must happen in community. It is only as each person in the church is serving brothers and sisters, including "speaking the truth in love," that the body can grow to maturity. It is even implied that the body of believers itself can become mature, that a local body of Christ can more or less accurately reflect a mature image of Christ.[19]

There is a certain ambiguity in this passage with regard to how much of this "maturity" is possible in this age. On the one hand, Paul calls for us to stop being immature children. On the other hand, phrases like "the measure of the full stature of Christ" (Ephesians 4:13) and "grow up in every way into him who is the head" (Ephesians 4:15) seem to imply perfectly reflecting the image of Christ. At this point, Paul's use of the term *teleios* may be breaking down under the weight of the glory of Christ. It is one thing to say a person is "complete" or "whole" or "mature" *(teleios)* if they conform to the pattern of normal adulthood. It is quite another thing to think that any human being will in this age be perfectly conformed to the pattern of the Son of God. Since Jesus is not just your everyday human being, there is a limit to how well human beings who have not yet been glorified can be conformed to his perfect image. Yet in his other writings, Paul uses *teleios* to refer to something that believers can attain in this life. Perhaps he is using the word in a completely different way here, but that is doubtful. Most likely, what he means here is that we need to reach some basic level of knowing Jesus and living like him so that we can continue to grow up into the "full measure" of Christ. Indeed, that is just how Paul uses *teleios* in Philippians 3. Although he has not yet reached the goal of perfect union with Christ, it is because of his mature understanding and practice of the gospel that he can run after Christ with such joyful abandon. Perhaps we can summarize what Paul means in Ephesians 4 this way: "become mature together so that together you can more and more accurately reflect the perfect image of Christ."[20]

The exhortations that follow suggest that for Paul, maturity included living a new life that was in keeping with the "new self, created according to the likeness of God in true righteousness and holiness" (Ephesians 4:25). Instead of lying, speak the truth (4:25). Instead of stealing, work and give some of your earnings to those in need (4:28). Instead of evil talk, let your words impart grace to those who hear (4:29). Instead of indulging "bitterness and wrath and anger and wrangling and slander" be "kind to one another, tenderhearted, forgiving one another" (4:31-32). Although they are not perfect, the mature are those who are actively putting off the old self and putting on the new self in these and many other ways. Mature Christians display godly character by living their lives in self-sacrificial love of others (Ephesians 4:17–5:2).

And it is especially interesting that Paul does not set the bar unreachably high in these examples. Mature followers of Jesus may not have reached the pinnacle of selfless love he demonstrated on the cross (Ephesians 5:2), but they have stopped lying, stealing, and verbally abusing others and have replaced those relationship-destroying behaviors with their opposites. They are actively building up rather than tearing down their fellow Christians. Even these basic changes in character and behavior cannot be accomplished without the new creation in Christ (Ephesians 4:24) but Paul assumes they *are* possible in this life. The "works of the flesh" and "fruit of the Spirit" found in Galatians 5 serve a similar function and emphasize the internal character qualities that produce the kind of loving behavior Paul describes in Ephesians 4. Most of the "works of the flesh" and "fruit of the Spirit" have a relational dimension: "enmities, strife, jealousy, anger, quarrels, dissensions, factions, envy" vs. "love . . . peace, patience, kindness, generosity, faithfulness, gentleness, self-control." The character qualities that the Holy Spirit produces in the mature follower of Jesus are especially oriented toward building loving human relationships. Mature followers are becoming the kind of people who can love others in the way each situation requires. As a minimum, they are in the process of putting away blatant sins that harm their brothers and sisters in Christ.

In 1 Corinthians Paul makes use of words related to human development to correct and guide his readers in ways similar to the passage in Hebrews. Paul is especially concerned that the Corinthian Christians divided themselves into factions: "I belong to Paul"; "I belong to Apollos" (1:10-13). They were also taking pride in special knowledge or "wisdom" or perhaps rating their favorite teachers on how eloquent or profound they seemed (1:17-20). Paul rebukes this divisive, prideful approach to Christian teaching by insisting that the gospel of Christ is not some kind of impressive worldly wisdom, but in fact is "foolishness" in the world's eyes — yet a powerful foolishness through which God brings low the proud of this age (1:17-31). After insisting that he never preached the kind of "wisdom" that the Corinthians are using to inflame their pride and create divisions, Paul says, "Yet among the mature we do speak wisdom, though it is not a wisdom of this age or of the rulers of this age, who are doomed to perish. But we speak God's wisdom, secret and hidden, which God decreed before the ages for our glory" (2:6-8). Most likely Paul is referring to the unexpected wisdom of God's plan to become human in Jesus Christ and through his humiliating death to bring salvation to all. Paul then switches from the word "mature" to a contrast between "spiritual" and "natural" people. This move implies that he equates mature with "spiritual" and immature with "natural" (sometimes translated "unspiritual"). What distinguishes "spiritual" (mature) people from "natural" (immature) ones is the Holy Spirit-imparted ability to discern, understand, and accept God's truth (2:10-14). "Spiritual" Christians are not insecure in their beliefs or confused about what is truly important: "Those who are spiritual discern all things, and they are themselves subject to no one else's scrutiny" (2:15). They don't need to prove their spiritual credentials (and indulge their pride) by claiming to be followers of the best teacher or possessing superior knowledge not available to others.

Paul did not leave his readers to wonder which kind of Christians they were: "And so, brothers, I could not speak to you as spiritual people, but rather as people of the flesh, as infants in Christ. I fed you with milk, not solid food, for you were not ready for solid food. Even now you are still not ready, you are still of the flesh. For as long as there is jealousy and quarreling among you, are you not of the flesh and behaving according to human inclinations?" (1 Corinthians 3:1-3). This passage reinforces the parallel between these sets of paired terms in Paul's thinking: infant versus adult, immature versus mature, natural versus spiritual, flesh versus spirit. These parallels are revealing. Mature Christians not only discern, understand, and accept the truth as revealed by the Holy Spirit; they also put it into practice in their lives. Rather than living according to the "flesh" (the old sinful nature or the "merely human" — see 1 Corinthians 3:4), they are led or ruled by the Holy Spirit living in them (see also Romans 8:1-11). The key signs of immaturity that Paul points out in his readers are their jealousy and quarreling, ultimately rooted in pride. Ironically, these same people looking down on others from a supposed lofty perch of superior wisdom were in fact spiritual babies who needed to re-learn the basics. Behavior that destroys the unity and love of the church is a clear sign of spiritual immaturity, no matter how "spiritual" or enlightened those doing it believe themselves to be.

It seems that the believers in Corinth were especially plagued by pride and misunderstanding regarding the "manifestations of the Spirit" (1 Corinthians 12:1; 13:1-2). In his discussion of the proper attitudes toward and use of these manifestations, Paul again makes use of the metaphor of growth to adulthood. After working his way through a catalogue of the gifts or manifestations of the Holy Spirit, Paul emphasizes that God gives these gifts so that recipients can build up and care for each member of the body of Christ. As in a human body, all parts are needed and all parts take care of each other. No one says to another, "I don't need you," and none says, "I'm not part of the body" just because they don't have the "right" gift or role (1 Corinthians 12:4-30).

It is in this context that Paul discusses the "more excellent way" of love. After his extensive description of the many ways that love cares for and serves others, he concludes that the gifts of the Spirit, wonderful as they are, will only be used in the present age, whereas love will exist forever (1 Corinthians 13:8-9). To illustrate this difference between this life and the next, he invokes the analogy of human growth to adulthood: "When I was a child, I spoke like a child, I thought like a child, I reasoned like a child; when I became an adult, I put an end to childish ways. For now we see in a mirror, dimly, but then we will see face to face. Now I know only in part; then I will know fully, even as I have been fully known" (1 Corinthians 13:11-12). Here Paul is saying that what we see and know of God now and what we will experience when we see Christ "face to face" in the age to come are as different as the capacities of a child and those of an adult. But in the context of the passage, we see that there is also a crucial continuity between these two states — in particular, the character quality of love that we can begin to experience even now. True, in this passage Paul is using the metaphor of "adult" to refer to a state that will only be reached in the age to come. But even here, there is a subtext that suggests that it is because he is mature and has "put an end to childish ways" that Paul is able to instruct the Corinthians in the way of love which their childish approach to "knowledge" and spiritual gifts has caused them to neglect.[21] And even though perfect knowledge of God would not be attained until the age to come, there is no reason to believe that Paul had low expectations for how well his readers could learn to love one another in this life.

Later in this same section on spiritual gifts, Paul returns to his more common use of the child-adult metaphor: "Do not be children in your thinking; rather, be infants in evil, but in thinking be adults" (1 Corinthians 14:20). Paul is using the metaphor of child versus adult to rebuke them for their shallow thinking about and misuse of speaking in tongues. Just as infants or young children have little firsthand experience with evil, so they should not be engaged in it. But when it comes to thinking well about the things of God and how to behave in his church, they should be mature adults. Here, as in most other places in which Paul uses this analogy, "mature" or "adult" especially refers to the ability to think well about the things of God. The Greek word used here for "thinking" is only used this once in the New Testament and refers to "mature reflection as opposed to childish emotionality."[22]

This "mature reflection" or "adult thinking" is available to all, not just to those who have been following Christ for decades or who have advanced degrees in theology. Anyone with basic competence in the Christian life would know that all things should be done in love or that speaking to people in a language they don't understand will not help them glorify God. Mature Christians have the knowledge and discernment to use the things of God for the loving purposes he intends. To do that, one needs to know, for example, what "manifestations of the Spirit" are and why God gives them (1 Corinthians 12), what love is like (1 Corinthians 13), and how to apply those truths to the use of the gifts in corporate worship (1 Corinthians 14). No doubt the Corinthians thought they knew what love was, as do many immature believers. But those who excuse themselves and claim to love others when they do not betray the fact that they are immature. They cannot discern what is wrong in their behavior nor can they discern how to apply the "law of love" correctly, especially in a situation in which they are tempted to self-indulgence. And the specific problems in Corinth make clear the dangers of a self-centered "spirituality" that runs eagerly after emotional experiences but ignores loving care for fellow Christians. The emotional dimension of faith and supernatural manifestations of the Spirit can be wonderful things. But when people caught up in these things sin against others in the name of being "spiritual," they reveal their immaturity. And they raise the possibility that the very elements of their spirituality that they value the most may be empty and meaningless (1 Corinthians 13:1-3).

When children are held up as exemplars for adults in Scripture, it is not their immaturity that is to be imitated. In Jesus' famous saying about the "little children" it is the children's acceptance of their lowly position that is praised as necessary for adults who would enter the kingdom of God.[23] As we have already seen, children were often assumed to be less experienced in sin, and adults were exhorted to disengage from evil in a similar way. In Proverbs, every reader is addressed as "my child" and is expected to be a lifelong learner of wisdom. That is because the "discipline" or "instruction" (the same word in Hebrew) found in Proverbs is for people of all ages, not just children. Yet the very structure of the book as well as much of its content clearly assumes that one can become a wise adult who is able to live well.[24] Paul sometimes compares himself to a child to indicate that, far from lording it over his spiritual children, he takes a humble, even vulnerable position toward them. Once he even compares himself to an "orphan" (abandoned child) if they reject him.[25] Scripture never uses the child-adult analogy to exhort adults to become immature, especially in their ability to think and live well according to God's truth. In contrast, the child-adult analogy is frequently used to exhort Christians to reach a state of competence in the Christian life.

Maturity and Holiness

Maturity and holiness are closely related, but not identical. Confusion on this point plagues efforts to foster spiritual maturity. The New Testament material on holiness has generated plenty of controversy and confusion over the centuries, and this makes it harder for people to understand the relationship between maturity and holiness. At root, many of these debates seem to be about how much holiness can be expected in this life. Unfortunately, as is often the case, these legitimate debates among theologians have generated considerable confusion among ordinary believers. Among the victims of this confusion were my students who insisted that "we can't be holy in this life." Their view of holiness and its relationship to maturity was wrong at such a basic level that we can correct it without needing to resolve all of the deeper controversies surrounding holiness. A simple review of some of the most widely accepted interpretations of the New Testament teaching on holiness will suffice.

Most interpreters agree that the New Testament writers have several meanings in mind when they apply the words for "holy" to living Christians.[26] First, all those who belong to Jesus Christ are already holy; hence they can be called "saints" (holy ones). Paul often addressed the recipients of his letters this way: "to the saints . . . at Colossae. . . ." (Colossians 1:2). In these same letters, Paul often rebuked the "saints" for their sins. So "saint" as a title for all believers means that all those who have experienced redemption in Christ are "holy" in the sense that they are set apart to belong to God and have been cleansed of their sins. But this *status* of holiness does not mean that they are perfectly righteous. So in other passages, the biblical writers exhort believers to "be holy," that is, to devote themselves to the *process* of "sanctification" by which God is making them morally and spiritually pure. The *ultimate goal* of this process is perfect conformity to the image of Christ who is the perfect image of God. Thus for Christians holiness is a current *status,* an ongoing *process,* and an ultimate *goal* only reached in the life to come.

Most Christians over the centuries have believed that the New Testament teaches that *some* moral and spiritual purity is possible in this life. That is, holiness is at least potentially not just a theological status, but a real change in who we are and how we live now. Most have also believed that *complete* purification and *perfect* conformity to the image of Christ will only be accomplished in the age to come.

In contrast, passages that exhort Christians to grow from spiritual infancy to maturity clearly assume that maturity is fully achievable in this life.

Maturity must therefore be a stage in the larger process of sanctification. When a person becomes a Christian, she is a spiritual "infant." After some reasonable season of nurture, growth, and challenge in the context of a loving community of Christ followers, she grows into spiritual maturity. From there, growth in greater and greater holiness continues throughout life.

In fact, spiritual maturity may be more than just an early stage of sanctification. It may actually be a crucial foundation for further holiness. The biblical writers seem to use the word "mature" in this way. The writer of Hebrews exhorts readers to stop revisiting the basic truths and skills that should be mastered by one who is "mature" *(teleios)* and go on to imitate Christ in their "struggle against sin" (Hebrews 5:1–6:2; 12:1-4). They are to do this especially by enduring their trials, which are God's discipline and produce "the peaceful fruit of righteousness" (Hebrews 12:5-11).[27] Paul tells the Ephesians they need to stop being doctrinally unstable children and instead start living and speaking the truth with each other so that they can put off the old person and put on the new person in Christ (Ephesians 4:14-24). He rebukes the Corinthian believers because their prideful squabbling about so-called "knowledge" or "wisdom" betrays the fact that they are infants who lack crucial spiritual capacities. In contrast, the mature are the truly "spiritual" who can know God, understand his truth, and apply it in relationships of genuine love (1 Corinthians 2:6–3:4; 13:1-13; 14:20). Similarly, Paul insists that it is the "mature" who can run hard after Christ the way he does and who will eventually reach the ultimate "goal" or "prize" of perfect communion with Christ (Philippians 3:7-16). Far from being the end point of spiritual growth, spiritual maturity is the base camp from which the ascent of the mountain of holiness can begin in earnest. Figure 2.1 on page 49 illustrates one way to conceptualize the relationship between spiritual birth, maturity, and subsequent growth in holiness. In real life, the upward path of growth is not this smooth, but the diagram shows the general trajectory we should expect.

Summary: The Shape of Spiritual Maturity

What does all of this mean? What do Christians need to know about spiritual maturity? First Christians need to have the right expectations regarding maturity. Spiritual maturity is ***desirable***. Maturity is the gateway to the kind of deep, powerful, experiential relationship with Christ that energized Paul. It is the path to a beautiful life of love. It is ***attainable***, something to be expected in the life of every believer after a normal period of training.

Figure 2.1 Idealized Relationship between Spiritual Maturity and Holiness

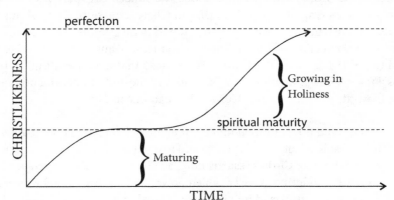

Finally, it is *visible*. People who fail to display the qualities of maturity are either spiritual infants or are slipping back into immature ways. And although no one can completely know the heart of another believer, exhorting certain believers to "grow up," as several New Testament writers do, only makes sense if some visible evidence can distinguish spiritual infancy from spiritual adulthood.

Christians today also need to know the content of spiritual maturity. First, mature believers *know the basic truths* of the gospel and the Christian way of life. Second, they *display discernment:* the ability to apply those basic truths to their lives. In particular, mature Christians are able to detect and stand firm against false teaching and they are able to recognize how to love others in everyday situations. Third, mature believers are *connected to the body of Christ* (the church) where they are *helping others become mature* and are *sharing with them in the mission* of the kingdom of God. Fourth, they *live a life of love*, displaying godly character qualities and avoiding sins that damage relationships. Fifth, they are actively putting off the old self and *growing to become more and more like Jesus.*

In all of this, mature Christians are living a *Christ-focused, cross-and-resurrection-shaped life*. They are not engaged in a self-help project. Their "self" is not something of ultimate concern for them. Indeed, they regard even some of their greatest qualities or achievements as worthless when compared to knowing Christ more deeply and becoming more and more like him. They accept the discipline of the Lord found in their trials and temptations. They know from experience that the deepest "relationship with

Jesus" comes from both the consolations and sufferings experienced in the process of serving others and sharing in Christ's mission. As Paul put it, mature Christians are always carrying around in their bodies both the death and the resurrection of Christ. They have at least begun to taste this life of dying and rising with Christ and are convinced that it is a beautiful, joyful, passionate life. It is anything but "serious and morbid." In commenting on Paul's words in Philippians 3, Gordon Fee had this to say:

> . . . he could throw himself into the present with a kind of holy abandon, full of rejoicing and thanksgiving; and that not because he enjoyed suffering, but because Christ's resurrection had given him a unique perspective on present suffering as well as an empowering presence whereby the suffering was transformed into intimate fellowship with Christ himself.[28]

Mature followers of Jesus may not have run very far yet in this race of dying and rising with Christ, but they are on the path.

Spiritual maturity is indeed beautiful and is the gateway to ever deepening closeness with Christ and conformity to his image. But it is not so difficult to reach that only a small group of the spiritual elite can hope to get there. Rather, it is what we might call *basic competence in the Christian life*, and is available to all those who belong to Christ. If the biblical authors wanted us to think that becoming spiritually mature was unusual or all but impossible, it is unlikely that they would have chosen the everyday analogy of growing from childhood to adulthood to describe it. To become spiritually mature definitely requires the power and grace of God, but it is not impossible and should not be unusual.

The Process of Growth to Maturity

"Growing up to maturity in Christ" does not tell the whole story of the Christian life, but it does tell an important part of that story that tends to be neglected by contemporary American Christians. And it is not enough merely to know that spiritual maturity is possible and even expected. Even knowing the traits of spiritual maturity does not by itself tell us how to get there. What do the Scriptures that use this metaphor teach about the *process* of becoming spiritually mature?

New Christians are spiritual "babies," and that is normal and good. There is nothing wrong with being a baby. Both babies and adults are valued members of the family. We would never say "adults are valuable but babies are not," so there should be nothing in the way we talk about or pursue spiritual maturity that implies that baby Christians are less loved by God or by the church than mature ones. Spiritual babies are hungry for and desperately need spiritual "milk" (1 Peter 2:2). That is, their spiritual mothers and fathers need to teach them the basic truths of the gospel and the Christian way of life. They need to be nurtured in the faith through affectionate relationships with people who help them eat the food of God's word. Paul even compared himself to a mother giving birth to (Galatians 4:19) and tenderly caring for (1 Thessalonians 2:7) his spiritual children. Spiritual growth to maturity happens in the context of a loving spiritual family and requires spiritual parenting. And in its early stages especially, the process may be quite intensive. Anyone who has ever lived in the same household as a newborn knows that frequent feedings are required.

After a reasonable period of growth, spiritual babies should develop into spiritual adults. In addition to regular "feedings" that help them learn the basics, immature Christians need to be connected to others who are "speaking the truth in love" into their lives (Ephesians 4:15). That means more than just telling them the facts about God. A literal translation might be "truthing in love," meaning not only verbally communicating truth, but also " 'maintaining,' 'living' and 'doing' the truth."[29] Paul thinks that Christians should be modeling the Christian life and coaching others in how to live it well. By observing mature Christians and talking with them about life, spiritual children learn the discernment they need; they begin to know how to apply the basic truths of God's word to life. They need "practice" (Hebrews 5:14) to develop discernment, and that practice must be done with help from others.

Just living in the family of God will put spiritual children in situations where they must practice loving others. Even spiritual children can be equipped to minister to others and help their brothers and sisters grow (Ephesians 4:12). And when members of the family sin against them, as will inevitably happen, spiritual children can learn to work for peace and to "bear with one another in love" (Ephesians 4:2). This suffering that happens as we share life with fellow Christians and spread the gospel can be an important source of growth. It is never easy to respond well to suffering of any kind. And when a person suffers at the hand of Christians, it is especially easy to get mad at God and distance oneself from God and the church. Christians who are not yet spiritually mature may be especially vulnerable to these negative outcomes from suffering. So they are especially in need of support, prayer, and guidance to be able to benefit from these difficult experiences (Philippians 2:1-11; Ephesians 4:2-3). But whether the opportunities are pleasant or painful, as spiritual children remain connected to a spiritual family, they will face situations that call for love. As they do, their spiritual coaches can guide them. As this happens, more and more the younger believers learn how to make good judgments about what love demands in most everyday situations.

It is not the teachers and coaches who change people from spiritual babies into spiritual adults. Paul reminds the Corinthians that although he "fed you with milk," he and all their teachers are "servants" through whom God works (1 Corinthians 3:2, 5). He then switches to an agricultural metaphor to capture the truth that God alone is the source of power to grow: "I planted, Apollos watered, but God gave the growth" (1 Corinthians 3:6). Yet spiritual mothers and fathers do have an important role to play. And that role even includes at times correcting spiritual children stuck in infancy when they should be growing up (1 Corinthians 3:1-4; Hebrews 5:11–6:2; Galatians 4:19-20). The spiritual parents in the early church realized that immature Christians would do immature things (quarreling, lying, stealing, becoming enraged, believing false teaching) that needed to be lovingly corrected.

Paul modeled this combination of nurture and challenge in his relationships with the churches he planted. Just after he compares himself to a "nurse tenderly caring for her own children," Paul reminds the Thessalonians that he also "dealt with each one of you like a father with his children, urging and encouraging and pleading that you lead a life worthy of God" (1 Thessalonians 2:7, 11). As with any good parent, a spiritual father or mother in Christ is motivated by a deep love for his or her children. That love motivates not merely an exchange of information but, as Paul expressed it, a deep self-giving: "So deeply do we care for you that we are determined to share with you not only the gospel of God but also our own selves, because you have become very dear to us" (1 Thessalonians 2:8).

In other words, spiritual babies need a good spiritual family. They need to be fed the right spiritual food. They need to practice loving and serving the other members of the family under the guidance of their spiritual parents. Growing up takes time, and even those who are doing all the right things to nurture their spiritual children cannot guarantee that they will develop properly. But growing to maturity is also what we might call a "normal supernatural" process that should work much of the time, because God wants to accomplish it in us.

Biblical Spiritual Maturity vs. Contemporary American Spirituality

We are now in a position to compare the biblical picture of growth to maturity with the traits of contemporary American spirituality. Table 2.1 summarizes those differences.

Table 2.1 Biblical Spiritual Maturity vs. Contemporary American Spirituality

	Spiritual Maturity	Contemporary Spirituality
Expectations	Desirable	Old, stuck, boring
	Attainable	Nobody's perfect
	Visible	Internal, subjective, vague
Content	Know basics	Doctrine hinders "relationship"
	Discernment	Whatever feels right
	Standing firm	Open-ended search
	Communal	If church helps you, great
	Missional	All about me and my needs
	Suffering and Comfort	Feel happy
	Like Jesus	Be myself
Process	Believe the Good News	Be good
	Learn truth	Seek experiences
	Practice in community	Self-defined and Self-directed

As Table 2.1 makes clear, biblical spiritual maturity is centered on Christ and grows in community, while American spirituality is too often focused on the self. It also becomes apparent how emotionally obsessive contemporary spirituality can be. Finally, when doctrine and discernment are left out of the picture, it becomes easy to justify oneself and ignore areas of life that need to change. Ironically, although the term "mature" has become synonymous with "old, stuck, boring," it is more often the spiritually immature who are "stuck." One way to help is to teach what the Bible says about spiritual maturity. God's word is powerful, and those who truly hear — who open their hearts and submit to God — will experience change. But even the reading, study, and preaching of the word of God cannot by themselves transform people from spiritual babies to spiritual adults. People need to be connected to the kind of nurturing and challenging Christian communities that can help them overcome juvenilization and grow up into Christ.

CHAPTER 3

Helping Adults Mature

Spiritual formation . . . is the process by which the human spirit or will is given a definite "form" or character. It is a process that happens to everyone. . . . Terrorists as well as saints are the outcome of spiritual formation. Their spirits or hearts have been formed.

Dallas Willard, *Renovation of the Heart*

I am arguing that thoughts and feelings always interact at some level and that, for the sake of growing to maturity, we should pay attention to this dynamic interaction much more than we do.

Stephen W. Rankin, *Aiming at Maturity*

What might be a good working definition of spiritual maturity?

Spiritual maturity is the foundational level of spiritual formation of the human heart resulting in thoughts, feelings, and choices that display basic competence in the Christian life.

I do not presume to offer this as the only possible definition of spiritual maturity. But identifying and teaching *some* biblically grounded definition of spiritual maturity is an important step in fostering maturity in a congregation, and I applaud anyone who attempts to do it, whether they use my definition or not.

This particular definition has several strengths that can serve us well as we try to foster spiritual maturity among contemporary American Christians. First, in keeping with the teachings of Scripture and the Christian tradition, it faithfully preserves the centrality of the human heart in the process of spiritual transformation. Second, it emphasizes the interaction between the mind, the feelings, and the will in responding to God's grace and truth. Only people who experience God's transformation in all three of these dimensions can achieve the competencies of a mature Christian as taught in the New Testament. Finally, this definition makes clear that spiritual maturity is to be understood as a foundational stage of spiritual formation. More abbreviated ways of describing maturity such as "being like Jesus" or "being a person who loves God and neighbor," while technically correct, assume too much and can therefore be misleading. A spiritually mature person is like Jesus and loves God and neighbor, but in a basic, introductory way. And such shorthand descriptions of maturity, although thoroughly biblical, often do not provide any help in knowing how maturity is to be achieved. Confused Christians quickly start thinking of these simpler formulations as unattainable ideals. Others get excited about the goal but become quickly frustrated when just knowing what they should be like and trying hard to achieve it do not seem to be working.

How are we to help Christians reach a spiritual maturity that impacts their thoughts, feelings, and wills? The New Testament passages that talk about maturity give general guidelines. Leaders must exhort believers to grow up in Christ. They must teach the basic truths of the faith. They must equip believers to speak the truth in love and do whatever else is necessary to help each other grow up into Christ. Communities of faith must become families in which spiritual mothers and fathers are helping their spiritual children practice how to discern right from wrong and truth from error not just theoretically, but in the daily decisions of life.

But these general guidelines still leave plenty of room for questions about implementation. What are the basic truths that every believer must master? How are we to equip Christians to be agents of maturity in one another's lives? How do we help people develop spiritual discernment? How do we help juvenilized adults escape their self-focused and emotionally stunted spirituality and instead value spiritual maturity enough to expend effort to reach it? These are crucial questions that must be answered if our churches are to make much progress in moving from juvenilization to spiritual maturity.

A Process for Growing Spiritually Mature Adults

If my interpretation of the New Testament teaching on maturity is correct, a first step in helping people grow toward maturity is to identify a core body of Christian teaching and help as many people as possible understand and internalize it. Churches and theological traditions will inevitably differ regarding the exact content of this basic teaching. One traditional approach teaches what to believe, how to pray, and how to live using the Apostles' Creed, the Lord's Prayer, and the Ten Commandments. Choices here will have significant impact on the spiritual formation of human hearts. Disagreements over these important matters have created different streams of Christian theology, spirituality, and even separate churches and denominations.

I cannot sort out all of these differences, nor is it my place to arbitrate among them. Fortunately, I do not need to do so in order to achieve the goals of this chapter. Instead, I offer more modest advice to church leaders. First, church leaders should identify the basic teachings of the faith as understood by their faith tradition and start teaching them. Second, I encourage everyone to include in their basic Christian teaching a description of spiritual maturity and some information about how it can be reached. Whatever we decide must be on the short list of foundational truths, we will still need to find ways to help people move beyond basic understanding of those truths. We must also help them embrace those truths and apply them to their lives. That is where having a working model of how people grow and how that growth can be encouraged becomes crucial.

Churches often have mission statements, vision statements, by-laws, and various other official descriptions of who they are, how they operate, or what they believe God wants them to accomplish. When it comes to programming, there is often a rush to offer specialized ministries for children and youth. Church people tend to think it is important to make young people into good Christians, even if exactly what that looks like might be left a bit vague. But clear and well-implemented plans for moving the adult members of the church toward spiritual maturity are rarer. Whatever the reasons for this neglect may be, it needs to stop if we hope to overcome the challenge of juvenilization. Quite a few people, after hearing about the juvenilization of American Christianity, have perceptively asked, "How do we form young people into mature believers if the adults in our church are not mature?"

At the risk of stating the obvious, the answer is to create and implement a congregational strategy for moving adults toward spiritual maturity. Such a strategy would need to include the following elements:

1. A **profile** of what a spiritually mature adult looks like.
2. A **process** or model that clearly explains how adults can grow into that profile.
3. A **plan** for implementing the process.
4. Communal **practices**.

Chapter Two provided a basic profile of the mature believer as well as general biblical teaching regarding the process of growth to maturity. Chapter Five will explain how church leaders can investigate the state of spiritual maturity in their congregations, discern which elements may need more attention, and create a pastoral plan to address those issues. Here our focus will be on explaining a specific model *(process)* of spiritual growth that helps us move from the general biblical guidelines toward specific ministry *practices* that can help adults mature.

There are many models of Christian growth and spiritual formation in existence. The very abundance of resources has perhaps contributed to confusion. Here are just a few of the words and phrases that get used to describe various perspectives on spiritual growth: discipleship, spiritual formation, spiritual mentoring, spiritual direction, spiritual friendship, spiritual disciplines, Christian education. Many of the books on subjects like these attempt to carve out a unique niche or create a "new" approach that is different than what anyone else has written before. Although no one intends it, the result can be that the process of spiritual growth seems complicated and possibly even inaccessible. Even worse, individuals and congregations can be tempted to flit from one approach to another. On the other extreme, some American Christians seem suspicious of any kind of "system" or "method" for spiritual formation. They think that any attempt to systematize the process of spiritual growth will inevitably be either superficial or oppressive.

Instead of getting caught in any of these traps, church leaders need to identify and teach a robust model for helping adults become spiritually mature. The model should then be made operational in regular church practices. Such a model should conform to the biblical teaching on how people mature. It should be flexible and adaptable. Many different kinds of people should be able to use it in different ways and in different settings. It should also be relatively easy to explain and use. If the approach is too complex, too few people will be able to master it well enough to be able to help others grow.

Understanding the VIM Model

The VIM model proposed by Dallas Willard in his book *Renovation of the Heart* meets these criteria. The acronym "VIM" in Willard's model of spiritual formation stands for Vision, Intention, and Means. To catch the *Vision* means to see the kind of person God wants you to become. The picture of a mature Christian should be clearly and compellingly set before each person's eyes, using Scripture to support each point. As people catch the Vision for who God wants them to become, they will be motivated to form the *Intention* to pursue the Vision. Intention means choosing to do whatever it takes to allow God to change me into the kind of person described in the Vision. Those who refuse to take steps or are not sure they really want to expend much effort have not formed the Intention. The answer in such cases is to return to the Vision stage to try to help them truly see and accept God's will for their life. Finally, *Means* are the spiritual disciplines that believers undertake in order to receive God's grace to change into the person God wants them to become. In order to be effective, those spiritual disciplines need to be tailored to the personality and needs of the individual as well as suitable for producing the particular trait of spiritual maturity that is being pursued. As an added benefit, the VIM model works not just for initial growth to spiritual maturity, but also for ongoing growth in holiness. Once they learn the VIM model, mature individuals can continue to listen to God and respond to God's action of spiritual transformation in their lives.

The first step in the VIM process is to listen for what God is doing in the individual's life. Spiritual parents need to listen carefully to those they are mentoring. How is God speaking through the person's story, past and present? What does that say about how God might be transforming the person in this current season of life? Spiritual mentors also need to listen carefully to God's word in Scripture as well as to the guidance and inspiration of the Holy Spirit in prayer. Similarly, those being mentored need to listen carefully to their spiritual parents and to God. More experienced believers get better at listening to God and to what God is doing in their lives to transform them. They become less and less dependent upon others in the process. Yet even the mature do better when they have dialogue partners, spiritual friends who can help them discern how God is forming them in holiness.

In the case of using VIM to help people toward spiritual maturity, the spiritual parent and the spiritual child should listen together to the biblical teaching on the content of spiritual maturity (see chapter two). Since the New Testament writers assumed that every Christian could achieve the traits of maturity, it could work to choose one particular trait together and start working toward it. But greater success is likely if the spiritual mentor and the mentee prayerfully consider together which trait God is working on in the mentee's life in this season. In particular, they should listen to the mentee's life. What do his current struggles, joys, and significant spiritual events say about what God is doing in his life to grow him toward maturity?

Times of listening together to God and to the mentee's life might look like this. After beginning with prayer, including asking the Holy Spirit to guide their speaking and listening, the mentor could say something like, "Tell me a bit about your spiritual life story. What has God done in your life to bring you to this point?" As the mentee shares her story, the mentor asks questions to clarify. "What do you mean by 'then I went through a hard time'? What was hard about it? What do you think was going wrong in your relationship with God at that point?"

The mentor should be careful to avoid offering advice at this stage. The goal is to listen to God and the mentee at the same time. The mentor can be looking for patterns of blessing and challenge in the mentee's life. Those patterns will be helpful later when it comes time to choose which element of spiritual maturity to pursue and how to pursue it. Also, it is good to be aware that spiritually immature people are not always very good at "diagnosing" their own spiritual maladies. So the "presenting issue" or symptoms may or may not determine the direction the VIM process takes. If the mentor starts to form opinions about what God might be doing in the mentee's life, she should wait to hear more before saying much about it. For now, the goal is to listen carefully for what God has done and is doing in this person's life. Rushing prematurely to advice is often ineffective because the mentor does not really know the person well. And even good advice is less likely to be received by a person who does not feel heard, known, and loved by the one dispensing the advice.

On the other hand, encouragement and naming good things in the mentee's life can be helpful even in this early stage of listening. For example, after the mentee shares a significant experience of encountering God, the mentor can say, "It sounds like God really worked powerfully in your life that time. That's great!" Similarly, the mentor can offer sympathy regarding struggles: "I'm sorry to hear about that difficult time in your life."

After some time of listening to the mentee's story, it is time to ask, "What do you think God is doing in your life right now? How might God be growing you?" This is the time to look at the list of traits of spiritual maturity together. The mentor can ask, "Which item on this list stands out to you as the one God may want to grow in your life right now?" Another good question to ask at this stage is, "What do you think of this idea of spiritual maturity? Which parts of it seem attractive or unattractive to you and why?" The aim in this kind of questioning is to begin to get a feel for how well the "Vision" of spiritual maturity presented in the New Testament has captured the mentee's imagination. Questions like, "How do you think your life would be better if it looked more like this profile of spiritual maturity?" can help the mentee articulate reasons why spiritual maturity is desirable. As he articulates those reasons, an emotional attraction to spiritual maturity may grow. Those who are indifferent to spiritual growth are unlikely to make much progress. When helping a person catch a vision for spiritual maturity, it is important to read the Scriptures about spiritual maturity together and discuss what they are saying. Don't just use a list of traits abstracted from those Scriptures. God's Word is powerful. It is only as we understand and accept God's truth that our thoughts and feelings and the inclinations of our wills can be transformed.

The Vision work is complete when the mentee sees what spiritual maturity is and sees it as desirable. But a general Vision of spiritual maturity should be further subdivided into individual Vision statements, with only one element of spiritual maturity as a focus of growth at any given time. This kind of Vision work should result in a simple vision statement that answers the question "What is God doing in my life right now to help me become spiritually mature?" For example, one vision statement might be "To become a person who understands the basic truths of God's word, someone who knows the 'basic elements of the oracles of God' and who has 'laid the foundation' of 'basic teaching'" (Hebrews 5:12, 6:1). As this example illustrates, a vision statement should provide a positive goal that is part of the overall biblical profile of spiritual maturity. It is also helpful to have a supporting Scripture quotation for each vision statement. In some cases, a vision statement like this may need to be subdivided into smaller steps. For example, a vision statement like "to understand the good news about Jesus well enough to explain it to another person" could be a first step in becoming someone who "understands the basic truths of God's word." Table 3.1 on page 62-63 suggests some possible vision statements, supporting Scripture quotations, and possible spiritual disciplines for each of the traits of spiritual maturity. But it is important to help mentees put the Vision into their own words because that will help them in the process of understanding what it is that God wants to do in their lives.

If Vision work is done well, the mentee should be ready and willing to form the Intention to pursue the Vision. A mother or father in Christ can ask questions like, "Are you ready to do what it takes to pursue this vision?" or "Are you ready to pray to commit yourself to this vision, to say an unconditional 'yes' to God?" If the answer is a sincere "yes" then the mentor can ask the mentee to pray such a prayer right then and there. If the mentor senses any hesitation, it is good to ask, "What concerns or reservations do you have about pursuing this vision?" If the mentee is worried about her ability to make much progress, encourage her with the truth of God's help and grace. But if the mentee seems unenthusiastic about the Vision itself, then it is best to circle back and discuss the Vision more. Perhaps the mentor and mentee picked the wrong element of spiritual maturity to pursue. Perhaps the mentee has more basic issues of personal conversion and commitment to Christ and needs to focus first on personally responding to the basic gospel message. For a person who acknowledges the importance of an area of growth intellectually, but has little desire to expend effort, the Vision statement may need to change to something like "to become a person who will *want* to know God's word."

Whatever the problem may be, it is crucial to make sure the Intention is in place before moving on to means. It is *largely a waste of time and may even be spiritually harmful* for a person to start trying to pursue a Vision without having formed the Intention (made a decision) to do so. They will almost certainly make no progress. And their failure to grow will discourage them from trying again. In extreme cases, people who have too many aborted attempts at spiritual growth sometimes decide that the faith is just "not for them." Willard calls his book *Renovation of the Heart* because it is the heart, the deep place in the person where fundamental choices about who I am and who I will become are made, that must say "yes" to God. If the person does not choose deeply from the heart to pursue the Vision, no change will happen.

After the person who wants to grow to maturity has formed the Intention to pursue the Vision God has given her, the next step is to help her identify suitable Means. Means are spiritual disciplines that believers practice in order to open themselves to receive God's grace to change. A spiritual discipline is something I *can* do right now which will allow me over time to receive God's grace so that I will be able later to do something I *can't* do right now. Like the sail on a sailboat, a spiritual discipline is not the source of power to change, but helps us receive more of the wind of God's Spirit.[1] Although I am an occasional recreational runner, I could not possibly go out right now and run a marathon. I would need to train over time and build up to that. But if I put in the training time wisely and diligently over

Table 3.1

Spiritual Maturity Element	Vision Statement and Supporting Scriptures	Spiritual Disciplines*
Know Basics	*To become a devoted follower of Jesus who understands, embraces, and stands firm in the Gospel and the Christian way of life that flows from it.* "It is he [Jesus] whom we proclaim, warning everyone and teaching everyone in all wisdom, so that we may present everyone mature in Christ." Colossians 1:28 ". . . the basic teaching about Christ . . . laying . . . the foundation" Hebrews 6:1	Bible Study Devotional Reading Discipling Meditation Memorization Mentoring Praying Scripture Spiritual Friendship Submission Teachability
Discernment	*To love God and neighbor well by being able to apply God's word to discern truth from error and right from wrong in the situations of everyday life.* "But solid food is for the mature, for those whose faculties have been trained by practice to distinguish good from evil." Hebrews 5:14 "Be transformed by the renewing of your minds so that you may discern what is the will of God — what is good and acceptable and perfect." Romans 12:2	Accountability Partner Confession & Self-Examination Contemplation Chastity Control of the Tongue Discernment Examen Fixed-Hour Prayer Journaling Mentoring Practicing the Presence Prayer of Recollection Rule for Life Spiritual Direction Spiritual Friendship Truth Telling
Communal	*To love the church and take my place in building up the other members of the body of Christ toward maturity.* "But speaking the truth in love, we must grow up in every way into him who is the head, into Christ, from whom the whole body, joined and knit together by every ligament with which it is equipped, as each part is working properly, promotes the body's growth in building itself up in love." Ephesians 4:15-16	Accountability Partner Celebration Conversational Prayer Community Covenant Group Discipling Holy Communion Hospitality Liturgical Prayer Mentoring Prayer Partners Sabbath Small Group Spiritual Direction Spiritual Friendship Truth Telling Unity Worship

Spiritual Maturity Element	Vision Statement and Supporting Scriptures	Spiritual Disciplines*
Missional	*To love Jesus and his mission so much that I actively participate with other followers of Jesus in bringing Christ's life to all people.* "As the Father has sent me, so I send you." John 20:21	Care of the Earth Compassion Intercessory Prayer Justice Prayer Walking Service Simplicity Stewardship Witness
Suffering and Comfort	*To become closer to Jesus and more like him by welcoming both his death and his resurrection power in my daily life and service of others.* "I want to know Christ and the power of his resurrection and the sharing of his sufferings by becoming like him in his death." Philippians 3:10	Centering Prayer Confession & Self-Examination Contemplative Prayer Detachment Breath Prayer Fasting Holy Communion Humility Inner Healing Prayer Rest Retreat Secrecy Self-Care Service Silence Simplicity Slowing Spiritual Direction Submission Unplugging Witness

*Adele Ahlberg Calhoun, *Spiritual Disciplines Handbook* (InterVarsity Press, 2005), provides definitions, descriptions, and ideas for practicing each of these spiritual disciplines.

several months, I probably could run a marathon. Learning to play a musical instrument or speak a foreign language are everyday experiences that work in a similar way. To acquire these skills requires intentional, sustained effort over time.[2] At the beginning, one cannot do much at all. But over time, most people can make real progress. In the case of spiritual disciplines, more than our human effort is at work. Imagine if going out for my daily run somehow connected me to a supernatural source of power to become a stronger, faster runner than I have ever been before. That would be closer to what is possible when God sends down his fire from heaven to consume the sacrifice on the altar of our spiritual disciplines. That's why some of the activities we call "spiritual disciplines" today were traditionally called "means of grace."

Many problems that seem to be about the Means are really Vision or Intention problems. Those who try to embark on a program of spiritual disciplines without a strong Vision that they firmly choose to pursue (Intention) seldom stick with the disciplines long enough to grow. Those who choose Means not well suited to the Vision or not well suited to how God has created them as a person also typically fail to grow. In many cases they just stop doing their spiritual disciplines because they find no spiritual life in them.

In contrast, those who are devoted (Intention) to a goal that God has for this season of their life (Vision) are much more likely to find a way to reach it. If the first spiritual discipline they try doesn't work, they'll drop it and try something else. The focus is not on the Means, but on the goal. If I try to force myself to get excited about long training runs, playing scales on the piano, or wrestling with French pronunciation, it is unlikely I will make much progress. Instead, I need to focus on how great it will be to cross the finish line or play my favorite song on the piano or talk to a new friend in a café in Paris. Vision is fundamental to spiritual growth. It seldom works to tinker with the Means when Vision and Intention are not in place.

For example, many people when asked, "How would you like to grow spiritually?" say something like "I'd like to pray more." This sounds good at first, but it is a trap for inexperienced spiritual mentors. Instead of jumping into the details of the Means such as "When do you pray?" or "What techniques do you use?" it is far more helpful to ask, "*Why* do you want to pray?" or "What is it that you would like to see God do in your life through prayer?" Only after answering the "why?" question well is it possible to choose the correct methods for prayer. In some cases "I want to pray more" just reflects something that the person has been told to do and is not really a desire of the heart at all. Deeper work may need to be done to identify and love the Vision God wants to accomplish in the person's life at this time.

As we saw in chapter one, a good many Christians in American today may be wrongly equating spiritual maturity with the practice of certain spiritual disciplines. Meanwhile, they are not at all clear on what the character of a spiritually mature person is like. This confusion is yet another example of the spiritual harm that comes from focusing on Means apart from a clear Vision.

Assuming the Vision and Intention parts of the process have gone well, the mentor and mentee should begin to discuss possible spiritual disciplines that are likely to contribute to the vision. The mentor should ask something like, "What steps do you think might help you to grow toward this vision?" After the mentee offers some ideas, the mentor can offer additional ones. One resource I use in my teaching and mentoring is the *Spiritual Disciplines Handbook* by Adele Ahlberg Calhoun. This reference book on spiritual disciplines provides brief descriptions of more than sixty spiritual disciplines. The disciplines are organized by category and by the spiritual "desire" (similar to Willard's concept of Vision) to which they correspond. It is helpful for spiritual mentors to use resources like this that provide a greater variety of possible spiritual disciplines than most of us have practiced personally.

A common mistake in spiritual mentoring is to push the mentee to engage in exactly the same spiritual disciplines that have helped the mentor in the past. Table 3.1 shows spiritual disciplines listed by Calhoun that might be helpful for fostering each of the elements of spiritual maturity. The variety of spiritual disciplines listed for each element allows flexibility. Many different spiritual disciplines can potentially help a person move toward each element of maturity.

After identifying a list of possible spiritual disciplines, the mentor and mentee should discuss which ones seem to fit the mentee. In addition to anything that might be indicated by the nature of the Vision itself, they should consider which disciplines are likely to work well given the mentee's personality, current life circumstances, and commitments. For example, extraverts will find it easier initially to learn about God's Word by joining a good Bible study group, while introverts will more quickly and easily benefit from reading the Bible on their own. Parents who are raising very young children will need to think carefully about how they are going to find a time and place to practice their spiritual disciplines. If the mentor has listened well to the mentee's spiritual life story, she will have learned some things about what kinds of spiritual disciplines have worked well for the mentee in the past. The goal is to identify one or two specific and helpful spiritual growth practices that the mentee can really do on a regular basis. It is not always necessary to add a new practice. If the person is already praying and reading the Bible regularly, perhaps the best thing to do is to make the current Vision a focus of that prayer and Bible study. For some of my students over the years, just attending Sunday worship and trying to connect with God and others there has been a simple but profound spiritual discipline. Such a simple practice might be a baby step toward having the communal and missional spirituality that characterizes the mature believer.

It is also important to help the mentee think through the specific details of when, where, and how she will practice these spiritual disciplines. Saying something like "I will pray" is like saying "I will play sports." It leaves many important questions unanswered. *Which* sport will you play? *Where? When?* Do you even know *how* to play that sport? Is that the right sport to develop the particular strengths and coordination that you are trying to develop? Do you have a team? People who are unable to answer these kinds of questions have not finished the process of choosing the *right way for them* to pray, engage God's word, or practice any of the other possible spiritual disciplines that the VIM process has suggested might help.

In addition, spiritually immature people are especially unlikely to have developed skill in practicing spiritual disciplines. After the mentee chooses a spiritual discipline and decides on some particular methods for practicing that discipline, the mentor will need to provide ongoing coaching. A good coach does not just say, "Go out there and make more baskets!" Telling must be combined with showing, watching, correcting, and even drilling if it is to become effective coaching. The mentor also needs to help the mentee discern when to persevere in a given discipline and when to make changes or switch disciplines completely.

Although there is a place for tailoring spiritual disciplines to the individual, mentors should be careful to discourage the idea that spiritual disciplines are totally a matter of personal preference. This is true for at least two reasons. First, Christians need a range of spiritual disciplines in order to grow and may need different practices in different stages or seasons of life. Robert Mulholland has helpfully noted that each person, by virtue of his or her personality, has certain preferred modes of spiritual growth. It is fine for people most often to engage in spiritual disciplines that work easily with their personality. But everyone also needs to develop what Mulholland calls his or her "shadow side" by at least occasionally participating in spiritual growth practices that are not comfortable or easy.[3] For example, an introvert may find it easy to connect with God through individual contemplative prayer, and this mode of prayer will naturally and appropriately become one of the staples of her spiritual life. But to grow spiritually in all dimensions, she will also need at least occasionally to engage in corporate spiritual disciplines like a group Bible study.

Second, some corporate spiritual disciplines are foundational to what it means to be a Christian — a member of the body of Christ and the family of God. In a world in which people are tempted to view spirituality as a self-focused and self-directed journey, it is important to remember that Scripture does not support this view of the mature believer. Scripture makes it clear that prayer, learning God's Word, Holy Communion, serving others, corporate worship, and possibly a few other practices should be part of every Christian's life. And at least one of the passages on maturity, Ephesians 4, teaches that ministering to others in the body of Christ is absolutely essential to individual and corporate maturity. Christians can legitimately practice some private spiritual disciplines in various ways that are best suited to their personalities and current spiritual needs. But to be in Christian community the way that the Bible commands requires that we conform to some corporate patterns of prayer, worship, and learning. The person who says, "I like to pray alone, but worshipping with others at church is not for me" has misunderstood how individual and corporate spiritual disciplines differ. They may also have misunderstood what it means to be a mature follower of Jesus.

Implementing VIM in a Congregation

There are many possible ways to implement the VIM model in a congregation. A first step should be looking at what the church is already doing to see where VIM might already be happening. Does the preaching and teaching on spiritual growth that is done in the church make use of the VIM model when explaining how believers can grow? The "application" section of a sermon is an especially good place to provide a bit more help than is often provided regarding the process of growth. Even if the acronym "VIM" is never mentioned, advice at the end of a sermon about receiving God's grace to change could be structured around that pattern. It could also be helpful to have a series of sermons or a class on spiritual growth to maturity that includes an explanation of the VIM model.

Leaders can also examine existing programming to see where VIM could be helpful. For example, what might VIM look like as applied to an annual cycle of corporate worship? What about VIM as a model for understanding what is happening or what should be happening in adult Christian education? VIM could also be used to teach the process of growth in new members' classes, baptism preparation, marriage preparation, confirmation classes, youth ministries, and even in children's ministries.

The most obvious way to implement VIM is through a program of mentoring in one-on-one or small-group settings. But this is the most intensive, and therefore the most demanding approach. In order for that to happen, sufficient numbers of church members need to understand the model and how to use it to coach others. So the first step in a strategy for implementing VIM in mentoring or small groups in a local congregation would be to gather a group of potential mentors or small-group leaders and teach them the model. The people in those classes would discuss the basic process outlined above and then practice implementing it with one another. As these first church members learned how to use the model, they could then become leaders of future VIM groups. If small groups already exist in a church, group leaders could be trained in the model and then encouraged to make use of it as a tool to help each group member in his or her spiritual growth.

Another way church leaders can facilitate the VIM process without necessarily creating an elaborate mentoring structure is to make spiritual disciplines more accessible to members of their congregations. What spiritual disciplines are already happening in the church, and what qualities of spiritual maturity are those activities producing in church members? What spiritual disciplines are not currently common, but would likely help many church members take their next steps toward spiritual maturity? Making use of Table 3.1, church leaders could prayerfully discern which element of spiritual maturity is most needed among their congregation members at this time. Then they could choose a few of the disciplines listed next to that element of maturity and provide teaching or written information that would help interested church members begin to practice one or more of those disciplines. In introducing that information or announcing a class on how to practice these disciplines, it would be helpful to explain that these spiritual disciplines are being promoted to help church members grow in a particular dimension of spiritual maturity. In other words, lay out a Vision that is likely to convince a good many church members to give one of these disciplines a try. Church leaders should be quick to identify church members who already practice these disciplines well and could serve as teachers, coaches, or advisors. As noted above, many people are lost when they hear an exhortation from the pulpit like "pray" or "read the Bible." The spiritually immature especially need practical teaching and sometimes even individualized coaching in order to learn how to engage in these and other spiritual disciplines effectively. By identifying and mobilizing congregation members or guest speakers with expertise in certain spiritual disciplines, leaders can help interested church members learn how to engage in practices that help them mature. In all of this, leaders should be thinking not just about creating programs but about building a community that understands, values, and talks freely about growth to spiritual maturity.

Like any model of spiritual growth, VIM will only work for people who care enough about spiritual maturity to put forth some effort. But as we saw in chapter one, a good many contemporary American Christians may not be highly motivated to pursue spiritual maturity. How can we help more people desire to grow?

A Change of Heart

Spiritual growth to maturity requires that thoughts, choices, and feelings all work positively together under the influence of God's grace and truth. If one or more of these dimensions of the person is uncooperative or actively rebelling against God, spiritual growth is either difficult or impossible.[4] A further problem is that since these three elements of the person are so intertwined, working on one in isolation from the others is often ineffective. As we saw in chapter two, the biblical teaching on maturity highlights the cognitive dimension of spiritual growth: knowing the basics and being able to discern how to apply them in real life. But having the will to learn and apply the truth and the feelings that support such choices can make or break the process.

When it comes to sorting out why some people are devoted to God and become more and more like Christ while others do not, the Bible and the Christian tradition often make use of the word "heart." This important word is used over 1,000 times in Scripture and refers to the core of the person, their deepest values, choices, and identity. There is a debate among Christians regarding which human functions are included in the biblical conception of "heart." Some prefer to emphasize that the "heart" refers especially to the will, the human capacity to make choices, especially those fundamental choices about who I am and who I will become. Others note that some Scripture passages speak of the heart as including thoughts and even feelings.[5]

In modern times, further confusion arises because of the way people commonly use the word "heart." In popular usage, even among Christians in church, "heart" refers *only* to emotions and is often contrasted with "head," which *only* includes thoughts and reasoning. As many have noted over the years, it is unbiblical and spiritually harmful to see the heart as *only* emotional, and we should do all we can to root out this sloppy way of thinking and speaking. It is also devastating to spiritual growth to see feeling and thought as fundamentally pitted against each other, as if we must choose which one will "win" in every situation. Similarly, ignoring the close relationship between our most powerful, life-shaping emotional patterns and the core of who we are does violence to what the Bible, the Christian tradition, and our everyday experience say about how human beings work.

Fortunately, this is another case where we do not need to definitively resolve a perennial theological debate in order to foster spiritual maturity. We can help people overcome many common obstacles to maturity so long as we learn how to work constructively with the dynamic interaction of thoughts, feelings, and will. The VIM model and what I will have to say about emotions below work whether one believes the heart is more or less synonymous with the will or whether one thinks it is a more complex reality that includes will, thought or even some kinds of feelings. Even in my definition of spiritual maturity I use "heart" in a way that is compatible with different views about which human capacities are included in it.

Figure 3.1 illustrates the proper relationship between the will, thoughts, and feelings as rightly ordered under God.[6] As the diagram illustrates, God rules the person through the will, and the will, thoughts, and feelings ideally cooperate to help the person make godly choices that result in godly behavior and spiritual growth. Although the will when necessary must regulate or even reject certain thoughts and feelings in order to obey God, the will also needs thoughts and feelings in order to operate. Imagine trying to make a choice that is completely detached from thought or feeling. No human being ever makes any such choices. In some cases feelings may seem to dominate a decision; in others thoughts may seem to predominate. But in all human choosing, thoughts and feelings are present and are highly influential on the outcome.

Figure 3.1

For example, imagine a person who goes on a retreat and experiences a powerful encounter with God through close relationships, singing, and teaching. In response to her encounter with God's love and truth, she deeply and sincerely prays to give herself more fully to God. Things she had heard about Jesus before suddenly seem more real and more emotionally powerful for her. She returns home and begins reading the Bible and praying daily. She finds a new level of joy in Christ and begins to look forward to daily times with God in prayer. She starts attending church more faithfully and finds herself feeling more affection toward fellow Christians. After hearing a sermon on serving Christ and his kingdom she rearranges her schedule to serve as an adult volunteer in the youth ministry.

How has God made these changes in her life? On that retreat her experience of God (feeling) and caring relationships with other Christians (feeling) combined with the preaching of God's word (mind) to motivate her to make choices (will) to give herself to God and to engage in spiritual disciplines after the retreat. Those spiritual disciplines in turn exposed her to more of God's truth (mind) which started to reshape her attitudes (feeling) and actions (will). All of this reshaping of her mind, will, and emotions was empowered by the working of the Holy Spirit, but it also required her active participation. My attempt to label some of these experiences as "thought" and others as "feeling" or "will" probably seems arbitrary — and rightly so. Although it is helpful to distinguish the particular roles that thought, feeling, and will play in our lives, they most often function as an integrated whole, and this is certainly true when God is at work in a spiritual awakening like this.

As this example illustrates, one of the most important ways that God works through the human will is to motivate it to choose to participate in spiritual growth practices that fill the mind with truth, retrain the body, and reshape the emotions along godly patterns. And it must be noted that one of the most important choices anyone makes is the choice to commit to growing with other Christians in community. Yet even in the best Christian environments, some people get "stuck" and others refuse to grow. Why? Often it is because emotional experiences do not translate into a transformed will that rearranges the person's life to pursue further growth. Older patterns of thinking, feeling, and choosing take over again after the retreat or mission trip.

Emotions as Resources and Obstacles to Growth

When mind, will, and feelings are working together properly in Christ, spiritual growth runs relatively smoothly. But when they persist in their sinful state of conflict and continue to sabotage one another, growth is often thwarted. Among contemporary American Christians, it seems that feelings are too often obstacles rather than resources for spiritual growth. Table 2.1 makes it clear that emotions loom large in contemporary American spirituality, but not in ways that foster spiritual maturity. American Christians tend to think that spiritual growth and spiritual maturity are primarily internal, emotional matters. They don't have positive feelings toward the word "mature" because it sounds like someone who is old, stuck, or boring. They value a sense of emotional connection with God and feel that doctrine might get in the way of that relationship. They value church, their faith, and perhaps even God himself because these things help them feel better about their problems or feel happy. They think that the way to grow closer to God is to seek new and better emotional experiences. Because of self-absorption, pride, or emotional neediness, they sin against love and destroy the unity of the church, all the while justifying themselves and blaming others.

Some who have read my earlier work on juvenilization and spiritual maturity have accused me of taking a negative view of emotions or of wrongly equating being emotional with being immature.[7] Let me be clear: Emotions are powerful and created by God for our good. We would be less than human and life would be less than good if we had no emotions. The difference between immature and mature Christians is not that immature Christians have powerful feelings and mature ones do not. Rather, mature Christians have or are developing godly emotional patterns while immature believers are stuck in emotional patterns that hinder spiritual growth. Thus in order to help contemporary American Christians grow toward spiritual maturity we need to understand how emotions work and how an individual's most life-shaping emotional patterns develop.

Emotions are inner urges that arise in us because of what we think is happening or might happen in a particular situation.[8] Rather than seeing thought and feeling as fundamentally opposed, it is more helpful to realize that they are always linked. As Dallas Willard notes, every thought evokes a corresponding feeling.[9] So, for example, when I see my young child reaching out to touch a pot of boiling water, I feel fear. Why? First, I know from past experience that burns are painful and damaging. I perceive that this pot is hot and will therefore cause harm to my child. My feeling of fear is based on a correct judgment about the danger present in this situation. All this thinking and feeling happens in an instant because I have over the course of a lifetime formed the habit of perceiving hot things as dangerous and to be feared. Why does my child reach out to touch this dangerously hot pot? Because she does not yet know about hot things and burns, so she feels no inhibiting fear. In her case, ignorance and inexperience are preventing her from having the appropriate feeling that could be a big help in this situation.

So emotions and thoughts work together to shape both our inner life (heart) and our actions. If my thoughts and feelings about a given situation are in alignment with each other and with the truth, then emotions become a source of strength to act and may even contribute to clearer thinking. The fear I feel in the moment my child reaches for the hot pot can focus my attention and action to prevent a serious injury. At a higher level, my ability to empathize with others and perceive what is happening emotionally with them is crucial to thinking well about how to lead them or help them grow in Christ. Those with low emotional intelligence typically make worse decisions based on incomplete or incorrect thinking about how their decisions will affect other people.[10]

When it comes to *emotional patterns,* more is at work than just a judgment or perception about an individual situation. Human beings typically respond to the circumstances of their lives in patterns of thoughts and emotions that are rooted in their deepest values and priorities, their underlying life orientation which, according to Scripture, dominates the "heart."[11] And that life orientation is the product of a lifetime of experiences that have shaped their thoughts, feelings, and choices into recognizable patterns. Suppose that I see my child touching a hot pot with a stick. I may still tell her to stop, but I probably won't feel the same fear I did when she was reaching to touch the hot pot with her hand. Why? The tip of the stick is not as important to me as my child. Therefore danger to the stick does not evoke fear in me. In contrast, my deep love for my child causes all things related to her to have more emotional power for me. When she shows me affection, I experience joy. When she is disobedient, I feel anger. In fact, when something is important enough to us, we can experience strong emotions just by thinking about good or bad things happening to it. Emotional patterns are shaped by our deepest loves, the people and things to which we are most deeply committed and with which we most deeply identify — the things to which our hearts are most deeply attached.

Thus emotions give us valuable, if not always completely reliable, information about reality. My feeling of fear about the hot pot alerts me to real danger for my child. On the other hand, if I suddenly feared that purple elephants would trample my child in our backyard, my emotional response to that thought would not correspond to reality. At times we need to think twice about a situation and our emotional response to it before we act. Often our feelings are disproportionate or even misleading because our perception or judgment about the situation is incorrect. Of course, realizing that something is not a real threat does not necessarily remove the feeling of fear. But it might give just enough perspective to allow me to resist the urge to run and instead stay to help.

Even if my individual emotions do not always provide reliable information about the world *outside* me, my patterns of emotional response over time can tell me something true about what is *inside* me. My pattern of fear when I see my child in danger says something about my underlying love for her and the high value I place on her happiness and safety. If, on the other hand, I regularly felt joy when I saw my child about to injure herself, that would say something horrifying about the moral formation of my heart. My emotional patterns provide important information about who I am as a person and what I deeply value, about what my heart has chosen to love over time. Far from being unimportant, secondary matters, emotional patterns are the outflow of my heart produced by a lifetime of experiences, thoughts, choices, and actions. Those patterns of emotional response are now part of who I am, and those parts of me play a crucial role in fostering or hindering spiritual growth.

Helping People Develop Mature Emotional Patterns

Those who are maturing in Christ have come to love God and deeply desire to grow. Those who are stuck in immaturity love something else more than they love becoming like Christ. In Dallas Willard's terms, the spiritually immature person is experiencing entanglements of the will. They have chosen too many things, or the wrong things, to be at the core of their lives.[12] A lifetime of choices has given their heart a particular shape that resists change.

Self-deception often stiffens this resistance to change. We deceive ourselves into believing we love God first when in fact we love several other things just as much. And such self-deception is especially likely when we sense that the emotional cost of recognizing who we really are is so high. Such Christians are often the ones who wreak havoc in families and churches all while claiming to be spiritual. They "know" that Christians are supposed to be loving, but they excuse their own community-destroying sins because they are blind to the warped shape of their hearts. Their false image of who they truly are is in turn jealously guarded by their long-standing emotional patterns. This is what went wrong with the Christians in Corinth to whom Paul wrote.

Even when Christians begin to recognize the malformation of their hearts and desire to be transformed in Christ, old emotional patterns regularly hinder their progress. According to Scripture and many Christian theologians throughout the centuries, one of the most important ways God changes our emotions is by helping our minds and wills be captured by God's truth.[13] The writers of Scripture assumed that knowing God and God's truth held the key to emotional healing. That is why so many Scripture passages that teach about emotional matters provide good reasons to feel certain ways. For example, Scripture tells Christians they can feel joy because God made us and claims us (Psalm 100:3), God is good, loving, and faithful (Psalm 100:5) and has saved us (Psalm 51:8, 12), we have brothers and sisters in Christ (Philippians 4:1), we know that our suffering is producing holiness in us (James 1:2-4; Romans 5:1-5), and God has blessed us in many ways so that we always have something for which to be grateful (1 Thessalonians 5:16-18). These same Scripture passages usually suggest a course of action — often praising, thanking, or worshipping God — as a way to grow in joy. Thus thought, feeling, will, and action all come together to receive and experience God's gift of joy, including an emotional uplift.[14]

Similarly, Scripture passages that tell us to love God and others, fear not, have hope, and so on typically give good theological reasons why those responses correspond to reality no matter what our internal experience or external circumstances might be. It is certainly true that Christian love must be put into action even when the feelings of the moment are not cooperating. Yet it is equally true that God wants us to regularly feel love toward those we are serving. In fact, transformed emotional patterns will make us better at loving others. In the parable of the Good Samaritan, presumably the priest, Levite, and Samaritan all knew that the loving thing to do would be to help the man who had been robbed, beaten, and left for dead. But only the Samaritan was "moved with pity" (Luke 10:33) and so took loving action. On the other hand, it would have also been in keeping with biblical teaching if the priest had stopped to help even though he did not feel compassion in that moment. Indeed, doing so might have been one step in the process of God transforming him into the kind of person who regularly experienced compassion for those in need. As one of my intellectual mentors once put it, "expressing love increases love." What we do with our bodies can over time reshape our thoughts, feelings, and choices.[15]

At this point it is important to be cautious and realistic. Knowing good reasons to be joyful and engaging in actions appropriate to joy does not always quickly or easily produce a new emotional pattern of joy. It is only as our thoughts and our will become more and more conformed to God's reality over time that our emotional responses will conform more and more to God's original intention. Spiritual transformation of emotions happens indirectly, and it often takes time. This makes sense given our normal experience of emotions. It is often impossible to stop feeling a certain way in a given moment. Only less powerful, relatively easy to change emotions are typically subject to the exercise of our wills in the moment. But when we are talking about immature emotional patterns that are hindering our growth, we are dealing with precisely the kind of emotional responses that are the hardest to change in the moment of temptation or of emotional turmoil — what Dallas Willard refers to as "on the spot."[16]

So the way to change negative emotional patterns is through godly training "off the spot." We need to allow God to change the underlying condition of our hearts that is producing the ungodly emotional pattern. This happens as we engage in spiritual disciplines that retrain our mind, will, emotions, and even our bodies. The person must practice the right spiritual disciplines "off the spot," that is, outside of those moments when he is most tempted to yield to the old immature, sinful emotional pattern. Over time, God will work through those spiritual disciplines to transform the person into someone who has a new heart with different loves. Those changes in life orientation will create new patterns of emotional response. The Christian will regularly feel love for brothers and sisters in Christ and hatred toward evil, rather than struggling with the opposites of these emotional patterns.

Thus the VIM model can be used to facilitate God's transformation of our emotions. First, identify the hindering emotional pattern. Second, using Scripture, identify the opposite, godly emotional pattern and the truths and actions that support it. Third, using questions aimed at uncovering entanglements and duplicity of the will, probe the underlying heart condition that is producing the negative emotional pattern. Fourth, create a Vision statement that expresses the desired change in what the person loves (heart), names the old emotional pattern to be replaced, and describes the new emotional pattern God wants to create. Fifth, pray, asking God to change the heart, surrendering the negative emotional pattern to God, and committing to do whatever it takes to allow God to create the new emotional pattern. Read, study, meditate on, and memorize key Scripture passages that support this Vision for the new emotional pattern. Finally, in light of the results of the earlier interrogation of the will, identify and practice other spiritual disciplines that are likely to open that particular dimension of the heart to God's transforming power.

For example, many contemporary American Christians have an emotional aversion to the word "mature." A spiritual mother or father in Christ could ask such a person, "What thoughts and feelings come to mind when you hear the word 'mature'?" and "What thoughts and feelings do you think God wants you to have toward spiritual maturity?" The mentor and mentee could then read and discuss Scriptures about spiritual maturity to see why it is desirable. For example, they could discuss Paul's burning desire to "know Christ" found in Philippians 3 as well as other passages that use the word "mature" in order to find the reasons why maturity is better than immaturity. They could examine episodes in the life of Jesus that show how wonderful it would be to be more like him, reflect on how their life would be different if "the fruit of the Spirit" rather than "the works of the flesh" dominated (Galatians 5), or ponder the description of love found in 1 Corinthians 13. These and many other Scripture passages make it clear that spiritual maturity is beautiful and more to be desired than whatever has entangled their heart.

Next they could discuss probing questions in order to reveal the underlying heart condition that is making spiritual maturity emotionally unattractive. What are the things that I love more than spiritual maturity? Why do I love those things? What does God want me to do in response to this new knowledge about the sources of my negative feelings toward maturity? It can also be helpful to identify the underlying good that the person's heart is seeking and explore better ways to pursue that good. Since sin and the devil cannot create anything new, but can only pervert the good things God created, most entanglements of the will are attachments to something good. The problem is that the person loves that thing more than God. The desire for that good thing or the fear of losing it is pushing the person to sin. Some probing questions can help. What is the underlying good thing that you are seeking through this negative pattern of thinking, feeling, and acting? What are the results of pursuing this good thing in the way you are currently pursuing it? How do you think God wants you to pursue that good thing? What is preventing you from believing and acting on what Jesus said, "Those who want to save their life will lose it, and those who lose their life for my sake will find it" (Luke 9:24)? The result of this process would be a Vision statement such as "To love God more than I love being 'cool' so that I no longer feel afraid of becoming more like Jesus but instead regularly get excited about it."

Such a person might benefit from spiritual disciplines designed to help him reprioritize his loves, such as detachment or pursuit of simplicity. The practice of examen, which asks the individual to ponder the events of each day looking for moments of closeness and distance from God, could raise awareness that moments of "feeling cool" are not in fact life-giving. Or perhaps fasting from image-enhancing practices such as looking in the mirror a lot or taking a long time to choose the day's clothing could discipline the desire to look cool. Intentionally choosing to serve in hidden ways, such as setting up chairs or emptying wastebaskets, could help with the prideful desire to be the center of attention. The possibilities for spiritual disciplines are endless, and should be adapted to the personality, life history, and particular sinful emotional patterns of the individual.

Table 3.2 on page 79 shows some connections between transformed emotional patterns and growth in the elements of spiritual maturity as taught in key New Testament passages. Many of the biblical terms listed in Table 3.2 should be seen as not *exclusively* emotional. However, all the terms listed in Table 3.2 have an important emotional component, and until the underlying heart conditions change, those sinful emotional patterns will continue to block growth. There is a two-way relationship between the traits of spiritual maturity and the emotional patterns listed in Table 3.2. Those who are growing in one of the traits of maturity will begin to experience a corresponding change from sinful to godly emotional patterns in that area of their lives. Looking at the relationship from the other direction, those who experience sinful emotional patterns may need to engage in VIM along the lines suggested above in order to remove that obstacle to growing in a particular trait of maturity.

Given that I have defined spiritual maturity as "basic competence in the Christian life," what level of godly emotional patterns should be expected in a spiritually mature person? A spiritually mature believer will not have conquered all negative emotional patterns or developed a full and consistent set of godly emotional patterns. She will still struggle at times against feelings that are at odds with what she knows to be right and true. And she will also sometimes fail to have the right feelings of love, joy, peace, or hope (or anger at injustice or sin, for that matter). But she will have understood and accepted God's ideal for our emotional lives and will have started on the path toward godly emotional patterns. She will have had a change of heart that produces a genuine love of Christ and a desire to become more and more like him. That heart change will be deep enough such that when convicted by the Holy Spirit or corrected by a sister in Christ, she will quickly admit her sin, repent, and try to repair the effects of her wrongdoing. The mature believer will begin to develop emotional patterns that push her to love God, learn the truth, and put it into practice in her life. In contrast, the immature believer is typically stuck in old emotional patterns that blind him to his own

Table 3.2 Emotional Patterns and Spiritual Maturity

Sinful Emotional Patterns	Godly Emotional Patterns	Maturity Scripture	Elements of Maturity
Complacency	Zeal Love for Christ	Phil. 2:1-16	Know Basics (Gospel) Desirable, Attainable & Visible
Pride Self-righteousness	Humility Joyful "loss of all things" Love for Christ Love of righteousness Love of true wisdom	Phil. 2:1-16 1 Cor. 1–3	Know Basics (Gospel) Discernment Suffering & Comfort Jesus centered, not self-centered
Bitterness Wrath/sinful anger Malice	Forgiveness Kindness Gentleness Compassion Patience Love of brothers and sisters	Eph. 4:2, 31	Discernment Communal
Instability Confusion	Love for God Love of truth Love of brothers and sisters	Eph. 4:14-15	Missional Know basics Discernment
Confusion	Love of truth	Col. 1:28	Standing firm
Jealousy Quarreling	Humility Love of brothers and sisters	1 Cor. 3:1-4	Discernment Communal
Despair Fear	Hope Joy in suffering	Heb. 5:11–6:11	Suffering & Comfort Standing firm
Laziness Indifference	Desire to learn Love of righteousness	Heb. 5:11–6:8	Know Basics Discernment

sin and kill his motivation to love God and others. He has to keep re-learning the basics because he never really came to love God enough to apply himself to learning and loving the truth. For the immature believer, the dynamic interaction of thought, feeling, and will often pulls him away from God and from spiritual growth. In contrast, the mature believer has been transformed by God so that thought, feeling, and will now work together much of the time as an engine of spiritual growth.

If spiritual maturity is the job of the whole church, then emotional maturity is, too. Fortunately, anything that is done to help people's minds and hearts embrace the biblical vision for spiritual maturity will also help heal their emotional patterns. A congregation that makes spiritual maturity a priority will find that such efforts "spill over" into emotional transformation of church members. Yet given the power and brokenness of emotions in so many people's lives, more specific help will be needed in many cases. That means that churches need to become intentional about providing teaching, practices, and safe places for people to engage in the work of emotional growth. Implementing VIM as a congregation model for growth could help. Teaching on emotions and God's plan for emotional transformation will also help. A good many people find their emotional patterns improve just by being connected in friendships with loving brothers and sisters who are encouraging them in Christ.[17]

Spiritual transformation of emotional patterns will be messy at times, and only the kind of love that is willing to "bear one another's burdens and so fulfill the law of Christ" (Galatians 6:2) will pay the price. One church that determined to become an emotionally maturing body of believers showed their love by providing a structured sabbatical for their youth pastor so she and her husband could work on the negative emotional patterns that were tearing apart their marriage.[18] In the end, some church members will refuse God's offer of emotional healing, and so will remain mired in immaturity. Those individuals deserve our love and care. But it is also fine for them to feel a bit of healthy discomfort that comes from being in a community of Christians who are actively challenging each other to grow to spiritual maturity. Thankfully, because God wants to heal our hearts and our emotions, we can expect many wonderful things to happen as we begin together to take steps toward emotional maturity.

CHAPTER 4

Reaching the Tipping Point:
Youth Ministries That Help the Whole Church Mature

A s I tried to show in *The Juvenilization of American Christianity,* youth
ministries are constantly reshaping the church, sometimes revitalizing
it, other times juvenilizing it, and often doing a bit of both at the same time.
It is in their work with young people that churches grope their way toward
what will become church-wide responses to emerging cultural trends. If I
am right about how juvenilization works, then it is crucial for churches to
help teenagers catch a vision for spiritual maturity. Otherwise, they may get
stuck in spiritual adolescence and become the next generation of immature
adults.

But youth ministries are not just a good investment in the future maturity of the church. They are also one of the best ways to produce spiritually
mature adolescents and adults *now.* A growing body of research shows that
the right kinds of youth ministries can help the whole church grow up. We
no longer need to guess or hope for the best when it comes to youth ministry.
Armed with research-based insights, adults and young people can work together to create not just better youth ministries, but congregational cultures
of spiritual maturity.

I am using the phrase "youth ministries" to include the entire range
of possible relationships, structures, activities, and ministry philosophies
that intentionally or unintentionally form young people in a local church.
In this sense, every church has a "youth ministry," whether it hires a youth
pastor, eliminates all age-specific activities, or just lets young people suffer
from benign neglect. As we shall see, the forms that youth ministries take
do matter, but one of the recurring mistakes in the history of youth ministry is to look for the "magic bullet" — the perfect structure, system, or

person that will solve all problems and make youth ministry easy. In fact, history, research on youth ministers, and personal experiences confirm that churches can take opposite paths to the same bad destination. For example, some churches that hire a youth pastor and other churches that eliminate specialized youth ministries both experience the same unintended negative consequence: most adults in the congregation ignoring the spiritual nurture of youth.[1] No model of youth ministry or set of practices can substitute for a congregation-wide commitment to young people. And although adults may be reluctant to shoulder this burden together, it is in fact one of the best ways for them to grow spiritually too. One reason some churches have so little impact on the spiritual maturity of their young people is that so many of their adults are absorbed in endless identity quests or are struggling to cope maturely with the demands of life. Little do these adults know that some of the best potential partners for their spiritual growth are the teenagers sitting at the other end of the pew.

Setting the Right Goal: Devoted vs. Maturing Teenagers

A first step in creating youth ministries that help the whole church mature is to determine what maturing Christian young people should be like. Two important national studies provide portraits of the most devoted Christian teenagers in America today. A comparison of these studies shows that teenagers can be "devoted" to their faith without necessarily being on the path to spiritual maturity. More positively, these studies also show that some churches in America are succeeding in forming young people into mature followers of Jesus. It can be done. Finally, these studies help us identify and apply the right criteria for success in youth ministry.

The National Study of Youth and Religion (NSYR) found the following traits in the most religious group of teenagers in America, the top 8 percent that researchers named "The Devoted":

> Attends religious services weekly or more.
> Says faith is very or extremely important in everyday life.
> Feels very or extremely close to God.
> Currently involved in religious youth group.
> Prays a few times a week or more.
> Reads Scripture once or twice a month or more.[2]

The good news here is that many Christian parents, youth leaders, and young people themselves are already working hard to help the teenagers they know experience these things. We should all keep doing so, because as we shall see below, teens who score high on these kinds of measures are more likely to stay strong in their faith after they leave high school.

Less encouraging is the fact that only about one-quarter of all church-going teenagers experience these elements of faith at a high level. Compare the traits of the devoted with those of the next most religious group of teens in America, the 27 percent that researchers labeled "The Regulars":

Attends religious services two to three times a month or weekly.

Faith ranges from very to not very important in everyday life.

Closeness to God, youth group involvement, prayer, and Scripture reading are variable but less religious than for the devoted.

Not surprisingly, statistical analysis revealed that the faith of devoted teenagers was making a bigger impact on their daily moral choices (they don't abuse substances; they do volunteer) than the weaker faith of the regulars was making in their lives.[3] Being only *sometimes* interested in attending youth group, growing in faith, or getting closer to God does not do much for American teenagers. The regulars, although they can often be found in church, are less likely than the devoted to be growing toward maturity.

Further, the NSYR researchers applied statistical analysis to identify the following factors that positively correlated with teenagers being among the devoted:

- Say parents tend to understand, love, or pay attention to them.
- Say they would like to attend church more often than they do.
- Have more close friends who are involved in religious youth group with them.
- Parent says teen's friends are a positive influence.
- Involved in more organized activities outside of church.
- Evangelical or Mormon.
- Female.
- White.[4]

They also identified parental factors linked to teenagers being among the devoted:

– Attend religious services often and say faith is important to them.
– Married.
– More educated.[5]

We should be cautious about interpreting and applying these findings. First, statistically significant factors like these should not be taken as deterministic. It would be a mistake to conclude, for example, that it is impossible for an African American male whose parents are not married to be among the devoted. Rather, these lists tell us that some kinds of internal and external factors seem to be more favorable to teenage religious devotion than others. Second, these kinds of statistically significant correlations tell us nothing about the mechanisms by which these factors may be encouraging teens to be devoted to their faith. Why are girls more likely to be among the devoted than boys? These findings cannot tell us. Even where the connection between a particular factor and religious devotion seems obvious, such as "would like to attend church more often than they do," we still don't know *why* some teenagers feel this way and others do not.

The most important caution for our purposes flows from these first two. It is possible for a teenager to score high on the measures of being devoted and have many of the supporting factors yet not be maturing in his or her faith. The NSYR interviews confirmed that at least some teenagers who are in church all the time and say faith is "extremely important" to them are nevertheless inarticulate about the content of their faith. Thus they do not display the biblical maturity trait we have named "know the basics." Similarly, NSYR did not often find what we have called "discernment" among American teenagers. Even otherwise highly religious teenagers tend to think that religious and moral beliefs are largely matters of personal preference or are "just how I was raised." They have no idea why they believe what they believe and are not sure how to apply the truths of their faith in everyday life.

So the traits that place a teenager among the devoted could be fully compatible with juvenilized spirituality. For example, a teenager could report feeling "extremely close to God" and yet agree that "doctrine gets in the way of relationship." He could pray and read the Bible sometimes while wrongly equating the practice of these disciplines with spiritual maturity. He could affirm that his faith is "extremely important" to him but be thinking of it as source of personal, individualistic comfort rather than as a source of strength for joining in mission with the church.

Rather than complaining about the study, we would do better to use its findings to challenge our *own* criteria for success in youth ministry. Who wouldn't be thrilled to see young people attending church and youth group regularly, saying they feel close to God and find their faith to be extremely important to them, and at least sometimes praying and reading the Bible? The problem is, even these very positive signs may not be *sufficient* evidence of a true transformation from juvenilization to spiritual maturity.

Fortunately, another study gives us a more detailed list of criteria for measuring strong faith in teenagers. The Exemplary Youth Ministry (EYM) Study investigated 131 churches in seven denominations, including Evangelical, Mainline Protestant, and Roman Catholic churches.[6] The churches selected were identified by representatives from that church body because of their reputation for successfully producing "vital, maturing faith" in the lives of teenagers. Table 4.1 on page 86 lists the traits of "vital, maturing faith" as identified by both young people and adults in these churches and compares these traits to the traits of biblical spiritual maturity from chapter two.[7]

This comparison reveals that American teenagers can become spiritually mature *while they are still teenagers*. Young people who consistently display the seven traits of vital, maturing faith are in fact spiritually mature as the New Testament defines it. These mature teenagers are not finished growing. And they are not yet fully prepared to live as spiritually mature adults. Given the long and winding road to full adulthood in America, they will need to learn how to stand firm in their faith in the wilderness of emerging adulthood. Nevertheless, according to biblically sound criteria of spiritual maturity, these churches are achieving real success.

The EYM research team also helpfully identified the thirty-three specific items that formed the basis of the seven characteristics of vital, maturing faith listed in Table 4.1 (see Appendix A). That longer list tells us that young people of maturing faith can be observed actively participating in faith-related activities and speaking with others about their faith. For example, maturing teens "are heard referring to having prayer, devotions, and meditation times" and "are heard referring to seeking help from Scripture in deciding what is right and wrong." It is easy to see how teenagers like these become active shapers of their churches' intergenerational cultures of spiritual maturity. EYM concluded that in these churches, "youth ministries often lead the way." For example, in these churches not only do adults try to adapt corporate worship practices to help young people connect with God, but "the worship life of the young people often inspires adults to worship in fresh ways."[8] In these churches,

Table 4.1 "Vital, Maturing Faith"*
Compared with Biblical Traits of Spiritual Maturity

Vital, Maturing Faith	Definition: Youth are . . .	Biblical Spiritual Maturity
1. Seeking Spiritual Growth	Pursuing spiritual growth through conversation, study, reading the Bible, prayer, small groups, retreats.	Desirable (godly emotional patterns) Know the Basics Discernment Communal
2. Possessing a Vital Faith	Keenly aware of God present and active in their own life, the lives of others, and the life of the world	Suffering & Comfort (godly emotional patterns) Communal Missional
3. Making the Christian Faith a Way of Life	Recognizing God's "call" and integrating their beliefs into the conversation, decisions, and actions of daily life.	Discernment
4. Practicing Faith in Community	Actively practicing their faith in Christ, privately and publicly, through participation in the congregation's worship, ministries and leadership.	Communal Missional
5. Possessing a Positive Spirit	Reflecting loving and hopeful attitudes toward others and life.	Suffering and Comfort (godly emotional patterns) Missional
6. Living a Life of Service	Involved in activities caring for others, reaching out to others in need, and addressing injustice.	Missional
7. Exercising Moral Responsibility	Living with integrity utilizing their Christian faith in making moral decisions.	Discernment

*Roland Martinson, Wes Black, John Roberto, *The Spirit and Culture of Youth Ministry: Leading Congregations Toward Exemplary Youth Ministry* (St. Paul, Minn.: EYM Publishing, 2010), p. 28.

teenagers become agents of spiritual maturity, not passive consumers of juvenilized programs.

In contrast, if teenagers do not seem to be devoting much time, effort, or conversation to their faith, then they are probably not maturing. It is crucial not just to talk to teenagers about faith, but to get them talking about it with adults and with each other. Maturing teens "speak publicly about their relationship with Christ," "bring up topics of faith" in conversation, "offer comfort or support to a friend or neighbor in the event of a death or tragedy," "defend a friend or acquaintance who is being talked about when he or she isn't there," and "actively seek to discourage friends from cheating at school."

Exemplary youth ministries are full of young people who are talking with each other about faith and challenging each other to grow.[9]

Churches that help teenagers grow in these characteristics of "vital, maturing faith" are successfully overcoming the immature, counterfeit Christianity that the NSYR labeled "moralistic, therapeutic deism." Adults and teenagers are working together to reverse the effects of juvenilization. But how do they do it?

How Churches Are Fostering Spiritual Maturity in Teenagers

The research team that conducted the Exemplary Youth Ministry study gathered reams of data and identified forty-four different church-based "assets" that help youth mature. But they summarized it all in one important conclusion:

> It is the culture of the whole church that is most influential in nurturing youth of vital Christian faith. The genius of these churches seems best described as a systemic mix of theology, values, people, relationships, expectations, and activities. It appears that a culture of the Spirit emerges with its pervasive and distinct dynamics and atmosphere that is more powerful than its component parts.[10]

In particular, they found that in churches with exemplary youth ministries, the entire congregation worked together to make youth and youth ministry an "essential priority." These churches provided high-quality age-appropriate activities for youth. But they also worked hard to integrate the generations. The entire pastoral staff advocated for youth and youth ministry and devoted themselves to building a congregational culture that encouraged spiritual maturity in people of all ages.[11]

All of this sounds good, but what can be done to cultivate this kind of community of faith? Here is where all those specific assets become important. The Congregational Faith Assets are qualities that EYM determined to be contributing in some way to helping teenagers find a "vital, maturing faith." Researchers grouped the assets into four categories: Congregational Faith and Qualities (eighteen assets), Youth Ministry Qualities (six assets), Family and Household Faith (five assets), and Leadership (four traits of pastors, six traits of youth ministers, five traits of youth and adult leaders).

These assets are of two types. Some of the assets are things that any healthy Christian congregation should be doing or aspiring to become. For example, the "Congregational Faith" assets include "Experiences God's Living Presence," "Emphasizes Prayer," "Focuses on Discipleship," "Emphasizes Scripture," and "Makes Mission Central."[12] The fact that general traits of the church as a whole seem to make a difference in the lives of young people confirms the argument of the first three chapters of this book. Churches that want to promote spiritual maturity need to prioritize it, teach it, and cultivate practices that encourage it. Although we can be quick to pass over these general assets or to assume they are in place, EYM pushes us to take a hard look at our congregational cultures to see if we are really living the faith well together.

These church-wide assets also confirm that, in a sense, everything a church does is "youth ministry," because for good or for ill, the wider church culture forms young people. Looking at this relationship from the other direction, churches with a high commitment to youth and helping them mature also turn out to be good at helping *everyone* mature. That is, EYM supports the claim made at the beginning of this chapter: the right kinds of congregational investment in youth can help the whole church mature.

The second type of congregational asset identified by EYM relates more specifically to work with youth. Several of these assets seem especially likely to promote the traits of spiritual maturity listed at the end of chapter two. These assets are also the ones most likely to be lacking in juvenilized churches or in churches where youth ministry is not a high priority. Churches that find themselves neglecting spiritual maturity in favor of other activities, programs, or goals or that realize they have allowed young people and adults to become isolated from one another especially need to consider ways to foster the following assets.

Congregational Assets

7. *Supports Youth Ministry:* youth and ministry with young people are high priorities for the congregation.
8. *Demonstrates Hospitality:* congregation values and welcomes all people, especially youth.
10. *Encourages Thinking:* welcomes questions and reflection on faith and life.
14. *Fosters Ethical Responsibility:* encourages individual and social moral responsibility.

15. *Promotes Service:* sponsors outreach, service projects, and cultural immersions both locally and globally.
17. *Participate in the Congregation:* Youth are engaged in a wide spectrum of congregational relationships and practices.
18. *Assume Ministry Leadership:* Youth are invited, equipped, and affirmed for leadership in congregational activities.

Youth Ministry Assets

20. *Develops Quality Relationships:* authentic relationships among youth and adults establishing an environment of presence and life engagement.
21. *Focuses on Jesus Christ:* youth ministry's mission, practices, and relationships are inspired by the life and ministry of Jesus.
22. *Considers Life Issues:* values and addresses the full range of young people's lives.

Family and Household Assets

26. *Promotes Family Faith Practices:* Parents engage youth and the whole family in conversations, prayer, Bible reading, and service that nurture faith.
28. *Equips Parents:* congregation offers instruction and guidance that nurture parental faith and equips parents for nurturing faith at home.
29. *Fosters Parent-Youth Relationships:* congregation offers parent-youth activities that strengthen parent-youth relationships.

Pastor Assets

32. *Supports Youth Ministry:* understands, guides, and advocates for youth ministry.
33. *Supports Leaders:* affirms and mentors youth and adults leading youth ministry.

Youth Minister Assets

34. *Provides Competent Leadership:* reflects a superior theological, theoretical, and practical knowledge and skill in leadership.
35. *Models Faith:* a role model reflecting a living faith for youth and adults.
36. *Mentors Faith Life:* assists adult leaders and youth in their faith life both one-on-one and in groups.
37. *Develops Teams:* reflects a clear vision and attracts gifted youth and adults into leadership.

Youth and Adult Leader Assets

40. *Equipped for Peer Ministry:* Youth practice friendship, care-giving, and outreach and are supported by ministry training and caring adults.
41. *Establish Adult-Youth Mentoring:* Adults engage youth in the Christian faith and life supported by informed leadership.
42. *Participate in Training:* Youth and adults are equipped for ministry in an atmosphere of high expectations.
43. *Possess Vibrant Faith:* Youth and adult leaders possess and practice a vital and informed Christian faith.
44. *Demonstrate Competent Adult Leadership:* Adults foster authentic relationships and utilize effective practices in youth ministry with a clear vision strengthened by training and support.[13]

One reason for selecting these particular assets is that they reflect some of the most powerful dimensions of these churches that set them apart from others. First, these congregations prioritize making mature disciples of Jesus, not just making converts or engaging in any number of other worthy causes. Typically they have clearly articulated mission statements or other official documents that spell out these discipleship goals in some detail. And there is a high congruence between the mission and values of the church as a whole and the mission and values of the youth ministry. Second, these churches help both young people and adults deeply engage the content of the gospel, understand the Bible, and apply their faith to concrete situations in their lives. These are learning communities. Third, intergenerational relationships go beyond being "friendly" to become a key location for meeting God and for mutual growth in spiritual maturity. These churches expended significant effort to help the generations worship, serve, lead, and learn together. Fourth, everyone who attends these churches learns that being a Christian means joining the mission, and most are actively serving others. Fifth, because youth are integrated into the congregation, they come to see the church as their church. Young people become active contributors to the church's intergenerational culture of spiritual maturity. Sixth, pastors and youth ministers model the church's mission and values and equip others to do the same.[14]

The EYM researchers provide helpful guidance in making use of their assets approach. They suggest that an assets approach encourages church members to nurture the overall health of the church, not just the specific programs serving youth. In addition, no one needs to view either adults or young people as "problems to be solved," since all can provide assets upon which to build. They also outline a process for applying the assets approach. The members of a church should identify assets that are strong in their congregation and other assets that seem to be ripe for improvement, then pick one or two assets and try to strengthen them. The authors provide questions that leadership teams can use to assess their congregational culture and assets. They provide examples and guidelines for growing assets in each of the four asset categories. Finally, the authors remind us that the assets are cumulative and mutually reinforcing. So as a congregation continues to add more and more of these assets, they will at some point reach a "tipping point" resulting in a life-giving congregational culture of maturity in which the whole seems to be greater than the sum of its parts.[15]

EYM affirms the efficacy of what some are starting to label the "hybrid" approach to youth ministry. That is, a combination of age-specific and intergenerational activities and relationships can provide a powerful synergy that helps young people mature.[16] A growing body of research supports the claim that bringing the generations together for friendship building, worship, service, or learning in genuinely mutual ways can help people of all ages grow in Christ.[17] The phrase "genuinely mutual" is meant to remind adults to include younger people in choosing, planning, and leading these intergenerational experiences whenever possible. If we want young people to see the church as theirs, then we must be careful to make sure that adult concerns, dreams, or agendas are not the only ones that are treated seriously. Although it is common for adults to believe that young people need them, the reverse is equally true. Adults need young people in order to grow up in Christ.

As is true with the assets as a whole, there may be a "tipping point" with regard to intergenerational spiritual formation. Contact between generations that is infrequent or superficial might not make much difference in anyone's life and could even reaffirm intergenerational fears and prejudices. Some advocates of intergenerational spiritual formation suggest that a church will need to make a fundamental change in its ministry philosophy in order to make significant progress.[18] EYM confirms that intergenerational ministry is most effective when it becomes commonplace in a congregation. In some of the exemplary youth ministry congregations, it actually became hard for both church members and researchers to draw a strict boundary between what counted as "youth ministry" and the rest of church life.[19]

"Standing Firm": Six Faith-Sustaining Factors in the Lives of Teenagers

One drawback of the EYM assets approach is that it can be overwhelming to think about fostering ten congregational assets, let alone forty-four. Where should we begin? By integrating the findings of EYM with those of NSYR we can identify six faith-sustaining factors in the lives of teenagers that are especially likely to lead to stronger faith in emerging adulthood. Churches should prioritize helping as many teenagers as possible experience as many of the six faith-sustaining factors as possible and at the highest level possible.

Spiritually mature Christians stand firm in the face of false teaching and suffering (Colossians 1:28; 4:12; Ephesians 4:14; Hebrews 6:4-12). This particular trait of spiritual maturity should be a high priority for youth ministries in America today. Even teenagers who seem to be strong in faith will soon be wandering in the spiritual wilderness of emerging adulthood. NSYR found that among the group of teenagers who ranked in the top 25 percent among their peers in church attendance, importance of faith in their lives, and frequency of personal prayer, one in four declined in these same measures after age 18. Among those only moderately devoted to their faith while in high school, more than half declined in these measures between the ages of 18 and 23. Even the devoted, the most religious 8 percent of all teenagers, stood only about a 50 percent chance of remaining among the top 25 percent most religious emerging adults.[20] Despite the overall story of decline, about 15-20 percent of all emerging adults stay reasonably strong in their faith between the ages of 18 and 23.[21] What makes the difference?

Statistical analysis of the NSYR data showed that *particular combinations* of six faith-sustaining factors during the teenage years correlated with stronger faith in emerging adulthood, at least as measured by high church attendance, felt importance of faith, and frequent personal prayer. Figure 4.1 on page 94 shows the six pathways to strong emerging adult faith discovered by NSYR.

These are not the only factors that showed some correlation with a lasting faith. Individual teenagers could experience all of these factors and still decline in faith. Or other factors not listed might be more important in helping a particular teenager stay strong. But these six combinations of the six faith-sustaining factors show a high probability of helping the "average" Christian teenager stay strong in his or her faith. There are many other paths to strong emerging adult faith, but these six paths are especially common.

One or two faith-sustaining factors might be enough to help young people be strong in faith during their teenage years. But Figure 4.2 on page 95 shows that teenagers who had only one or two of these factors at a high level were more likely to decline in their faith as emerging adults, *even if other faith-sustaining factors were present at a moderate level.* As in Figure 4.1, it was *particular combinations* of factors that created three different pathways from higher teenage faith (top 50 percent of all teenagers) to lower faith in emerging adulthood (bottom 50 percent).[22] The factors that support a lasting faith seem to be cumulative. Taken together, Figure 4.1 and Figure 4.2 suggest that there is a critical "tipping point" of faith inputs during the teenage years.

In my experience of over ten years of visiting some of the best youth ministries in the country, some of these faith-sustaining factors are more common than others. Much youth ministry is oriented toward helping teenagers have powerful religious experiences, and the NSYR results confirm the importance of those efforts. Think, for example, of experientially powerful worship times, retreats, and mission trips. Further, it is likely that teenagers who are immersed in youth ministries that are helping them have frequent moving religious experiences will also say that their faith is "very" or "extremely" important in their lives. Indeed, the implied goal of much youth ministry is to generate these kinds of positive feelings toward the faith.

But not all religious experiences are alike. Teenagers who fit into the NSYR category "Teen has many religious experiences" claimed *all four* of the following to be true in their lives: 1) had committed life to God 2) had prayers answered 3) experienced a miracle 4) had a moving spiritual experience.[23] It is not surprising that this relatively high level of religious experience makes a difference. The cumulative effect of such experiences probably reassures a teenager that her faith is true and important. Another implication of this list of four kinds of experiences is that making a commitment to God is valuable, but probably not sufficient by itself to create a lasting faith. NSYR findings about the timing of first commitments to God seem to support this interpretation. Of the 69 percent of all emerging adults in the study who had at some point committed their lives to God, 59 percent did so for the first time before age 14.[24] This finding suggests that churches should encourage students to build on their early commitments to God by helping them find ways to continue to experience God in everyday life. Imagine a nineteen- or twenty-year-old whose last memorable religious experience happened six to ten years ago. It is not very likely that faith will still be central to his life. Compare that experience with the life of a second emerging adult who had moving experiences of God through worship, prayer, or relationships with other Christians sprinkled throughout her high school years.

Figure 4.1 Paths from Strong Teenage Faith to Strong Emerging Adult Faith

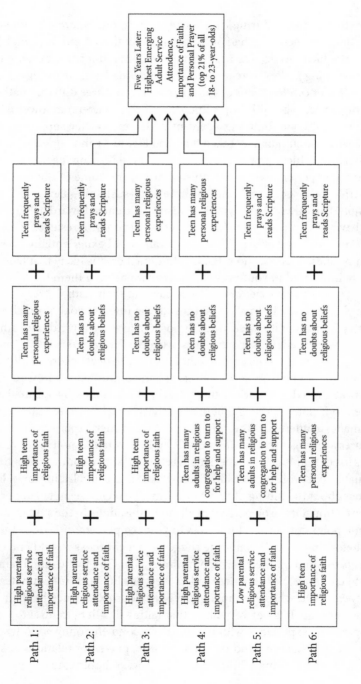

Source: Christian Smith with Patricia Snell, *Souls in Transition: The Religious and Spiritual Lives of Emerging Adults* (New York: Oxford University Press, 2009), p. 226.

Figure 4.2 Paths from Strong Teenage Faith to Weak Emerging Adult Faith

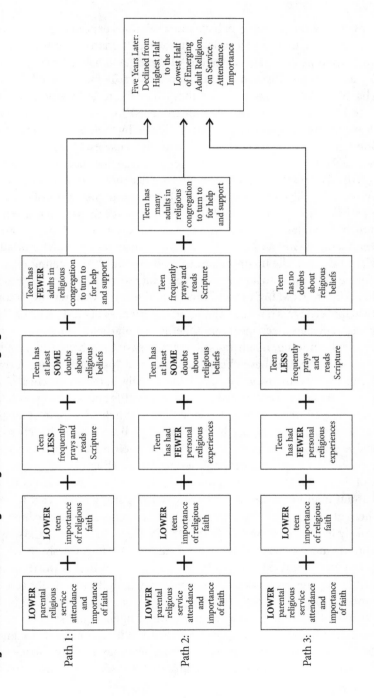

Source: Christian Smith with Patricia Snell, *Souls in Transition: The Religious and Spiritual Lives of Emerging Adults* (New York: Oxford University Press, 2009), p. 230.

How can we help teenagers have more religious experiences like these? First, we can teach them about godly emotional patterns as described in chapter three. Then we can make use of the VIM model to help them experience God's transforming power in their emotional lives. Teenagers need to move from having isolated religious experiences to enjoying godly emotional patterns. Those who do not make this shift are at risk for declining in faith once they leave the nurturing environments provided by their families, churches, and youth ministries. It is *not* enough just to tell teenagers, "Your faith should not be based on your emotions." No matter how true that statement might be, it is equally true that people whose hearts are deeply committed to God will be developing godly patterns of emotional response to the events of life. And those godly emotional patterns will in turn encourage them to stand firm in the faith. In emerging adulthood, young people must have the inner resources to keep pursuing God and attending church largely on their own initiative. In order to do that, the inner dynamic of will, thought, and feeling must be transformed by God into an engine of spiritual growth.

In addition, EYM highlighted ways that the entire congregation's spirituality helps teenagers have life-changing experiences of God. In exemplary churches, adults and teenagers join together regularly for worship services that are "enlightening, inspiring, interesting, easy to understand, and relevant in daily life." In these churches prayer is a "pervasive, core activity attached to every dimension" of church life. Finally, in these churches "God's presence is named and celebrated in the everyday life and work of youth and adults." These churches engaged in practices that helped people of all ages encounter God and recognize his work in their lives. These churches had a palpable sense of God present and active in their midst. Although EYM researchers did not go into detail about how these churches cultivated this sense of living together in God's presence, they did say that leaders talked often about it and modeled it.[25] The Sticky Faith study found that teenagers who had regular, positive experiences of intergenerational worship were more likely to remain strong in their faith in college. In contrast, those who grew up in churches where high school students seldom worshipped with adults or even interacted with them did not fare as well. It is worth noting that just being present in a worship service in which they were not actively welcomed did not necessarily help.[26]

It can be threatening for a congregation to open a conversation about how well they are experiencing God together. But it can be deadly to ignore problems in this area. One reason that teenagers may not experience God much when they join adults for worship is that *nobody* is experiencing God much in worship. If we suspect that the entire congregation's spirituality has become dry, it can help to gather a group of people to pray regularly for spiritual renewal and an outpouring of the Holy Spirit. Another obvious move is to evaluate what is being done in corporate worship and make prayerfully discerned changes. Chapter five describes a process for evaluating elements of church life and their contributions to spiritual maturity using worship music as one example.

The best youth ministries in the country also typically have a strong team of adult volunteers who are meeting regularly with small groups of young people to help them grow in their faith. Several other studies confirm the NSYR finding that teenagers who have at least one mentor during high school tend to have stronger faith in emerging adulthood.[27] Youth ministers with a strong adult volunteer team have typically invested considerable effort in recruiting, training, and encouraging these leaders. Unfortunately, the Study of Protestant Youth Ministers in America (SPYM) found that many youth ministers felt ill-equipped for and unsuccessful in mobilizing volunteers.[28] Church leaders that want successful youth ministries need to help their youth ministers learn how to build a strong volunteer team and send potential volunteers their way.

In addition, both NSYR and EYM suggest that young people who have *multiple* friendships with different adults in their church do the best at becoming strong in their faith. The churches in the Exemplary Youth Ministry study devoted effort and creativity to fostering faith-enhancing relationships between teenagers and adults outside of specific "youth activities." One church established a surrogate grandparent ministry and created opportunities for these pairs to share their faith stories and serve together. Other congregations created prayer partnerships between adults and teenagers. The teenagers felt connected to a caring adult who they knew was praying for them often. The leaders of these congregations equipped not just youth ministry volunteers, but a wider group of adults to provide a safe, welcoming place for teenagers. Teenagers knew they could talk about anything with the adults in their church and be challenged, yet not rejected.[29] These congregations were good at helping adults engage in what Richard Dunn calls "pacing" with young people: walking through life beside a young person and listening well before offering advice.[30] The Sticky Faith study found that teenagers who enjoyed a web of spiritual friendships with many adults had stronger faith in college. Not surprisingly, those teenagers who got the impression that the adults in their churches wanted nothing to do with them had weaker faith when they went to college.[31]

Coaching teenagers into a life-giving pattern of personal prayer and Scripture reading needs more attention in many churches. It should come as no surprise that Exemplary Youth Ministry churches were teaching teenagers how to pray.[32] More commonly, youth ministers and other church leaders *tell* teenagers to read the Bible and pray without providing the kind of one-on-one and small-group coaching over time that can help them develop those skills. Probably one reason for this deficit is that a good many adults struggle in this area of their lives as well.

As we saw in chapter three, often people give up on their spiritual disciplines because of Vision or Intention problems. Youth leaders should be teaching about the biblical vision for prayer and Scripture reading. Why are these disciplines so wonderful? What powerful changes can young people expect in their lives through these disciplines? If this vision work is done well, more and more teenagers will want to learn how to pray and read the Bible on their own because they will understand the biblical reasons for these disciplines. For those who seem reluctant, mentoring conversations about underlying heart attachments — entanglements of the will — can help.

Youth leaders must present a variety of methods for prayer and Bible reading and help students practice them. Instead of just telling teenagers to try it at home, teach a particular prayer technique at a youth meeting. Then have each teenager practice this method of prayer during the youth meeting. Bring the students back together in small groups to discuss how it went and how to overcome obstacles that might arise as they try to implement this method at home. For adult volunteers to be effective guides, they may need to be taught how to pray and read Scripture first.

Most importantly, the youth leadership team needs to recognize that helping teenagers establish a life-giving pattern of prayer and Scripture reading will take considerable investment over time. Keep asking teenagers how that pattern is going, and keep coaching until it works for them. Remind teenagers often that there are many good ways to pray and encounter God's word and encourage each person to keep searching until they find methods that work for them. Youth leaders can encourage a culture in which adults and teenagers feel free to ask each other, "How are your times of prayer and Scripture going?" and "How can I help?"

If we don't stay with them over time, teenagers will miss the chance to learn how to navigate transitions in their prayer lives. Even if one set of prayer or Scripture practices works well for a particular student, she will at some point face a transition. Sometimes a set of prayer practices becomes dry. Other times, a particular way of praying is not right for helping with the new vision God has placed in a person's life. Even more commonly, changing life circumstances, such as moving from a school-year schedule to a summer schedule, will cause times of prayer and Scripture reading to disappear. We need to teach teenagers skills for rebooting prayer in their lives. Warn them that these transitions are coming. Ask them to talk to one of the adults in the youth ministry if they are experiencing a transition. Have adults share their stories of rebooting their prayer lives after life transitions. Most importantly, remind everyone to try something new when transitions sabotage their existing prayer patterns. Whether they like routine or hate it, too many Christians labor under the mistaken idea that they will find one pattern of prayer and Scripture reading and practice it forever. That image of personal prayer is neither accurate nor helpful.

Teenagers who report having no doubts about their religious beliefs are also more likely to stay strong in faith later. For some, their lack of doubt may be due to just accepting what they are told and not thinking much about it. But given how inhospitable emerging adulthood is to fervent faith, it is unlikely that such a superficial lack of doubt in the teenage years would be enough to sustain faith later. The NSYR researchers believe that a more likely explanation for why the factor "Teen has no doubts about religious beliefs" helps create a lasting faith is that such teens have embraced "a belief system that explains lived reality and provides direction for [their] life."[33] That kind of deeply embraced belief system sounds a lot like the traits of spiritual maturity we have named "know the basics" and "discernment."

When it comes to helping teenagers embrace a set of life-changing beliefs, the content of chapters two and three can help. Helping teenagers learn about the foundational truths of their faith and begin to experience them using the VIM model can make a big difference. The young people in the EYM churches strongly agreed that their youth ministries helped them understand their faith better, apply faith to daily life, and make serious life choices about future relationships and values. The EYM youth ministries accomplished these feats by first establishing a clear goal: helping youth become mature disciples of Jesus. Typically they listed five or six qualities they hoped to instill in young people under the heading of "disciple of Jesus." Then adult and student leaders worked together to create environments where young people could begin to experience God and grow in these qualities. In particular, the best youth ministries placed adults and teenagers in small groups to discuss the Bible and learn how to apply it to the everyday situations of their lives. Teenagers met regularly with peers and adults who knew them, cared about them, and challenged them to grow in understanding and living their faith.

These students raved about how well the youth ministry served as a "spiritual support group."[34]

In the process of developing a set of firm convictions, many high school students will probably face some doubts. It is important for parents, youth ministers, and other concerned Christian adults to create an atmosphere in which teenagers can express their doubts and receive help. The Sticky Faith study found that students with stronger faith in college tended to come from homes in which they felt free to talk about their doubts with their parents. Their parents did not get defensive or engage in high-pressure attempts to convince their child to believe the "right" things. Instead, parents listened carefully, offered their ideas, and asked probing questions that pushed their child to think more deeply about the issues. These were homes in which faith matters were frequent topics of conversation. These parents even talked about their doubts with their children and explained how they had lived with them and overcome them. The Sticky Faith study also found that the number one thing graduating high school seniors wished had been more available in their youth ministries was "time for deep conversation."[35]

Finally, parents proved crucial in four out of six possible pathways to strong emerging adult faith. Parents of strong faith attended church often and said that their faith was "very" or "extremely" important in their lives. Even in path six, which seems to exclude the influence of parents, researchers found that the parents of those teenagers were often religious too, just not as strongly so as the parents who contributed to paths one through four.[36]

The power of parental faith highlights the critical need for congregations to be fostering spiritual maturity in adults. In addition to implementing a congregation-wide model of spiritual formation like the VIM model presented in chapter three, church leaders would do well to consider some of the qualities found in churches with exemplary youth ministries. Youth, parents, and adult leaders in these churches testified that their churches were *both* welcoming and challenging. In particular, adults strongly agreed that their congregation "challenges my thinking," "encourages me to ask questions," "expects people to learn and think," "helps you make decisions about what's right and wrong," "teaches members about Christian perspectives on moral questions," and "helps you learn how to apply your faith to everyday decisions."[37] These exemplary congregations invested heavily in helping adults achieve the core competencies of Christian maturity: "know the basics" and "discernment." And parents like these are more likely to be able to help their teenaged children process their doubts in a spiritually healthy way. They will be confident enough in their own faith to initiate faith conversations with their children.

These churches also equipped parents to be a positive spiritual influence in the lives of their teenage children. Past research reported in EYM showed that parents who talk with their teenagers about faith, pray with them, and serve with them are the most likely to encourage strong faith in their teenage children.[38] The churches in EYM taught parents how to have conversations with their teenagers about matters of faith and morals. They provided resources and training to help parents establish patterns of family prayer, Bible reading, and other faith-enhancing family traditions. Exemplary churches also provided opportunities for families to engage in service together. The youth ministries in these churches provided classes for parents on the typical struggles of adolescents, including training in how to have parent-teen conversations about these topics.[39] Youth ministry leaders included parents as partners in the youth ministry. Many parents and grandparents served as volunteers. Youth ministers consulted these and other parents when planning and assessing the church's youth ministry activities. Individual comments from parents showed a high level of trust and respect between parents and youth ministers.[40]

Youth ministries in EYM churches also provided opportunities for parents and teenagers to interact as part of the yearly cycle of youth activities. One youth ministry not mentioned in the study invites parents to attend the youth meeting once a month. Parents and teenagers listen to the same teaching together, then discuss it together in small groups. Families take home a handout that provides ideas for continuing the faith conversation throughout the next month.

Unfortunately, SPYM found that many youth ministers believed they were not very effective at helping parents in these ways. Youth ministers felt especially ineffective at helping parents have better relationships with their teenage children. But the same study found that many youth ministers already have too many competing demands and struggle to meet the unrealistic expectations their churches place on them.[41] Other leaders in the church need to take the initiative to equip parents and to equip the youth minister to help parents.

Attentive readers will note a potential discrepancy in this chapter. Earlier I questioned the measures of strong teenage faith used by NSYR, but in this section I have been more accepting of similar criteria when applied to emerging adults. On the one hand, we should not assume that every emerging adult who reports frequent church attendance, says her faith is very important to her, and claims to pray often is spiritually mature. However, emerging adults who are connected to the body of Christ and praying are the ones who have the best chance of becoming spiritually mature if they are not already. Those who have stopped these external practices are at risk for losing their internal convictions. As confirmation of this hypothesis, NSYR found that very few emerging adults who stopped going to church, praying, or reading the Bible still said that faith was "very" or "extremely" important in their daily lives.[42] Still, many emerging adults will need more than these basic practices in order to thrive in their faith. What can be done to help them?

Youth Ministry and Emerging Adulthood

Emerging adulthood presents churches with a difficult set of challenges. Emerging adults are living through a season of life that is inhospitable to faith and filled with life-shaping decisions and competing demands. Many emerging adults stop going to church, so it can be hard to connect with them or to know how to help them. In addition, many churches hire emerging adults to serve as youth ministers. At least some of these good Christian young people are still figuring out how to grow up and are working through their ambivalence toward the church. Churches, seminaries, and theologians are just beginning to grapple with the realities of the new emerging adulthood. The best we can do at this point is to give an overview of the landscape that must be more carefully explored in the future if we want to help emerging adults mature.

If more and more churches focus on growing teenagers of "vital, maturing faith" along the lines suggested by EYM and NSYR, then it is likely that more emerging adults will be strong in faith and present in church. But there will still probably be a large number of people in their twenties who lose interest in their faith and drop out of church. As a result, church leaders and parents who care about these young people will need to start thinking of "youth ministry" as something that continues beyond the high school years.

Helping Emerging Adults Mature

Since emerging adults in America are much more religiously diverse than American teenagers, it is harder to make use of social science research to identify a few key factors that can help them thrive spiritually. In part because of this religious diversity, NSYR did not identify factors during emerging adulthood that enhance faith. One study that surveyed a smaller sample of emerging adults found two sets of factors to be significantly related to higher church attendance during emerging adulthood. The emerging adults in this study had all been active church attendees as teenagers, but varied greatly in their current interest in faith.

Relational Factors during Young Adulthood and Young Adult Church Attendance

1. *Attendance of friends:* If their friends don't go to church, young adults don't go to church.
2. *Spiritual depth of friends:* If young adult friends are shallow Christians, young adults are less likely to attend church.
3. *Number of older adult Christians:* Those with two or less older adult friends attend church less often.
4. *Spiritual life of other adults:* If older adult friends (teachers, coaches, employers, neighbors, co-workers, etc.) are shallow Christians, young adults are less likely to attend church.

Young Adult Religious Practices and Young Adult Church Attendance

1. *Bible study groups:* Participation in a Bible study, prayer group, or worship service other than those at church (such as a campus ministry or parachurch group) during young adulthood is associated with higher church attendance.
2. *Number of church programs:* Those who attend more programs tend to attend church more often.[43]

Similarly, the Sticky Faith study found that college students who found Christian friends and who had parents and other Christian adults reaching out to them tended to stay stronger in their faith. On the other hand, many college freshmen in the study struggled to find a church and had no idea how to go about it. Many experienced suddenly being on their own with regard to faith matters and felt ill-equipped to deal with the challenges.[44]

These findings confirm several principles that college ministry workers have known for years. First, don't expect emerging adults to show up at church just because you are offering a program you hope will appeal to them. Instead, those who hope to reach emerging adults need to go find them and provide faith-enhancing activities on their turf. Coming to church is rarely the first step in an emerging adult's journey back to strong faith. More often, church attendance is the fruit of a long process of friendship building and faith encouragement.

Second, spiritual friendships between older Christians and emerging adults may be even more crucial than they were for these same young people during the teenage years. Churches need to create structures and provide training to encourage adult mentors of high school students to continue the mentoring relationship for at least a few years past high school. A growing body of research suggests that such lasting mentoring relationships make a big impact on emerging adults during the first few years out of high school even though face-to-face contact becomes less frequent.[45] Jana Sundene and Richard Dunn have written an outstanding book on how to mentor emerging adults that could be used for training.[46] In my experience, many emerging adults would like to have a mentor but have no idea how to find one. Meanwhile, many adults who would be open to such a spiritual friendship assume that they must wait until a younger person approaches them. As part of the training process, church leaders should encourage potential mentors to take the initiative and provide ideas for how to begin such mentoring relationships.[47]

Finally, the spiritual lives of emerging adults will be largely determined by the spiritual lives of their closest friends. After I was involved for a few years in campus ministry at Michigan State, the University of Michigan, and the University of London, it became easy for me to spot which freshmen would stay strong in their faith. Those who chose to join a campus ministry and establish their main friendships there would thrive in faith. Those who chose instead to primarily identify with a group of friends who ignored faith not only stopped going to church, they sometimes stopped even believing in God. The Sticky Faith study confirmed the importance of friends. Many of the college students from Christian backgrounds whom they interviewed testified to intense loneliness in the early days of college. Since they perceived that "everyone" was partying and they wanted friends, they too began to party. The first two weeks of college seem to be especially pivotal.[48] Another study found that friendship groups arise organically in the first few weeks of college life. Seemingly trivial factors like living in the same dorm and having compatible schedules seemed to disproportionately determine friendship groups.[49]

Those who care about emerging adults must provide them opportunities to connect in friendship with other Christians. Sticky Faith researchers Powell and Clark provide helpful suggestions for how parents and youth leaders can prepare high school students for the difficult transition to college, especially the crucial first few decisions about friends, church, and other faith priorities.[50] We must challenge emerging adults with the seriousness of what they are doing when they choose the small group of peers with whom they will be spending most of their time over the next several years. The call to discipleship for today's emerging adults is a call to choose to invest in spiritual friendships.

Emerging adults who do not go to college will also face difficult transitions. Some evidence suggests that these young people are even less likely than college students to attend church. They may also be more isolated from supportive relationships and institutions that can help them through life-altering crises such as unplanned pregnancies, cohabitation and shattering romantic breakups, substance abuse, and financial hardship. Some of the most heartbreaking stories that appeared in *Souls in Transition* were stories of young people who chose not to go to college or for whom personal crises interrupted their education.[51] One study of a small town in Iowa found that young people who grow up there experience very different transitions to adulthood. The college-bound overachievers experience the entire community of adults rallying behind them to launch them in life; adults encourage them to go out into the world, succeed, and not return. In contrast, young people who are not college bound get the leftovers of adult investment during high school and even less help in transitioning to adulthood after high school.[52] Churches can and should invest in emerging adults who are not college bound. Unfortunately, ministry with these emerging adults is even less well developed than ministry to college students.

One way churches can help all varieties of emerging adults is to think creatively about how to help them cope with multiple transitions and competing demands. Setran and Kiesling identify the key dimensions of life in which emerging adults need help: spiritual formation, identity, church, vocation, morality, sexuality, and relationships.[53] Churches can help emerging adults by providing deep teaching and safe places to discuss these life issues. We should not assume that our church is good at providing the intellectual environment that emerging adults need. Kinnaman's research on emerging adults who have left the church suggests that as teenagers, some of these young people did not experience their churches as safe places to discuss difficult questions. Instead, they remembered shallow teaching and judgmental, anti-intellectual adults who displayed a fortress mentality and reacted defensively to tough questions.[54]

Setran and Kiesling explain the challenges facing emerging adults in each of the key areas of their spiritual development. They also offer thoughtful theological analysis and practical guidelines for helping emerging adults grow to maturity in each of these domains. They note that emerging adults stand at a critical juncture of life in which the cost of discipleship looms high, identity is in flux, and the big decisions of life are made by isolated individuals and are too often based on random feelings and events.[55] Several times a year I find myself sitting in my office listening to a student who is telling me about how he is about to change his college major based on one conversation with a friend or an offhand comment from a professor. These are bright, motivated Christian young people who do not seem to know any other way to make an important decision. Churches can serve emerging adults by providing communities of discernment that can help them make godly decisions in the key areas of their lives.

But how can we help emerging adults when so many of them never show up at church? Emerging adults often complain that churches provide no age-specific programs for them. When emerging adults attend churches that invest heavily in ministry with children, youth, and older adults, but have no ministry for their age range, they conclude that the church does not care as much about them as about those in other life stages. Meanwhile, churches find it hard to attract the critical mass of people that could sustain an age-specific ministry with emerging adults. As a result, emerging adults tend to gravitate either toward parachurch college ministries or churches that are entirely shaped around their preferences. Unfortunately, these age-specific ministries may not do much to overcome juvenilization and may merely delay the difficult transition to adult church membership. Age-specific ministries play a crucial role in sustaining faith in the wilderness of emerging adulthood, but such ministries are at their best when they also help emerging adults grow to spiritual maturity and develop an adult connection with a Christian congregation. Congregations with few emerging adults in attendance should consider partnering with an existing campus ministry or other age-specific emerging adult ministry. As they serve the needs of that group, church members will find natural opportunities to build friendships with emerging adults and contribute to their growing maturity.

Fortunately, not every church needs to create an age-specific in-house ministry with emerging adults in order to make a difference in their lives. Churches that invest in genuinely mutual intergenerational activities will both appeal to emerging adults and help them grow. If a church is good at helping all ages connect with each other and with God in intergenerational settings, then emerging adults will feel "normal" and included in the church. If these intergenerational activities draw on their leadership skills, expertise, and life concerns, emerging adults will be empowered, challenged, and equipped by the church rather than becoming passive consumers who drift away. And emerging adults especially need to learn to value and grow in relationships that are "given," not chosen, and intergenerational, not age-segregated — just the kinds of relationships they can find in a Christian congregation. Although intergenerational friendships might be an acquired taste for many emerging adults, beneath their initial resistance often hides a deep relational hunger.[56]

EYM provides guidance for helping young people feel included in the church through intergenerational ministry. Several of these principles apply equally well to emerging adults and to teenagers. First, make sure that the congregational culture is welcoming to young people. Leaders can give teenagers and emerging adults opportunities to be "up front" and publicly celebrate their accomplishments and life milestones. Leaders should speak positively and use positive metaphors to describe young people, rather than perpetuating stereotypes of young people as a "problem." Second, evaluate all activities to see if they are welcoming to young people. For example, do the music, prayers, metaphors, sermon topics and applications, and other elements of worship reflect the diversity of ages and life experiences present? Do teenagers and emerging adults serve as leaders in the church? How can we help them take on leadership roles? Third, actively promote intergenerational participation in existing activities. For example, invite teenagers and emerging adults to the church work day and include them in planning the tasks to be done. If the mission trip has traditionally been mainly a youth activity, invite more adults to go this year and hold the trip over a holiday weekend so more adults can attend. Fourth, offer new intergenerational activities that are intended to help the entire church move toward important goals together. For example, create an intergenerational spiritual maturity retreat that equips everyone from teenagers to retirees to use the VIM model. Other congregations use intergenerational learning experiences to teach families how to pray and discuss the Bible together at home.[57]

Since emerging adults are consumed with life transitions and need discernment, churches could establish intergenerational discernment groups or an intergenerational class on discerning God's will. In such settings, older adults can share their stories of discerning God's will and emerging adults can describe their current concerns. Getting to know Christians of different ages in these groups or classes could spark ongoing mentoring relationships. And everyone in attendance would have an opportunity to grow in the spiritual maturity trait we have named discernment.[58]

As these examples illustrate, leadership, planning, and evaluation of intergenerational activities should include people of different age groups in meaningful ways. And people of all ages need to learn about the value of intergenerational ministry so that they are willing to pay the costs that come with it in an age-segregated society. A good way to begin the process of building interest in intergenerational activities is to teach about some of the many Scripture passages that encourage the generations to grow together in Christ.[59]

Helping Emerging Adult Youth Ministers Mature

One complication for the church's work with youth is that some youth ministers are entangled in extended adolescence. Parents and church leaders still assume that the best youth workers are young adults who supposedly can relate better to teenagers. Further, many take it for granted that youth ministry is a temporary stage on the way to a "real" adult leadership role. Poor pay, low status, and low levels of volunteer support have sometimes conspired to make this a self-fulfilling prophecy. I have had the privilege of teaching, mentoring, and befriending many of these young men and women over the years. They have much to contribute to the church and its work with youth. They deserve better support of all kinds from the churches that hire them than they sometimes get. In particular, other church leaders need to guide and support these emerging adult youth ministers in their transition to full adulthood.

Many youth leaders start their work during their twenties, the very years in which the transition to adulthood is most demanding. A few are at least initially drawn to youth work because they don't want to grow up. Others want to be taken seriously as leaders in the church, but feel uncomfortable relating to older adults. Some of these aspiring youth ministers even have a negative image of the church and see many of its ways as obstacles to authentic Christianity. Melissa Wiginton in her work with the Fund for Theological Education has had contact with numerous young people preparing for ministry. She contends that "most bright, capable, passionate young people entering theological education or preparing for ministry are not deeply committed to the church as an institution even as they recognize the need for and gifts of community in the life of faith."[60] Like their peers, a good many emerging adult youth ministers may be ambivalent about the church.

I have met more than a few freshmen youth ministry majors over the years who informed me, "I want to work with youth, but not in a church." When I ask for their reasons, very few claim that the church has harmed them personally. But they believe that such negative experiences are common. Or they just sense that working in a church will somehow restrict their ability to pursue their passion. Fortunately, most of these students grow out of their immature view of the church as a result of their coursework in our department and their culminating seven-month internship working in a healthy church.

A sense of distance from the adult church is not all bad. It sometimes provokes young leaders to ask probing questions which can lead to positive reforms in the church. In an age-segregated society, teenagers sometimes have a hard time identifying with older adults, so it is helpful to have role models who are closer in age. When those young leaders demonstrate Christian character and love for the church, they can motivate teenagers to embrace the best elements of the faith. But when youth leaders are stuck in extended adolescence, they are not well equipped to help teenagers aspire to Christian maturity and to love the church. By all means, churches should continue to hire emerging adults to lead their youth ministries. But they should commit to helping these young leaders transition well to full adulthood.

The Study of Protestant Youth Ministers in America tells us that emerging adult youth ministers need more support than they are often receiving. Youth ministers who are twenty-nine or younger, who have three or less years of experience, or who are serving in churches with youth groups of forty teenagers or less tend to be especially at risk for personal and professional struggles. Those leading groups of forty students or less are more likely to be concerned about a disconnect between youth and the rest of the church, to find that parents are less involved in the youth ministry, to struggle with apathy among the youth, to believe that they are not doing well at helping youth grow in faith, and to feel a general lack of respect and support from the adults in the church.[61] Youth ministers who are twenty-nine or younger or who have served less than three years in youth ministry are more likely to struggle with feelings of inadequacy and to be declining in their confidence as leaders, even when it comes to their core goal of nurturing the spiritual growth of teenagers. They struggle more with balancing the time demands of their jobs and with being organized. These same youth ministers are also more likely to feel ineffective at recruiting and training volunteers, involving parents in the youth ministry, and helping parents improve relationships with their teenage children.[62]

What can be done to help emerging adult youth ministers thrive? Both EYM and SPYM conclude that a congregational climate of support for the youth minister and youth ministry is crucial. Both of these studies recommend that church leaders develop the kinds of assets that EYM identified, particularly good working relationships between paid and volunteer leaders at all levels.[63]

SPYM further established that the youth minister's relationship with the senior pastor is critical.[64] One of the most important things a pastor can do is to advocate for church-wide support of the youth ministry. In addition, the senior pastor should make sure that the youth minister has opportunities for professional development. SPYM found that youth ministers most desired training for understanding and communicating biblical truth, understanding adolescent development and counseling, finding effective ministry strategies and new ideas, developing skills to help parents and families, and administrative skills.[65] Churches do not need to provide all this training on their own, but they should provide time and money for the youth minister to receive such training. Since time and money are always in short supply in churches, it is best to guide younger, less experienced youth ministers toward training opportunities in the areas that are typically weaker for them: effective teaching, counseling youth, developing volunteers, and helping families.

SPYM also found that youth ministers of all ages desired more peer mentoring relationships. Younger youth ministers especially wanted to "be mentored by someone outside of my ministry" and "have close staff relationships that develop and challenge me professionally."[66] Connecting a new youth pastor with a more experienced youth pastor in the area can be helpful. The senior pastor or another experienced leader in the church should also actively mentor the youth minister. The mentor could make use of the VIM model as a basis for conversation with the youth minister. The mentor could also read *Shaping the Journey of Emerging Adults* by Dunn and Sundene and make use of its advice on mentoring. Both mentor and youth pastor could read *Spiritual Formation in Emerging Adulthood* by Setran and Kiesling and discuss the topics it raises as they apply it to the youth minister's life.

There is one topic that emerging adult youth ministers might not raise themselves but should probably be part of any mentoring relationship with them. Emerging adult youth ministers do not typically need help loving teenagers, but they often need help loving the church, especially when the face of the church is a difficult or intimidating adult. Over the past ten years of conducting evaluative visits of undergraduate youth ministry interns, I have often found them to be extremely patient with the failings of teenagers but more easily angered and disillusioned by the failings of adults.

Mentors should ask emerging adult youth ministers whether they are growing in their love for people of all ages in the church, not just teenagers. Then they should use the VIM model of spiritual formation to help the youth ministers pursue that vision. Numerous Scripture passages talk about the significance of the church and the deep love God has for it. Paul's love for the churches he planted shines through all his letters. I like to use Ephesians 5 when teaching undergraduate youth ministry students about the significance of the church. If the church is the bride of Christ, then those who say they love Christ should also love his bride. I ask my students to imagine how I would react if they told me, "Dr. Bergler, I want to be your friend, but I can't stand your wife." Mentors should encourage emerging adult youth ministers to meditate on the biblical vision for the church and how ministers should love it.

Mentors should also ask probing questions that will help youth ministers examine the entanglements of their wills and the patterns of emotional response they have to the church. Why are they reluctant to choose to love the church when people fail or hurt them? Why do they find it easier to forgive teenagers than adults? What spiritual disciplines can open them up to God's grace to love all members of the church in spite of their flaws? As numerous Scriptures attest, we become most like God when we love those who seem undeserving of our love because they do not love us, or do not love us well (Matthew 5:43-48; Romans 5:6-8; 1 John 4:9-11). Without excusing or ignoring faults in the church that need to be corrected, emerging adult youth ministers need to confront what their negative patterns of emotional response to the church are saying about who *they* are as followers of Jesus.

The "Tipping Point" and a Lived Theology of the Church

Whether we look at congregational culture, strong faith during adolescence, or faith that stands firm in emerging adulthood, there seems to be a "tipping point," a cumulative set of circumstances with great potential to produce spiritual maturity. But none of the research studies can tell us exactly where the tipping point will be in a particular young person's life or in the overall life of a congregation. This fact should not surprise us, since one plants, another waters, but God gives the growth (1 Corinthians 3:5-7). The spiritual maturity of an individual or a congregation is not something that we can produce by human effort alone. What these studies can tell us is that churches that prioritize the spiritual nurture of young people and build an intergenerational culture of spiritual maturity will be more likely to see spiritual growth among adolescents, emerging adults, and adults alike. And the possibility that there may be a tipping point sometime in the future should be encouraging as we take small steps to build congregational assets.

This chapter has focused on sociological evidence regarding the building blocks of effective youth ministries and has said little about theology. Theology does matter, and some Christian beliefs probably encourage healthy youth ministries and a congregational culture of spiritual maturity more than others. But the research studies cited in this chapter also suggest that "vital, maturing faith" is compatible with many different Christian theological systems.

So how does theology contribute to a congregational culture that produces spiritual maturity? First, theology provides the basic truths and principles of discernment that every mature Christian must embrace. And these "basics" are probably more shared among Christians from different traditions than many realize. If differences of opinion regarding these matters were so extreme, it is unlikely that the EYM researchers would have found such unity regarding the traits of "vital, maturing faith." Both the biblical and sociological evidence confirm that churches that help people learn, love, and live theology (as opposed to just having uninformed good feelings about God) tend to produce more spiritually mature Christians. And this seems to be the true whether the theology they learn comes from an Evangelical, Reformed, Lutheran, or Catholic theological tradition.

Second, theological reflection can help church leaders identify the barriers to spiritual maturity in their congregations. Often it is not the official theology of the church that hinders spiritual maturity; rather, it is the lived theology of the congregation that gets in the way. This lived or "implicit" theology is not necesssarily well articulated and may even be unconscious. Nevertheless it shapes attitudes, actions, and expectations. We have already noted that people who misunderstand spiritual maturity and the process of spiritual growth are not likely to grow. The evidence presented in this chapter suggests that lived beliefs about the nature and purpose of the church also need to be carefully examined. When churches find it hard to get adults to care about the youth ministry or to get young people to care about the rest of the church, a lived theology of the church that does not challenge American individualism and age segregation may be one of the causes. In the next chapter, we will explore a process that church leadership teams can use to evaluate everything they are doing in light of their theological beliefs. This process can help leaders identify which changes are most likely to promote spiritual maturity in their congregation.

CHAPTER 5

From Here to Maturity

The purpose of this chapter is to explain a process that congregations can follow to move from where they are to spiritual maturity. Most simply stated, the process is

1. Assess the state of spiritual maturity in the congregation.
2. Create a plan.
3. Implement the plan.
4. Monitor progress and make changes via an ongoing cycle of reflection and action.

This process must be done in community and requires prayerful, theologically informed discernment. No process like this can guarantee results. Only God can provide the spiritual power to renew a congregation — the life that causes the plants to grow, the Spirit who turns a pile of stones into a temple. But God works through faithful, skillful gardeners and builders (1 Corinthians 3:5-17).

Assessing Spiritual Maturity

Congregations need to assess their progress in spiritual maturity in at least two dimensions: 1) how individuals are doing and 2) how well the church is helping people grow. When it comes to assessing how individuals are doing, the traits of spiritual maturity identified in chapter two can be a good starting point. A church leadership team might discuss the following questions together:

A. **Expectations:** What do people in our church expect with regard to spiritual maturity?
  1. What evidence do we have that they see it as desirable?
  2. What evidence do we have that they see it as attainable?
  3. What evidence do we have that they see it as possible to know if they are mature?
B. **Content:** In what ways do people in our church display the traits of spiritual maturity?
  1. What evidence do we have that they understand and embrace the basic truths of the faith?
  2. What evidence do we have that they can discern how to apply God's truth to daily life decisions?
  3. What evidence do we have that they stand firm in their faith in the face of false teaching and suffering?
  4. How do they understand and relate to the church?
     a. Can they explain what the church is and why it is important without mentioning its personal benefits for them?
     b. Can they explain why being a mature follower of Jesus must include being connected to his body the church?
     c. Does their behavior demonstrate a love for the church despite its flaws?
  5. How do they understand and relate to the mission of the church?
     a. What do they think the mission of the church is?
     b. Can they explain why being a mature follower of Jesus must include participating in his mission?
     c. What evidence do we have that they have personally embraced the mission of the church and taken their place in it?
  6. How well are they doing at developing godly emotional patterns?
     a. Which godly emotional patterns that support maturity and unity in the church are common? (See Table 3.2)
     b. Which sinful emotional patterns that undermine maturity and unity are common? (See Table 3.2)
  7. Which of the behavior changes in Ephesians 4:25–5:2 are most common, and which are least common? (for example, from evil talk to speech that builds up, v. 29)
C. **Process:** How well do people in our church understand the process of growth to spiritual maturity?
  1. What evidence do we have that they understand the relationship between the gospel and spiritual growth?

2. What evidence do we have that they understand the importance of learning God's truth for spiritual growth?
3. What evidence do we have that they understand and embrace the importance of growing together in community with other believers?
4. How do they think suffering and comfort work together to help a person become more like Jesus?

By discussing these or similar questions, leaders should be able to get a general sense of the state of spiritual maturity among the members of their congregation. Such discussions might also produce consensus about which elements of spiritual maturity seem strongest and which seem weakest in the congregation as a whole. But since individuals vary so much in their spiritual maturity, a congregational survey could also be helpful. For example, leaders could prepare a congregational survey based on the thirty-three traits of maturing Christian youth identified by EYM (Appendix A). For each statement, ask church members to rate themselves on a scale of 1 to 5, with 1 meaning "not true of me" and 5 meaning "extremely true of me." In addition, it could be helpful to ask respondents to rate the church on how well it is helping them to achieve each of the thirty-three items. Collect the results and note which statements seem to consistently get the lowest scores. An average score of 3.5 or lower might indicate a possible area of concern. Pay attention to which of the 7 categories of "vital, maturing faith" contain the most items with low average scores. Then use Table 1 in chapter four (p. 86) to identify which traits of maturity might need attention in the church.

Another survey I have used in discipleship groups is "The Christian Life Profile Assessment Tool" created by Randy Frazee.[1] His survey covers thirty areas of Christian discipleship (beliefs, practices, virtues) from an Evangelical theological perspective. Leaders from other theological traditions might find his list of topics valuable as a starting point for thinking about what their list would be. Frazee also encourages participants to have a trusted Christian friend assess them using the same survey items and then compare the self-assessment and peer assessment results. The peer assessment is helpful because some people rate themselves too harshly in some areas and too optimistically in others. In addition, The Christian Life Profile books provide a curriculum that can be used to help individuals take steps in personal spiritual growth in response to the results of the assessments.

When using a survey for personal spiritual development, it is important not simply to gather anonymous information, but instead to provide pastoral guidance to help people avoid common pitfalls. For example, many people dislike the idea of completing a survey to measure their spiritual health. Leaders should reassure them that no survey can perfectly capture who they are in Christ. Stress that it is just a tool to help them begin to think about their spiritual growth needs and to open a conversation with God and others about those needs.

It is also helpful to explain that just because a particular item receives a low score does not mean that area is the person's highest priority for spiritual growth. For example, the college students I have asked to complete this survey have commonly scored low on giving money to the church. While this is an important area for them to begin to work on even now, when they believe they "have no money," it might not be the first area of growth to tackle. Something like the VIM process should still be used to identify what God's priority is for a person's spiritual growth. Since no survey can perfectly measure reality, an individual may need to depart completely from the items on the survey to discover God's priority growth area in her life.

Because of these pastoral concerns, using surveys for personal development should probably be done under the guidance of an experienced leader in venues like Christian education classes, new members' classes, or discipleship groups. Those who will be leading these classes and groups should be trained to help people use the tools in a wise manner. As a minimum, they should have practiced using the tool on themselves under the guidance of another leader in the church.

In addition to evaluating how well individuals are doing in their growth toward maturity, congregational leaders need to evaluate how well their church's culture is promoting maturity. The Exemplary Youth Ministry team created a survey that churches can use to assess how they are doing in each of the forty-four congregational assets. For each asset, church members are asked to rate both how highly they perceive their church to be prioritizing that asset and how effective they believe their church is at fostering it.[2] Using the results of this survey, leaders can identify one or more assets that need work. When choosing which assets to pursue, keep in mind the six faith-sustaining factors for teenagers: strong parental faith, multiple religious experiences, a strong belief system, frequent prayer and Bible reading, and several adult friends in the congregation. Focus on assets that are likely to make the biggest improvements in those six areas of teenagers' lives. As we saw in chapter four, churches that provide these faith-sustaining factors for teenagers are more likely to succeed in helping adults grow to maturity as well.

The six faith-sustaining factors can themselves serve as criteria for assessing spiritual maturity in a congregation. It can be especially helpful to survey or interview parents, youth leaders, and teenagers separately and compare their responses. Do not assume that adults really know how young people are doing. Be especially careful to provide a forum likely to elicit honest responses from teenagers. Either focus groups led by trusted adults or an anonymous survey could work. Items like those listed below could be used in a survey, with respondents rating the church on a scale of 1 to 5.

1. Our church helps teenagers have many experiences of God.
2. Our church helps teenagers in our congregation experience *all four* of the following: a. Has committed life to God, b. Has had prayers answered, c. Has experienced a miracle, d. Has had a moving spiritual experience.
3. Our church helps teenagers have a faith that is extremely important in their daily lives.
4. Our church helps teenagers understand and believe their faith so strongly that they have few doubts about it.
5. Our church helps teenagers pray and read the Bible often on their own.
6. Our church helps parents to pray, talk about faith, and serve with their teenage children.
7. Our church helps teenagers have several adult friends in the congregation with whom they feel comfortable talking about their lives.
8. Our church helps adults become good spiritual friends and mentors to teenagers.

All groups should rate the church on a scale of 1 to 5. Additional helpful information can be gathered from teenagers by re-writing these items as "I/me" statements and asking them to rate how well the church has helped them personally experience these things.

These are not the only ways to assess spiritual maturity in a congregation. For example, in his book *The Emotionally Healthy Church*, Peter Scazzero provides an inventory of Spiritual and Emotional Maturity that he has used with considerable benefit in his own multiethnic congregation in New York.[3] Other psychologists and theologians have developed their own faith maturity surveys or structured interviews.[4] Each attempt to measure faith maturity relies on some set of psychological and theological assumptions, so it is wise for a church leadership team to identify and evaluate those assumptions before using a particular survey. Some surveys measure important qualities but are hard to correlate with the biblical traits of spiritual maturity identified in this book. For these and other reasons, a survey might not be right for every congregation.

But every church leadership team should have a discussion about spiritual maturity and try to assess how well they believe their church is doing at helping people move toward it. It also makes sense for leaders to consult a wide variety of people in the congregation for their opinions on how well the church is helping people grow in Christ. Thankfully, since EYM points us toward a tipping point of assets that can produce widespread spiritual maturity in a congregation, much progress can probably be made without precisely measuring the spiritual maturity of individuals. Congregations will find honest self-assessment to be most valuable when all involved remember that their perceptions might not be accurate and that the goal is to build everyone up in Christ, not to label some people as mature and others as immature.

Planning for Maturity

Moving from assessment to specific ministry plans can look simple at first, but often becomes more complex the closer it comes to implementation. It can be simple because identifying an area of weakness often prompts general ideas for changes that might help. I hope the material in this book has already stimulated this kind of thinking. Congregational leaders should consider how to improve their churches' effectiveness in presenting the gospel in a way that produces expectations for growth, teaching the basics of the faith, teaching about spiritual maturity, implementing the VIM model of spiritual formation, and creating exemplary youth ministries by working toward a tipping point of congregational assets. One or more of these approaches to promoting spiritual maturity may emerge as the highest priority for a church.

Once some area of congregational life has been identified as a priority, try to come up with a list of specific action steps that could help the congregation grow in that area. A leadership team that is engaging in brainstorming on action steps is trying to answer the question "How?" How can we foster intergenerational spiritual friendships in our congregation? How can we help teenagers have all four kinds of experiences of God? Make sure that the answers to these "how" questions are not more general goals (e.g., "get teenagers talking to adults") but specific practices, such as "create an intergenerational Bible study group that studies Scripture passages on intergenerational relationships." It can also be helpful to identify practices that the church is already doing that are helping. How could these practices be improved to encourage even more spiritual maturity in more people? Similarly, it can be helpful to look for current practices that may be undermining this goal. How could those practices be modified so that they encourage this dimension of maturity?

When brainstorming, be sure to list all of the possible ministry practices that could help reach a goal without prioritizing or evaluating any of the practices yet. For example, "get every teenager in the church meeting weekly with an adult mentor to go through the VIM process" is a ministry practice likely to encourage spiritual growth through intergenerational relationships, but it also might be very difficult to accomplish. In brainstorming, neither the difficulty of doing something nor the fact that someone in the group does not like the idea should prevent it from making the list; one youth pastor I know calls these rules "no wimping" and "no blocking." Leaders should also locate books, articles, and websites that offer specific ministry ideas related to their area of focus. Appendix B lists some resources that provide specific ideas for fostering spiritual maturity in a congregation.

Next comes the hard part: choosing and implementing specific ministry practices that are right for a particular church at a particular time in its history. Some ideas can be ruled out because their relational or financial costs are unrealistically high. For example, "hire a staff person to coordinate intergenerational relationships" might be a great idea, but financially impossible for a given congregation. If brainstorming has gone well, there will still be a long list of possible action steps even after eliminating ideas that require excessive resources. How can a leadership team discern which ideas to try to implement? Here are some questions that can help, sorted by category.

God's Vision for the Congregation

1. Which of these ideas is in accord with what God has already called our congregation to be as defined by our vision statement, mission statement, or theology?
2. Which of these ideas may undermine a core element of what God has called our church to be?
3. Which of these ideas seem to be most in accord with what God seems to be doing with our congregation at this time? (Communal prayer for discernment will be required.)

Potential for Positive Change

1. Which of these ideas are likely to have the biggest impact in moving the most people toward the goal?

2. Which of these ideas could help us develop multiple congregational as-sets, elements of maturity, or faith-sustaining factors at once?

Congregational Resources

1. Which of these ideas can be implemented in existing ministries, pro-grams, activities, or relationships?
2. Which of these ideas will require new ministries, programs, activities, or relationships?
3. Which of these ideas could be combined?
4. Which of these ideas should not be combined because each idea's impact would be diluted?
5. Which of these ideas are likely to get widespread support quickly and easily? Why?
6. Which of these ideas would be harder for our congregation to embrace? Why?
7. What additional steps would be needed to help the congregation embrace these ideas?
8. What might we have to say "no" to as a congregation in order to say "yes" to these ideas? What will it take to get the congregation to make that change in priorities?
9. Who could lead this effort?
10. What are the financial costs and where will we get the money?

Asking these questions about a brainstormed list of possible ministry prac-tices can help a church leadership team discern which changes should be attempted first. It is important not to despise small beginnings. The assets approach reassures us that every action that we take to grow even one asset can be worthwhile. And gathering a leadership team that regularly engages in a process of prayerful reflection on spiritual maturity in their congregation is a significant step in itself. Churches that do not plan for maturity are less likely to experience it.

Maturity on Sunday Morning

Asking the right questions is crucial to effective ministry assessment and planning. But it is often hard to be sure that we are finding accurate and helpful answers. And since we are often uncertain about the "diagnosis" as well as the "prescription" for spiritual maturity, there are many ways for our efforts to go astray. One reason for this uncertainty is that congregational cultures, like all cultures, are complex, evolving, shared systems of meaning and identity. Cultures include relationships, words, symbols, metaphors, stories, practices, roles, physical objects, and more. Each of these elements of culture communicates messages and forms people in what the community believes and values, loves and hates. For example, Scott Wilcher observes that many churchgoing adults use animal, alien, or "closed door" metaphors to describe the young people in their midst. He believes that until adults change the metaphors they use to think about young people, the gospel, and the church, they will not be able to effectively welcome young people into the church and help them grow in Christ.[5] And it is not just *what* is said or done, but *how* it is said and done that communicates. Even what is *not* said or *not* done communicates something about the identity and priorities of a congregation. To complicate matters even further, different people can "hear" different messages being communicated through the same word, metaphor, or church practice. Some participants in a culture typically accept the whole package rather unreflectively and find it difficult to distinguish between essential and non-essential matters. But leaders must become skilled interpreters and cultivators of their congregational cultures.

Although it is probably impossible to eliminate *all* negative or unintended messages in a congregational culture, it can be valuable to honestly assess what the dominant messages seem to be. Congregational leaders must ask themselves whether spiritual maturity is among the highest priorities of their church as reflected in how the church spends its time, money, and energy. Would an outside observer or visitor be able to quickly see that this church prioritizes spiritual maturity? One way to be sure the answer is "yes" is to make sure that what happens in Sunday morning worship regularly encourages spiritual maturity.

In most churches, Sunday morning worship is the central activity. It is the one place where the most people will be present, hopefully to hear the most important messages and do the most important things. It is a time of worship in which the body of Christ comes together before God to honor and adore him. But if spiritual maturity is rarely mentioned or modeled on Sunday morning, then the leaders of the church are communicating that spiritual maturity is not central to the life of the church. If the singing, praying, preaching, and giving are done without reference to spiritual maturity or in ways that promote various forms of immaturity, then it is unlikely that many will mature. Sunday worship cannot do the whole job of growing Christians to spiritual maturity, but it must do its part.

What is the role of the church's weekly corporate worship gathering in promoting spiritual maturity? First, the teaching and preaching should regularly mention and explain spiritual maturity. Preachers should find memorable and attractive ways to describe spiritual maturity, and remind people often about it. Since spiritual maturity is so closely tied to knowing the basic truths of the faith and knowing how to apply them, Sunday morning worship should include compelling teaching about the gospel and the Christian way of life. As a result of attending Sunday worship regularly, a person should know that there are some core Christian beliefs and should be able to say what at least some of those beliefs are. Ideally, they should also be in the process of finding those beliefs to be attractive and life-giving.

Second, the way we teach about worship and the metaphors we use to describe it should promote spiritual maturity. We must think hard about how we describe worship and its benefits. For example, some people refer to corporate worship as a "filling station"; others describe it as a "hospital." But these metaphors focus on us and our needs. It is hard for us to remember that God is in fact the focus of worship. A more helpful, biblical image for worship might focus on entering the throne room of the King to honor him, offer ourselves to him as his servants, ask for his help and protection, and wait for his commands (1 Kings 8:22-61; Psalms 93; 95; 99; 100; 122; 123; 132; 134; Isaiah 6; Hebrews 4:14-16; 12:18-24; Revelation 4–7).

Third, the music and music leaders should promote maturity. Some church music leaders want to turn worship into a rock concert, while others want to turn it into a music appreciation class. Worship is neither. The people who lead the singing are, next to the pastor, the most important public face of the congregation. Whatever these people do and say from the front will be highly influential. The music they select, the words they speak, and the way they carry themselves will shape the congregation's spirituality as much as, or at times more than, whatever is said from the pulpit. So, for example, when a well-meaning worship leader introduces a song by saying "ignore everyone else around you — this time is just between you and God," he is teaching an individualistic or perhaps even self-absorbed theology of worship that might be hard for any sound teaching from the pulpit to undo. At the other extreme, I once attended midnight mass at a Catholic parish where the music leader decided to celebrate Christmas without singing a single traditional Christmas carol. This music leader's artistic sensibilities were not serving what should have been the pastoral and evangelistic goals of a Christmas mass.

Even worship practices that are central to our traditions and theologies of worship can send unintended messages. For example, the time-honored form of the Sunday morning sermon may communicate that religious knowledge is obtainable by only a few experts. Or it might communicate that church is a place we go each week to hear about another new thing to do that we have no intention of implementing in our lives. On the other hand, the way that the pastor prepares and delivers the sermon could communicate that this is a sacred moment in which God is speaking to the congregation.

It is fine to disagree with my particular interpretations of worship practices and the messages they may be sending. In fact, any such disagreements only serve to confirm my main point: interpreting congregational culture is difficult, yet important. Church leaders who care about spiritual maturity must carefully examine what happens Sunday after Sunday in their churches and ask, "Is a steady diet of our church's Sunday morning worship likely to produce a spiritually mature Christian?" A similar question should be asked of other church programs and activities.

But how can we know what various elements of our congregational cultures are communicating? And how can we know if those elements of our culture are forming people in spiritual maturity or not? We need more than just good questions. We need a process for finding good answers.

Monitoring Maturity

Church leaders who make an initial assessment of their congregation's spiritual maturity and implement targeted plans will probably see some progress. But leaders who commit to an ongoing process of discernment will be more likely to see long-term, significant growth in spiritual maturity among the members of their congregation. While it can be difficult to accurately interpret and effectively modify the key elements of congregational culture, an ongoing cyclical process of reflection on current practice that leads to new action can help. That process can then become the object of further reflection. Busy ministry leaders are often tempted to skip important elements of reflection and move straight to tinkering with ministry practices. At other times, prejudices or misinformation can lead to bad decisions because the leadership team did not take the time to carefully understand what was happening in the congregation and why. Even some kinds of success need to be critically examined, as the history of juvenilization and the uncertain spiritual life outcomes of the "devoted" teenagers in the National Study of

Youth and Religion both illustrate. To avoid these and many other possible pitfalls along the path to spiritual maturity, it helps to break the ongoing process of ministry discernment into four distinct steps: observe, interpret, evaluate, and act (see Figure 5.1 below). In order to illustrate how this process works and to delve deeper into the connection between corporate worship and maturity, I will use this discernment cycle to evaluate what I call "slow dances with Jesus" worship music.

Figure 5.1 Cyclical Process of Ministry Discernment

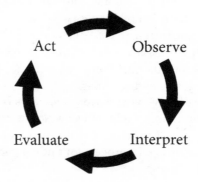

Act   Observe

Evaluate   Interpret

Listening to God Together

Monitoring maturity works best when a leadership team does it together, in consultation with God and with church members of all ages. Prayer and listening to the Holy Spirit are crucial elements of this cyclical process of discernment. Each of the four stages should be sustained and guided by prayerful interaction with God. Many Christians are not skilled in this kind of listening prayer. There are resources available that can help, but the most important thing is to begin to practice listening to God by giving God time and space to speak during team meetings.[6] It may be necessary for the group to study the topic of knowing God's will and discuss their beliefs about hearing God in order to reach some consensus about how to invite God's guidance into their reflective process. If members of the team do not have a shared understanding of the ways God's will is made known, it will be hard for them to exercise corporate spiritual discernment. Such a discussion can have the added benefit of raising awareness of the need to listen to God in many different ways throughout the cycle of reflection and action. Each time the team meets to engage in this process, they should take time for intercession and listening to God. If church leaders know congregants who are gifted intercessors or are especially good at listening to God, they should include these people in the discernment process.

Observe: What Is Happening?

Ministry decisions must be grounded in careful observations of both the internal life of the church and its external context. At this stage, it is important to ask "What is happening?" but not to rush to judgment about why it is happening or what should be done about it. The question "What is happening?" includes the question "What are some of the observable outcomes of our current practices?" This kind of observation can be done at various levels. For example, a youth ministry leadership team could gather observations about what is happening in their youth ministry and what effects the ministry's practices seem to be having in the lives of the young people involved. Church leaders could observe the culture of their congregation as a whole. Youth ministers or other church leaders could also narrow their focus to observe a particular aspect of their community life or ministry practice, such as worship or Christian education.

The Exemplary Youth Ministry team created two helpful tools for observing congregational culture: "Identifying Your Church's Culture" and "Investigating the Life of a Congregation." These tools ask questions like "What would an outsider, after sitting through several worship services, say your church values most?" and "Who are the heroes in your church — the members who are most celebrated, honored, or emulated?"[7] It is important to note that these tools created by the EYM team combine some elements of "observe" and some elements of "interpret." Appendix C also provides a list of questions to ask when observing congregational culture, with an emphasis on items that might bear on spiritual maturity.

What do we find when we observe the worship music found in many Evangelical youth ministries and churches? First, the music is often performed by a rock band that plays from a stage in the front of the worshipping group. In some cases, uses of lighting, gestures by the musicians, and cheers from the worshippers resemble practices found at a rock concert. When the musicians speak, they sometimes sound like pop artists introducing a song or pumping up the audience. Evangelicals tend to use the word "worship" to refer exclusively to singing songs of praise, and the younger they are, the more likely they are to use the term this way. Many worship songs are sung in the first person ("I") addressed to God ("you.") Promises of emotional fulfillment and declarations of love are common. The more the song attempts to communicate the intimacy between God and the individual Christian, the more likely the musical style resembles those used for slow dances at a prom or a wedding reception.

The words themselves sometimes draw explicitly on the language of romantic love as it is used in popular culture. For example, the opening stanza of Matt and Beth Redman's popular song "Let My Words Be Few" begins with the declaration, "You are God in heaven, and here am I on earth," then builds to the climactic phrase: "Jesus I am so in love with you." The second verse of Kelly Carpenter's song "Draw Me Close," which ranked in the top 25 worship songs in America between 2003 and 2006 on no less than eight different occasions, is typical of this genre of romantic worship:

> You are my desire
> No one else will do
> 'Cause nothing else
> Could take Your place
> To feel the warmth
> Of Your embrace
> Help me find a way
> Bring me back to You

A significant number of contemporary worship songs employ a slow-dance musical style and use words or phrases like "desire," "longing," "I need your touch," "hold me," "in your arms," or "you're beautiful."[8]

We can conclude that some contemporary worship music employs musical styles and words drawn from the North American culture of romantic love. And the musical ensembles that lead the singing draw on the cultural styles and practices of rock bands and pop music concerts. People who consume a heavy spiritual diet of such music tend to think of "falling in love" or "being in love" as good metaphors for their relationship with Jesus. I have run into many Christians of all ages who take it for granted that they should be "in love" with Jesus. For some, being "in love" with God is so central to their spirituality that they are not open to any criticisms of this metaphor.

A good many American Christians of all ages love this music. When they sing it, they feel close to God, spiritually energized, and ready to live another day in obedience to God. Some of the favorite chapel times at my Christian university are the "praise and worship" chapels, which have no speaker, only singing. Such worship music has become a primary way for many Christians to express and sustain their devotion to God. Singing is typically the only activity in Evangelical worship that actively engages our bodies. When my undergraduate students visit Roman Catholic churches, they often notice that the people there do not seem to be "into it" or "engaged" because they are not fervently singing to God. Pop music sung with passion has become a defining element of Evangelical Christian youth culture, and to some extent of Evangelical worship among adults as well.

Every process of observation is selective, and there can be no observation that does not include at least some interpretation. In this case, I chose to observe particular ways that certain contemporary worship practices mimic pop culture because I believe these adaptations may be problematic. But at this stage of the process it is important to avoid rushing to judgment. That is why I tried to identify some positive effects of this music as well.

Unfortunately, many leaders stop the discernment process here and decide to accept or reject a church practice without doing the hard work of interpreting what it may mean to the people to whom it speaks so powerfully. At the very least, a failure to interpret prevents leaders from really understanding and having compassion for the people they are serving. At worst, it leads to ministry failures of various kinds. Leaders who ignore the meaning and power of cultural forms may underestimate what it will take to tame or resist them. If they mistakenly reject a new ministry approach, they may block the creativity of the body of Christ and the work of the Holy Spirit. On the other hand, those who too easily accept a cultural adaptation may undermine spiritual maturity.

Interpret: What Does It Mean?

To interpret an element of congregational culture is to try to answer two important questions about it: "What does it mean?" and "Why is it happening?" If the practice is a Christianized version of something that is done in the wider culture, it is often revealing to investigate how it functions outside the church. Most likely some of those cultural functions and meanings will come with the practice when it is "baptized" and used in the church. Every cultural form enables certain ways of thinking and living, and hinders others.[9] So every translation of the Christian life into particular cultural forms highlights some aspects of the faith and makes it harder to remember and practice other aspects.

One reason youth ministries have contributed to the juvenilization of the church over the years is that youth ministry leaders typically held naïve views of the relationship between cultural forms and the messages they communicate. Many took an "ice cream scoop" approach to adapting elements of youth culture for use in church: simply take some element of youth culture, scoop out the "secular" content, and pour in some "Jesus" content. As we saw in chapter one, in the example of the young woman who described Jesus as being just like Elvis but better, this approach relies on the false assumption that cultural forms are neutral tools of communication.[10] A better approach is to realize that every form of communication reshapes the message to some extent, and to take steps to make sure nothing important in the message is lost.[11] This interaction between form and content cannot be avoided, so leaders who want to communicate God's truth clearly and effectively need to attend to it.

So how do we accurately interpret the meaning behind our congregation's cultural practices? The first step is to take the answers discovered using the "observe" questions from Appendix C and ask "Why is this happening?" and "What messages is this sending?" But that exercise will typically result in several possible answers. And all of those answers could be right, because practices and symbols tend to have multiple meanings and functions. In addition, different people will perceive different messages in the same practice or symbol.

When trying to interpret your congregation's culture, it is important to listen to as many different people as possible. Listen to people who love the practice as well as to those who dislike it. Listen to theologians and other scholars who have studied this practice or element of culture and tried to explain it. Listen to fellow leaders and church members of all ages. As team members listen to others and discuss possible meanings together, they can work toward a shared set of interpretations. Reaching some level of agreement about how to interpret a particular practice will prove crucial later when trying to unite around a particular response to it.

In some cases, it may be obvious that all or most of the possible messages being communicated by a particular practice are more likely to hinder than to encourage spiritual maturity. But in other cases, the meanings may be mixed or contradictory. What is to be done in such cases? For now, just list all of the possible meanings and causes of a particular element of congregational culture. Remember that every interpretation, including yours, is provisional and should be open to revision as further information becomes available. Appendix D provides questions that can help leaders discern whether a practice is mostly supporting or mostly undermining spiritual maturity.

How can you tell if your interpretation is correct? First, it should help you make sense of your observations by providing an "a-ha moment." Suddenly you see something new about why people are behaving a certain way. You begin to get a sense of what is important to people and what important functions a particular symbol, metaphor, or practice plays in their lives. Whenever possible, you should gain a genuine appreciation of the good in this element of congregational culture. Second, other outside observers should agree with your interpretation. Here is a good place to check your own observations against what researchers are saying about trends in society and in the church. Third, your interpretation should seem plausible to a thoughtful insider. It is important to note, however, that those who are immersed in a culture are not always able to see some of the reasons why they believe and behave the way they do. Your interpretation may still have some merit, even if insiders never noticed it before. Finally, a sound interpretation will seem promising as a basis for positively influencing congregational culture. Your interpretation might help you predict how people will act in particular situations. It might help you understand why people are "stuck" and not maturing. It might suggest possible changes that could help.

To return to our case study, what possible messages does "slow-dance" worship music communicate? How might it affect those who use it? Music is an important influence in many people's lives. Young people use music as a source of meaning, moral guidance, and identification. Adolescents and young adults use music for mood management. Two-thirds of college students report using music to help them deal with feelings of loneliness. "Light" music is especially used by young women to regulate emotions associated with romantic relationships and loneliness. Huge numbers of people use pop music as a sound track for romantic relationships, and the subject matter of popular music is heavily weighted toward emotional and sexual intimacy.[12]

Unfortunately, there has been little empirical research on music's effects on adults. But it is reasonable to suggest that Christians of all ages may use slow-dance worship music for mood management, especially since the most popular songs are so emotionally laden. Try this non-scientific experiment. Ask people who listen to a lot of praise and worship music to fast from it for a few days. If they are anything like the undergraduate students in my youth culture classes, they will miss the emotional comfort their music gives them. As we saw in chapter one, contemporary Americans of all ages need a lot of help dealing with difficult emotions. So it should come as no surprise that they turn to romantic music, both secular and Christian, to help them with their emotional needs. Some singing sessions in some churches may function as a kind of emotional triage. Singing these songs in the ways that some of our churches do may be keeping some emotionally critically-ill people functional — certainly a valuable and even praiseworthy thing to do. But further assistance will be needed to cure their chronic emotional health problems and help them reach spiritual maturity.

Music does affect us. According to some cognitive psychologists, as we grow up listening to music, our brains get "hard wired" to prefer particular sounds and to associate them with particular meanings. According to a well established theory of media effects called "priming," media products reinforce patterns of thinking and behaving in certain situations. These patterns are called "schemas," and once they are formed, an individual may use them to form judgments about real-life situations. Physiological and emotional arousal (of the sort commonly associated with music and music videos) make priming effects more powerful. Schemas that are primed through frequent exposure can affect me even if I know that they are unrealistic portrayals.[13]

The effects of priming have been demonstrated in experiments. One study showed college students music videos that portrayed stereotypical male-female interactions (sexual aggression by male, submission by female), followed by a video (not a music video) in which a female resisted a male's advances. Those primed by the music videos were more likely to evaluate the second woman negatively. In another study, male undergraduates who frequently listened to either violent heavy metal *or Christian heavy metal* were more likely to express negative attitudes toward women.[14] This latter study suggests that musical styles, not just words, are part of the priming effect. Even if the causality works in the other direction — certain kinds of people are drawn to certain styles of music — there may still be reason for concern. The music people love provides evidence about their patterns of emotional response. And these patterns in turn say something about their hearts.

There has been little or no empirical research on the effects of worship music, so we can't know for sure what its priming effects might be. But the media-effects research should warn us that popular music may be priming us to apply its schemas about love and romance to our relationship with Jesus. And it is likely that this effect is increased when the worship songs we sing draw heavily on the very same musical styles, words, and metaphors as their secular counterparts.

What are the messages or "schemas" about romantic love found in popular culture? We are all swimming in a sea of music, television shows, and movies that use "true love" as the agent of salvation and the solution to every problem. Our participation in this culture of "redemptive romance" probably makes it feel natural for Christians to use "falling in love" with Jesus as a metaphor for salvation. Among college students, three-quarters of men and half of women surveyed agree that "The right mate 'completes you' — filling your needs and making your dreams come true." Similarly, 94 percent of never-married respondents in their twenties agreed that "When I marry, I want my spouse to be my soul mate, first and foremost." Half of all college students agreed that "There is such a thing as love at first sight." In contrast to real life, in which infatuation is fleeting, the media relies on instantaneous "falling in love" as a permanent solution to all problems because it is a quick fix that can fit into not only a two-hour movie, but even a three-minute song. Also popular is the myth that "Your perfect partner is cosmically predestined, so nothing/nobody can ultimately separate you." If we believe these myths, for us love is "maneuvered beyond reason and choice — and beyond our responsibility." Research shows that those who believe such myths have more unrealistic expectations and are more dissatisfied in their real romantic relationships.[15]

But if the media myths about love and romance are not good for our human relationships, can they be good for our relationship with Jesus? Of course it could be that Jesus functions as the "perfect lover" who fulfills the longings that cannot be fulfilled by any human being. But the schemas of popular culture are unlikely to help us develop a realistic sense of what that means.

The content of pop music is weighted heavily toward explorations of being in and out of love and the emotions that go with those experiences in adolescence. Psychological research shows that especially for younger adolescents, romantic relationships are primarily about the individual's status, emotional needs, and identity search. The ability to develop genuinely mutual romantic relationships with staying power develops later. For some people, this ability is only just developing during young adulthood. Much pop music assumes and reinforces an immature approach to romantic relationships.[16] One psychologist's description of romantic love is especially revealing. The person who is "in love" thinks obsessively about the beloved. Lovers idealize their beloved and ignore that person's flaws. They experience "extreme energy, hyperactivity, sleeplessness, euphoria, mood swings." Obstacles or adversity can heighten their passion. Many become emotionally dependent on the relationship and rearrange their life to spend more time with that person. They will neglect other obligations and relationships in order to pursue their beloved. Above all, a lover "craves emotional union" with the beloved. But all this passion is "involuntary and difficult, if not impossible to control." And it inevitably fades.[17]

Both social-science research and my own observations of Christians immersed in romantic spirituality urge me to conclude that slow-dance worship songs are drawing on American cultural scripts about romantic relationships for their emotional impact. Those exposed to a steady diet of this music will be tempted to embrace the Christian life as a kind of romantic infatuation. Like an adolescent working out his emotional needs and identity issues, such Christians may develop a self-centered relationship with Jesus. Like a smitten lover, they may make extreme sacrifices to keep the emotional highs coming. Although they feel that they are ready to die for Jesus now, they might break up with him later. They will value the way Jesus makes them feel and will be much less concerned about the theological content of the faith. Too many slow dances with Jesus may reinforce immature forms of the Christian life.

Evaluate: What Does Our Christian Faith Say?

After we have identified and begun to interpret important elements of the culture in our youth ministry or church, we are ready to evaluate them in light of the truths of the Christian faith. Since our specific concern is juvenilization, it is crucial to evaluate elements of congregational culture using a well-developed theology of spiritual maturity. Chapter two can serve as a resource for such evaluation. Appendix E provides questions that church leaders can use to evaluate elements of congregational culture in light of their potential impact on spiritual maturity.

How are we to evaluate slow-dance worship music in light of the biblical teaching on spiritual maturity? On the positive side, it can help people feel that God loves them personally, just as the shepherd loves the lost sheep and the father loved his lost son (Luke 15). Through his death and resurrection, Jesus creates a close Father-child relationship between his followers and God (Romans 8:12-17, Galatians 3:23–4:7, 1 John 1–3), and this music emphasizes that closeness. These songs also resonate with the promises of peace, joy, encouragement, and rest found in the Scriptures (Romans 14:17; 15:4-6, Philippians 4:4-7, Matthew 11:28-30). God does want to help us with our problems, including our emotional problems (2 Corinthians 1:3-11). Those who feel "in love" with Jesus may even be motivated to make sacrifices for him. The music may help some people feel motivated to pursue spiritual growth.

Nevertheless, although the Bible makes clear that Christians have a close, familial relationship with God, that closeness is not described in terms of romantic love. There are passages that use marriage and marriage feasts as metaphors to describe the relationship between Christ and the church. But these passages teach about things like being ready for the Lord's return, the joyful celebration to follow, or Christ ruling the church and giving his life to purify it (Matthew 22:1-14; 25:1-13; Luke 12:35-38; Romans 7:4; 1 Corinthians 11:3; 2 Corinthians 11:2; Ephesians 5:21-33; Revelation 19:7; 21:2, 9, 17). None of these passages tell Christians they should be "in love" with Jesus. And they are corporate images, not metaphors for the individual believer's relationship to Christ.

These New Testament images are drawing on Old Testament passages that refer to God as the "husband" of Israel (Hosea 1–3; Isaiah 54:5-8; 62:4-5; Jeremiah 2:20; 3:1; 31:31-34; Ezekiel 16:8-22). These passages use the marriage metaphor to teach about God's faithfulness despite the unfaithfulness of his people. They are corporate images intended to help us understand and appreciate the goodness and covenant-keeping love of God. These passages do not tell us to feel "in love" with God.[18] These uses of the marriage image can probably be extrapolated to include the idea of emotional closeness between God and an individual believer, especially since the more prominent metaphor of sons and daughters of God includes that kind of closeness (Romans 8:15-16; Galatians 4:6). But "falling in love" as it is experienced in contemporary American culture has as many differences as it has similarities to God's covenant-keeping love for his people.

The sole possible exception to what I have been saying is the Song of Solomon. Because this poem offers few reliable clues that fix its place in history and because of its erotic subject matter, interpretations have varied widely. Yet two main approaches have emerged. The rabbis and Christians before the modern era interpreted the Song of Songs as an allegory of the love between God and his people or sometimes as an allegory between God and the individual human soul. But these interpreters typically spiritualized the desires depicted in the book. God desires his people and his people desire him, but that mutual desire should not be equated with ordinary human sexual desire or romantic feelings. Modern interpreters deny that the poem should be read allegorically, seeing it rather as a divine endorsement of human erotic love. One modern interpretation even sees this book as a satire on the reign of Solomon and his exploitation of women.[19]

The Song of Solomon is shaky ground on which to build a maturing Christian spirituality. If modern interpreters are right, then the book should not be read as teaching much about desire between God and his people. If traditional interpreters are right, then we must also allow not just the Song of Solomon but the entire canon of Scripture to reshape our distorted understandings of erotic love before we apply them to our relationship with God. It is God's love which is the original; the erotic love between a man and a woman is a pale reflection.[20] We can learn something about the relationship between God and his people by examining the best in human marriage. Yet we should also let Scripture teach us that erotic love is not the standard by which all loves are measured. And we must not take the worst of our culture's follies regarding romantic love and treat them as spiritual ideals. Although they agree on almost nothing else, both traditional and modern interpretations of the Song of Songs caution us in these ways. Finally, if God intended the Song of Solomon to draw a parallel between erotic human love and the love between God and the individual human being, why was that metaphor not picked up more prominently in the New Testament? After all, the New Testament writers make much of the fact that individual followers of Jesus enjoy a closer relationship with God their Father than was possible under the Old Covenant.[21] At the very least we can conclude that because of the shape of contemporary American spirituality, allegorical or metaphorical readings of the Song of Solomon can easily be abused to promote immature ways of relating to God.

What kind of relationship are the metaphors of "falling in love" or "being in love" likely to encourage between a contemporary American Christian and God? Such a person might be like the plant on rocky soil that springs up quickly, but withers when trouble or persecution comes (Matthew 13:5, 20-21). He may be tempted to believe a false gospel of emotion management or redemptive romance rather than the biblical gospel of the kingdom of God.

A disciple's relationship with Jesus the master involves training and submission, not just emotional comfort, and certainly not erotic excitement (Luke 6:40; Matthew 28:20). Followers of Jesus give up all claims to their own life and devote themselves to joining him in his kingdom mission. They exercise their wills to choose to follow him (Matthew 19:16-22). Mature Christians get stronger in their faith and better at sacrificially serving others over time (Philippians 3, Ephesians 4).

Slow-dance worship music also does little to grow mature Christian *communities*. With its emphasis on the one-on-one relationship between Jesus and the believer ("Jesus I am so in love with you") it does nothing to counteract the rampant individualism in American society. The particular brand of individualism found in this music emphasizes how God fits into my life and provides me what I need, not how I need to fit into God's kingdom. In other words, it reinforces the therapeutic or even narcissistic religion that is rampant in contemporary America: God exists to help me feel better about my problems. It at least potentially undermines a key element of biblical spiritual maturity: serving Christ's mission in community with other Christians.

People heavily influenced by romantic worship music may well come to value their local church only insofar as it meets their emotional needs. They may switch churches or drop out altogether when they no longer feel their needs are being met. The good of others and the unity of the body of Christ are not as important to these believers as their own sense of emotional fulfillment. Romantic love is regarded as a private affair in American culture, and lovers typically resist outside interference. In contrast, the Bible teaches that Christian growth to maturity cannot be achieved in an exclusive, private relationship between Jesus and the believer (Ephesians 4:11-16).

Thankfully, much of the contemporary worship music influenced by pop and rock styles is not "slow dance with Jesus" music. But many American Christians have at least implicitly decided that "falling in love with Jesus" is a helpful metaphor. What should we do with this metaphor and the music that supports it?

Act: What Should We Do to Encourage Spiritual Maturity?

A group of Christians who have done well at observing, interpreting, and evaluating a particular church practice will often already have a general sense for how they should approach it. But the group will still need to think carefully about what kind of action is appropriate. There are four clear options. A church could *accept* the practice and keep it as it is because they see no negative effects or they believe any possible negative effects are negligible. Second, a church could *eliminate* a cultural expression completely either because they believe it contradicts some important element of the faith or because it significantly undermines spiritual maturity. A third option is to keep the practice but *modify* it to minimize its negative effects. Finally, a church could keep the practice largely unchanged, but find ways to *compensate* for its negative effects through other practices.

Given that church leaders are not likely to spend a lot of time evaluating practices that they think are wonderful, it may be rare that they take the *accept* approach at the end of their deliberations. But those engaging in the discernment process should be genuinely open to that possibility. Sometimes even cultural practices that seem obviously sinful or theologically incorrect do not turn out to be so after more careful examination. For example, on the face of it, eating meat used in a pagan temple ceremony seems like an obvious violation of God's commandments against idolatry. Yet Paul insisted that Christians could eat this meat because of the freedom found in the gospel, because pagan gods are not real and because the meat could be purified by thanking God for it before partaking. He urged Christians on both sides of this issue to focus on more important matters: loving each other well and "righteousness and peace and joy in the Holy Spirit" (Romans 14:17). In practice, loving others well meant that neither those who ate this meat nor those who believed it was wrong to eat it got everything they wanted. Neither group could legitimately force everyone in the church to take their approach. Instead, everyone needed to put the good of others first. Those who ate this meat were to carefully avoid scandalizing those with weaker consciences, and those who believed it was wrong for them to eat this meat were not to condemn their brothers and sisters who did. The goal was for both groups to be able join together in communal meals, especially the Lord's Supper (Romans 14:1–15:13; 1 Corinthians 8–9; 10:23–11:1). God cares deeply about the unity of his church, and so should we as we try to promote spiritual maturity (Ephesians 4).

So how can we decide which of the four options is appropriate in a given instance? Appendix E provides some guidance by suggesting which of the four "act" options might be needed depending upon how a leadership team has answered the "evaluate" questions. As in each stage of the cyclical process of ministry discernment, corporate prayer and listening to the Holy Spirit are very important. But it can also help to imagine what each of the four options might look like in practice. Such a thought experiment can reveal whether a particular community of Christians has sufficient vision, unity, and resources to make particular changes.

Returning to our case study, we can imagine that those who decide to *accept* slow-dance worship music would do so because they see it as helpful, or at least not damaging, to Christian spirituality. They might see it as a legitimate way to welcome white, middle-class Americans who like contemporary music and help them feel connected to God. Such Christians will freely use this music and will make much of the analogy between romantic love and Christian discipleship. They might teach on the Song of Solomon or the marriage metaphors in Scripture and explain their relevance for understanding the love between God and his church.

Those who choose to *eliminate* slow-dance worship music would do so because they believe that this music distorts the biblical picture of discipleship and reinforces false gospels promoted in American popular culture. They might conclude that this music is not contributing to the culture of spiritual maturity that they are trying to build together in their church. They would most likely stop singing any songs that use key romantic phrases like "in love" or "I need your touch." They might also decide to avoid using the metaphors of "falling in love" or "being in love" in sermons or other teachings. They might recommend that Christians avoid this music even in their private lives, not just during corporate worship at church. They might explain how romantic spirituality hinders individual and corporate spiritual maturity. They might scrutinize all their music, not just the overtly romantic music, to make sure that words like "need," "feel," and "love" are used in biblically sound ways.

A church that chose to *modify* slow-dance worship music would keep singing it in public worship, but they might change some of the words in some of the songs. For example, some uses of "I" and "me" could be changed to "us" and "we." Some uses of the phrase "in love" could be modified to other verb forms. They could also choose to sing less of this kind of music and instead sing other contemporary worship music that does not rely so heavily on romantic imagery. They might avoid dimming the lights and eliminate DJ-style introductions of these songs to subtly signal that something other than a slow dance with Jesus is about to happen. They might also decide to teach about the Song of Solomon and the marriage metaphors in Scripture in ways that attempted to correct distorted perceptions of what it means to be "in love" with God.

A church that wanted to *compensate* for the harmful effects of slow-dance worship would look for ways to counteract the negative effects of this music, but without directly attacking it or eliminating it. They might sing more songs that talk about Jesus as Lord and ways that Christians need to follow him and be devoted to his kingdom purposes in the world. They might encourage artists to write new music that powerfully expresses other elements of biblical discipleship. They could find or write new songs that use "we" and "us" more than "I" and "me" — or dwell almost exclusively on God and not much on the worshippers at all. They would provide sound biblical teaching on God-centered worship. They would also work to make sure that preaching, prayer, the Lord's Supper, and other worship activities are forming people in spiritual maturity.

Those taking the *compensate* approach might also teach against the false gospels of "redemptive romance" and "emotion management" and explain how they differ from the gospel of the Kingdom of God. In particular, they would talk about sin and our need for forgiveness through Christ as a balance to the emphasis on emotional comfort found in much worship music. They would teach about other metaphors for the Christian life, such as servant, friend, or child of God, or brothers and sisters in Christ. Since they want to *compensate* for rather than *eliminate* romantic spirituality, they might not openly teach against the metaphor of falling in love. Instead, they might teach about elements of Christian faith and life that romantic spirituality tends to neglect, such as service, suffering, and our need for connection to the body of Christ. All these efforts would ideally be part of a broader culture of spiritual maturity in the church.

In practice, *modify* and *compensate* can look similar, and some combination of both is often helpful. The difference between the two approaches is that in a pure *compensate* approach, a church would leave the questionable practice unchanged and just add other practices or teaching to counteract its perceived weaknesses.

Both the *modify* and *compensate* approaches can be helpful in cases in which it is hard to reach consensus about the effects of a practice. In some cases, it is possible to see some positive effects and some negative effects that a practice may be having on the spiritual maturity of congregation members. Or congregation members may be divided, with some firmly convinced that a practice has mainly negative effects, and others thinking it has mostly positive effects. In such cases, the *modify* or *compensate* approaches allow congregational leaders to experiment with small changes to see if they make a difference in spiritual maturity without unnecessarily alienating congregation members who may like the practice.

After exploring the options, church leaders need to choose a course of action based on their theological convictions and their sense of what God is calling their church to do. I would argue that since romantic spirituality does little to promote the traits of spiritual maturity and tends to undermine quite a few of them, churches would be wise to eliminate the most blatant examples of slow-dance worship songs from their worship repertoire. This step keeps such music out of corporate worship and makes clear that the church is not promoting this spirituality. Teachers and preachers should also stop using the metaphor of "falling in love" with Jesus. In many cases, church leaders could eliminate these elements of worship without causing much controversy or provoking many complaints, although it might be hard to get some musicians to agree to these changes.

Yet quietly eliminating "falling in love" language from our singing and teaching might not be enough to counteract the juvenilization that comes through romantic spirituality. A larger subset of contemporary worship music is emotionally therapeutic, subtly romantic, or both. Romantic spirituality can be found in popular Christian books and on the lips of well-known Christian speakers.[22] American Christians are often as immersed as everyone else in popular entertainment that ceaselessly proclaims the false gospel of redemptive romance. Our silence on these matters might not speak loudly enough to be heard over the noise of popular culture. We may need to explicitly teach against romantic spirituality and its tendency to reduce Christian discipleship to an adolescent infatuation. At the very least, we need to make sure that we are offering compelling words, metaphors, symbols, and practices that can help people find other sources for mature identity in Christ.

After implementing some action steps to counteract romantic spirituality, a church leadership team should observe the results of those changes over time. From there, the cycle of discernment would continue, perhaps resulting in revised action steps. The same process can be applied to any element of congregational culture in order to monitor maturity and take informed action to promote it.

This process might seem overly mechanical to some readers. It is certainly analytical. But as we become more intentional in our pursuit of spiritual maturity, it is important to be humble and loving in how we form judgments and try to influence outcomes. It is easy to start finding immaturity or juvenilization everywhere. Instead of forming good judgments (discernment), we can become judgmental. Christians should not go running to their pastor or music leader every time they see something in worship that they think might promote immaturity. Becoming "maturity police" could easily turn into its own form of immaturity as we all try to impose our preferences on each other. That is what was happening in some New Testament churches with regard to meat offered to idols.

Another danger is that instead of finding hope in God's plan for spiritual maturity, we can feel overwhelmed by all the problems to solve in our own lives or in our congregations. And instead of welcoming outsiders, we could become closed communities full of people who think their stubborn refusal to change for the sake of others is a mark of maturity. I find several metaphors useful in providing spiritual perspectives that can help us avoid these and other dangers that may come from a heightened awareness of juvenilization and spiritual maturity.

Bridge Builders and Gardeners

Humans are finite creatures whom God created to rule over creation as regents (Genesis 1:26-28). We tend the garden; we don't create it (Genesis 2:15). And salvation comes not from us, but from God, who entered our world and changed everything (John 1, Ephesians 1, Philippians 2:1-11). Church leaders cannot control the destinies of their congregations, nor can they keep their distance from people as they figure out what is "best for them" and impose it without their knowledge or consent. Church leaders would do better to think of themselves as both bridge builders and gardeners.

We should be building bridges to those who do not yet know Christ and have not yet become members of his family, the church. This book has not been about bridge building, but considerations of spiritual maturity should shape how we design and manage bridges. A bridge must touch both sides of some gap that divides people. It must reach people where they are and speak to them in words, symbols, metaphors, and feelings that they can understand. Paul did this in Athens when he found an altar dedicated "to an unknown god" and used it as a starting point to tell the Athenians about the one true God and his Son. He began with their understanding of God, quoted their poets approvingly, and led them toward new understandings of God, worship, and salvation.[23] In extreme cases, some congregations could themselves be so immersed in immaturity that they are effectively on the "wrong side" of the bridge. In such cases, church leaders will need to build a bridge to a new land of kingdom living and encourage members of the church to follow them there.

As people cross our bridges and begin spending more and more time with God's people, they should begin to see that things are done a bit differently in this new family that lives in a new kingdom. They will need to learn to be bilingual — to speak the language of their own culture, but also the language of Christian faith.[24] This requires that they become immersed in words, images, metaphors, practices, and relationships that help them learn this new way of life and new language.

When we are planning, building, or maintaining bridges to faith and to membership in God's family, we must always ask, "What can we do to encourage the traffic to flow in the right direction?" Are visitors and young people entering the family of God and learning the language of faith? Or are the saints crossing back over the bridge to avoid growing to maturity? Paul visited the Aeropagus in Athens and spoke the language of Greek philosophy, but he did not go there to become a Greek philosopher and leave his calling as an apostle behind.

Leaders can influence, although they cannot fully control, which way the traffic flows. My wife and I visited Prince Edward Island on our honeymoon. There was no fee to cross the bridge onto the island, but when we left one week later, we paid a rather high toll. The people who created the bridge toll wanted to make it easy for tourists to visit. Of course if Prince Edward Island was not also a beautiful place to vacation, no bridge toll system would get people to come in the first place, let alone stay.

No one wants to cross a bridge that leads to an unattractive destination. That is one of many reasons why church leaders must also be skillful gardeners. The word "culture" comes from the Latin word for "cultivate," as can still be seen in the word "agriculture." Congregations, like all human communities, are more like gardens to be tended than they are like mathematical problems to be solved. Although we might prefer to find a "solution" that "fixes" things for good, that is not how gardens work. They need regular attention. But that sustained work yields a beautiful garden full of life-giving food.

The gardener's job is not to create the plants or even get them to grow, but to create the conditions that will encourage growth. Leaders need to plan the layout of the garden, prepare the soil, plant, water, weed, and wait. They need to watch for growth, transplant, and prune or thin the plants. Good gardening requires thoughtful planning, keen observation, and wise discernment about what the plants need. The results depend upon a complex interaction between the gardener, the plants, the soil, the weather, weeds, insects, and probably other factors as well. And many of these forces are outside the gardener's control or can only be compensated for to some degree. A good gardener works almost every day in the garden, although there will be times and seasons that require more or less intense work. A gardener does not begrudge this work, but often looks forward to it and takes joy in it.

Seeing themselves as gardeners can help church leaders confidently exercise faith, hope, and love in their work. They can trust God, who has re-created his people to live in flourishing, growing communities. They can work hard while rejoicing in the hope of seeing the harvest that God will send. Good gardeners love the individual plants, the whole garden, and the God who created them. And they do all this without taking full credit or laboring under a cloud of self-blame. An experienced gardener takes the long view. Some years produce better harvests than others.

Nurturing a garden in which Christians are growing to maturity is a noble calling. It is a privilege to work in God's vineyard whether it seems to be a good year or not. Your church is a beautiful creation of God. Nothing in this book is meant to condemn you or your church. Rather, this book is a gardening manual that offers help and hope for every church to thrive. May you now be better equipped to take your next steps together to cultivate the garden God has entrusted to you. One plants, another waters, and God gives the growth (1 Corinthians 3:5-9).

Thirty-Three Characteristics of Maturing Christian Youth That Combine to Form the Seven Characteristics of "Vital, Maturing Faith"

Characteristic 1: Seek Spiritual Growth

Youth are pursuing spiritual growth through conversation, study, reading the Bible, prayer, small groups, and retreats.

1. Are heard referring to having prayer, devotions, and meditation times.
2. Ask sincere and searching questions about the nature of a life of faith in God.
3. Prefer and attend gatherings where they can learn more about the Christian faith.
4. Accept opportunities for learning how to speak naturally and intelligently about their faith.
5. Are involved in Bible study and/or prayer groups.
6. Join Christian groups to build friendships and learn how to be a friend.

Characteristic 2: Possess a Vital Faith

Youth are keenly aware of God present and active in their own life, the lives of others, and the life of the world.

1. Speak openly about seeking or experiencing God's guidance.
2. Are heard asking each other about what God has recently done in their lives or the lives of others.

3. In times of trouble, reassure others that God is active to make things work out in the long run.
4. Occasionally speak of having been keenly aware of the presence of God.

Characteristic 3: Make the Christian Faith a Way of Life

Youth recognize God's "call" and integrate their beliefs into the conversation, decisions, and actions of daily life.

1. Speak publicly about their relationship with Jesus Christ.
2. When providing a rationale for their actions, will at times cite specifics of their faith.
3. In conversation with family and friends, bring up topics of faith or Christian living.
4. Pray for people especially needing God's help.

Characteristic 4: Practice Faith in Community

Youth actively practice their faith in Jesus Christ, privately and publicly, through participation in the congregation's worship, ministries, and leadership.

1. Regularly attend worship services.
2. Have willingly participated in two or more of the following:
    • Taught Sunday school, Bible class, or Vacation Bible School
    • Served with a group to improve conditions at school or neighborhood
    • Made a presentation before a faith group or in worship
    • Helped in raising money for a Christian project or mission trip
    • Served on a congregational or denominational committee or task force
    • Regularly contribute money to a congregation or faith project

Characteristic 5: Possess a Positive Spirit

Youth reflect loving and hopeful attitudes toward others and life.

1. Enjoy being together, as evidenced by their laughing, singing, and conversation.

2. Show a gracious, loving attitude to people not easy to like (for example, the difficult, rude, shunned, "loser").
3. Have friends of widely diverse socioeconomic, ethnic, and religious background or persuasion.
4. Have been heard describing the Christian faith as a necessary force in society, helping people develop attitudes of understanding, sympathy, and cooperation.
5. Are known for their general optimism, trust, and positive expectation of other people, being convinced that one person can do much to make the world a better place.
6. Are eager, responsive, and cooperative rather than unresponsive, disinterested, and apathetic.

Characteristic 6: Live a Life of Service

Youth are involved in activities caring for others, reaching out to others in need, and addressing injustice.

1. Give portions of time and money for helping people.
2. Attend conferences or workshops that present the challenge of service professions such as the ordained ministry.
3. Speak out publicly against specific social injustice.
4. Try to offer comfort or support to a friend or neighbor in the event of a death or tragedy either by talking or by action (personal presence, help with routine tasks, transportation, visit in hospital, and so on).
5. Defend a friend or acquaintance who is being talked about when he or she isn't there.
6. Organize and participate in study or action groups to address injustice or immorality.
7. Are involved in activities of service related to church, community, or world.
8. Are assuming responsibility for some aspect of their youth ministry.

Characteristic 7: Exercise Moral Responsibility

Youth live with integrity utilizing their Christian faith in making moral decisions.

1. Are heard referring to seeking help from Scripture in deciding what is right and wrong.
2. Actively seek to discourage friends from cheating at school.
3. Have a reputation for not participating in activities such as lying, stealing, substance abuse, etc., and have a reputation for honesty, integrity, hospitality, and acts of kindness.

Roland Martinson, Wes Black, and John Roberto, *The Spirit and Culture of Youth Ministry: Leading Congregations Toward Exemplary Youth Ministry* (St. Paul, Minn.: EYM Publishing, 2010), pp. 39-41.

Resources for Cultivating Congregational Cultures of Spiritual Maturity

Anderson, Keith R., and Randy D. Reese. *Spiritual Mentoring: A Guide for Seeking and Giving Direction*. Downers Grove, Ill.: InterVarsity Press, 1999.
Mentoring process and expectations
Beginning mentoring relationships

Calhoun, Adele Ahlberg. *Spiritual Disciplines Handbook: Practices that Transform Us*. Downers Grove, Ill.: InterVarsity Press, 2005.
Descriptions of over sixty corporate and individual spiritual disciplines
Self-assessment tools
Ideas for practicing each discipline

Allen, Holly Catterton, and Christine Lawton Ross. *Intergenerational Christian Formation: Bringing the Whole Church Together in Ministry, Community, and Worship*. Downers Grove, Ill.: IVP Academic, 2012.
Creating an intergenerational culture
Intergenerational worship
Intergenerational learning
Intergenerational story sharing
Intergenerational service and missions
Intergenerational small groups
Forty intergenerational ideas
Intergenerational ministry resources
Biblical passages that reflect an intergenerational outlook

Cloud, Henry, and John Townsend. *Making Small Groups Work: What Every Small Group Leader Needs to Know.* Grand Rapids: Zondervan, 2003.
Leading groups that help people work through negative emotional patterns and other obstacles to growth

Dunn, Richard R. *Shaping the Spiritual Life of Students: A Guide for Youth Workers, Pastors, Teachers and Campus Ministers.* Downers Grove, Ill.: InterVarsity Press, 2001.
Mentoring junior high and high school students

Dunn, Richard R., and Jana L. Sundene. *Shaping the Journey of Emerging Adults: Life Giving Rhythms for Spiritual Transformation.* Downers Grove, Ill.: InterVarsity Press, 2012.
Mentoring emerging adults

Martinson, Roland, Wes Black, and John Roberto. *The Spirit and Culture of Youth Ministry: Leading Congregations Toward Exemplary Youth Ministry.* St. Paul, Minn.: EYM Publishing, 2010.
Assessing congregational culture and assets
Developing a youth-friendly and youth-involving congregation
Evaluating youth ministry programming mix
Principles for family-friendly congregations and youth ministries
Strategies for family faith formation
Assessing and improving leadership (pastor, youth minister) to foster exemplary youth ministry
Individual tools available at www.firstthird.org/eym/tools.aspx?m=3929

Powell, Kara E., and Chap Clark. *Sticky Faith: Everyday Ideas to Build Lasting Faith in Your Kids.* Grand Rapids: Zondervan, 2011.

Powell, Kara E., and Brad M. Griffin. *Sticky Faith Teen Curriculum: 10 Lessons to Nurture Faith Beyond High School.* Grand Rapids: Zondervan, 2012.

Powell, Kara E., Brad M. Griffin, and Cheryl A. Crawford. *Sticky Faith, Youth Worker Edition: Practical Ideas to Nurture Long Term Faith in Teenagers.* Grand Rapids: Zondervan, 2011.

www.stickyfaith.org.
Parents helping teenagers have lasting faith
Youth ministers helping teenagers have lasting faith
Churches helping teenagers have lasting faith

Rankin, Stephen W. *Aiming at Maturity: The Goal of the Christian Life.* Eugene, Ore.: Cascade Books, 2011.
Accessible explanation of cognitive view of emotions and its usefulness in spiritual formation

Scazzero, Peter. *The Emotionally Healthy Church: A Strategy for Discipleship that Actually Changes Lives.* Grand Rapids: Zondervan, 2003.
Developing emotionally mature leaders and churches

Setran, David P. and Chris A. Kiesling. *Spiritual Formation in Emerging Adulthood: A Practical Theology for College and Young Adult Ministry.* Grand Rapids: Baker Academic, 2013.
Mentoring emerging adults
Creating communities, teaching, worship, service, etc., that welcome emerging adults and help them grow

Strommen, Merton, Karen E. Jones, and Dave Rahn. *Youth Ministry That Transforms: A Comprehensive Analysis of the Hopes, Frustrations, and Effectiveness of Today's Youth Workers.* Grand Rapids: Zondervan/Youth Specialties, 2001.
Supporting, training, encouraging youth ministers for effective youth ministry

Wilcher, Scott. *The Orphaned Generation: The Father's Heart for Connecting Youth and Young Adults to Your Church.* Chesapeake, Va.: The Upstream Project, 2010.
Using metaphors for gospel, church, youth, and adults that welcome youth
Helping adults become guides to young people
Combining age specific and intergenerational ministry with youth

Willard, Dallas, *Renovation of the Heart: Putting on the Character of Christ.* Colorado Springs: NavPress, 2002.
VIM model of spiritual formation
Dimensions of the person and spiritual formation (thoughts, feelings, will, body, social dimension)
Theory and some application of VIM model helpful for those training others in the model

Questions for Observing a Congregational Culture

Theology

1. What words, phrases, metaphors do people in the church most often use to describe
   God?
   Jesus?
   the Holy Spirit?
   the gospel?
   the ideal Christian?
   the church?
   spiritual maturity and spiritual growth?
   adults?
   teenagers?
   children?
   relationships between people of different ages?
2. Which biblical words or theological topics do people talk about the most or seem to value the most?
3. Which theological topics are never or rarely discussed either from the pulpit or in conversation among church members?
4. What topics would a person hear and what would a person be challenged to do as a result of the "average" month or year of sermons?
5. What topics are taught in Christian education settings, how are they taught, and by whom?
6. What are the Christian teachings that everyone is expected to understand and accept? How are those teachings communicated?

7. What are the most popular worship songs, and what theological truths do those songs seem to highlight?
8. What is weekly corporate worship like? Who does what and how do they do it?

Priorities and Values

1. Where does the church invest its time, money, and effort?
2. Which programs, activities, or people seem to get only the "leftovers" of congregational time, money, and investment?
3. What or who seems to be highly valued as evidenced by being highly visible or frequently praised or celebrated?
4. What kinds of people are most and least represented in the congregation, and how do the church's demographics compare to those of the surrounding community (e.g. gender, age, marital status, political views, race or ethnicity, income level, type of employment)?
5. Which programs or activities cannot be touched because they are so treasured that eliminating or modifying them would lead to a great outcry?

Physical Space/Building

1. How is the physical space arranged and decorated?
2. How comfortable are people with making changes to the physical space?
3. Where do different activities for different kinds of people take place, and how are they decorated and maintained?
4. What visible symbols (photographs, flags, crosses, works of art, etc.) decorate the worship space and other rooms in the church?

Questions for Interpreting an Element
of Congregational Culture

A. What does it mean?

1. What messages seem to be communicated by the words, metaphors, and symbols that make up a particular congregational practice?
2. What is *not* said or *not* communicated in this practice, and what messages might those silences communicate to congregation members?
3. If this practice parallels something in the wider culture, what meanings does it have in the wider culture that might influence what people see and hear when they engage in this practice in church?
4. Even if this is a practice unique to the church, how might people's assumptions, beliefs, or other ways of thinking that come from sources outside the church influence what they hear and see when they experience this church practice?
5. What kind of person is this practice likely to produce? Why do you think so?

B. Why is it happening?

1. Where did this practice come from?
   a. How was God involved in the origins and development of this practice?
   b. Is this practice rooted in some of the core theological beliefs of our church? Which ones?
   c. Who were the people who started the current version of this practice?
   d. What were the original purposes or goals for this practice?
   e. How well is it currently achieving those purposes or goals?
2. Why do people in our congregation react the way they do to this practice?

    a. Who loves it and why?

    b. Who dislikes it and why?

3. What needs or desires does this practice seem to be addressing for people?

    a. Which of the following (or other) desires lie behind this practice?

       Belonging

       Acceptance

       Emotional comfort

       Personal growth or challenge

       A sense of mission or purpose

       Hunger for truth

       Boundary maintenance ("us" vs. "them")

       Power/control

       A feeling of connection to God

       Love

    b. What causes the people in our church to feel especially strong needs or desires in those areas of their lives?

    c. Does this practice seem to be meeting those needs or fulfilling those desires in mostly healthy or mostly unhealthy ways? Why do you think so?

4. What might happen if this practice was eliminated? Why? What does that tell us about who values this practice and why?

Questions for Evaluating an Element of Congregational Culture in Light of Biblical Spiritual Maturity

Gospel

1. Which elements of the gospel does this practice tend to emphasize?
2. Which elements of the gospel does this practice tend to obscure or undermine?
3. Which of the messages communicated by this practice contradict some element of the gospel?

Spiritual Maturity

In what ways does this practice help or hinder people in
1. learning to value spiritual maturity?
2. learning how to grow to spiritual maturity?
3. learning the basic truths of the faith?
4. learning and practicing discernment?
5. understanding and valuing the church?
6. taking their place in the church and building others up in Christ?
7. understanding and valuing the mission of the church?
8. taking their place and serving in the mission of the church?
9. replacing sinful behaviors with loving behaviors?
10. replacing sinful emotional patterns with godly emotional patterns?

Theological Significance

1. False Teaching
   a. Does this practice or the messages it communicates contradict a core element of the gospel?
   b. Does this practice or the messages it communicates contradict a core element of Christian moral teaching?
   c. Does this practice or the messages it communicates contradict other core biblical teaching about God, Jesus, or salvation?
   (If the answer is "yes" to any of these questions, then *eliminate* or significantly *modify* the practice.)
2. Matters of Emphasis or Clarity that Could Influence Spiritual Formation
   a. Will people formed by this practice be likely to get better *(accept)*, become worse *(eliminate)*, or stay the same *(modify* or *compensate)* in how well they understand and live the gospel, Christian moral teaching, or other core theological truths? What makes you think so?
   b. Will people formed by this practice be likely to get better *(accept)*, become worse *(eliminate)*, or stay the same *(modify* or *compensate)* in their growth toward spiritual maturity? What makes you think so?
   c. Will people formed by this practice be likely to get better *(accept)*, become worse *(eliminate)*, or stay the same *(modify* or *compensate)* in how well they love God and neighbor according to the biblical teaching on what love should be like? What makes you think so?
   d. In what ways is this practice likely to mislead people? In its intended, clear, obvious messages? *(eliminate* or *modify)* Only by what it does not say? *(modify* or *compensate)* Or only when people misunderstand or misinterpret it? *(accept, modify,* or *compensate)*

NOTE: The items in parentheses suggest categories of action that church leaders should consider depending upon what answers they give to the evaluative questions. For explanations and examples of *accept, modify, compensate,* and *eliminate* see the section of chapter five entitled "Act: What Should We Do to Encourage Spiritual Maturity?"

Notes

Notes to Chapter 1

1. Mark Regnerus and Jeremy Uecker, *Premarital Sex in America: How Young Americans Meet, Mate, and Think about Marrying* (New York: Oxford University Press, 2011), p. 174.

2. For a description of the early Youth for Christ Movement and its role in the emergence of juvenilization, see Thomas E. Bergler, *The Juvenilization of American Christianity* (Grand Rapids: Eerdmans, 2012), pp. 49-54, 147-75, 198-205, 208.

3. For the full story of how juvenilization differed by faith tradition, see Bergler, *Juvenilization.*

4. For a more complete explanation of the relationship between juvenilization and church growth see Bergler, *Juvenilization,* pp. 209-19.

5. Theodore Caplow, Howard M. Bahr, and Bruce A. Chadwick, *All Faithful People: Change and Continuity in Middletown's Religion* (Minneapolis: University of Minnesota Press, 1983), pp. 19, 80-81. For more on how youth ministries played a key role in keeping Americans interested in religion, see Bergler, *Juvenilization,* pp. 209-11.

6. "The last time I saw Elvis," *Youth for Christ Magazine* (March 1960): 4. For more information on the costs and benefits of juvenilization, see Bergler, *Juvenilization,* pp. 208-25.

7. For a summary of the research on early puberty, see Steven D. Bonner, "Looking into Our Children's Eyes: Precocious Puberty — Adolescents before Their Time," *The Journal of Youth Ministry* 10:2 (Spring 2012): 7-18. Interestingly, Bonner reports a lesser known branch of medical research that finds a correlation between family disruption and early menarche for girls.

8. For descriptions of intentional marketing of cosmetics, revealing clothing, and racy entertainment to "tweens" see Alissa Quart, *Branded: The Buying and Selling of Teenagers* (New York: Basic Books, 2003), pp. 63-75. For the locker room teasing anecdote, see John Berard, James Penner, and Rick Bartlett, *Consuming Youth: Leading Teens through Consumer Culture* (Grand Rapids: Zondervan, 2010), p. 48.

9. For an extended treatment of the causes and effects of shrinking childhood, see Neil Postman, *The Disappearance of Childhood* (New York: Vintage Books, 1994).

10. Barak Goodman, director, *Frontline: The Merchants of Cool.* DVD. (Boston: PBS, 2001). For more on marketing to teenagers see the web site associated with the film, http://www.pbs.org/wgbh/pages/frontline/shows/cool/ and Quart, *Branded.*

11. Christian Smith with Kari Christoffersen, Hilary Davidson, and Patricia Snell Herzog, *Lost in Transition: The Dark Side of Emerging Adulthood* (New York: Oxford University Press, 2011), pp. 231-32.

12. Christian Smith with Patricia Snell, *Souls in Transition: The Religious and Spiritual Lives of Emerging Adults* (New York: Oxford University Press, 2009), pp. 33-87.

13. For detailed descriptions of each of these problem areas see Smith et al., *Lost in Transition.* For the strong commitment to "no regrets" among emerging adults, see Smith and Snell, *Souls in Transition,* pp. 41-42.

14. Smith et al., *Lost in Transition,* pp. 150-52. See also Smith and Snell, *Souls in Transition,* p. 57, and Regnerus and Uecker, *Premarital Sex,* pp. 169-204, 245-50.

15. For evidence that many emerging adults think they will be back in church or more serious about their faith in their thirties, see the interviews reported in Smith and Snell, *Souls in Transition,* pp. 14, 79, 149-50, 173, 193, 197, 200-201, 206, 208. For evidence that the percentage of young adults who return to church may be declining in recent decades, see Robert D. Putnam and David E. Campbell, *American Grace: How Religion Divides and Unites Us* (New York: Simon and Schuster, 2010), pp. 139-47. Putnam and Campbell were measuring percentages of people who had remained in the church tradition of their youth, so it is possible that overall the percentage of return could be the same if we take into account people who as adults became active in a different denomination than the one in which they were raised. But the only "religious group" that seemed to be increasing in its retention rate over time was the "nones" — that is, those with no religious background who stayed that way as adults.

16. Smith et al., *Lost in Transition,* pp. 11-16, 231-39. See also Mary C. Waters, Patrick J. Carr, Maria J. Kefalas, and Jennifer Holdaway, eds., *Coming of Age in America: The Transition to Adulthood in the Twenty-First Century* (Berkeley: University of California Press, 2011), and Katherine S. Newman, *The Accordion Family: Boomerang Kids, Anxious Parents, and the Private Toll of Global Competition* (Boston: Beacon Press, 2012). For reasons emerging adults give for delaying marriage, see Regnerus and Uecker, *Premarital Sex,* pp. 182-94.

17. For the early history of *Seventeen* and its advertising philosophy, see Grace Palladino, *Teenagers: An American History* (New York: Basic Books, 1996), pp. 102-8. For the quote about not wanting to grow up, see Louis de Rochement, "Teen Age Girls," *The March of Time* 11:11 (New York: Time, Inc., 1945), re-released in *The March of Time: American Lifestyles — American Youth* (New Line Home Video, 1987). See also Jean M. Twenge, *Generation Me: Why Today's Young Americans Are More Confident, Assertive, Entitled — and More Miserable Than Ever Before* (New York: Free Press, 2006).

18. Thomas Frank, *The Conquest of Cool: Business Culture, Counterculture and the Rise of Hip Consumerism* (Chicago: University of Chicago Press, 1997).

19. Liberal Mainline Protestants have been especially prone to idealize youth, but white Evangelicals, African American Protestants, and Roman Catholic adults all did it too. See Bergler, *Juvenilization,* for examples.

20. Barak Goodman and Rachel Dretzin, directors, *Frontline: The Persuaders* (Boston: PBS, 2004). See also the web site associated with the film, http://www.pbs.org/wgbh/pages/frontline/shows/persuaders/.

21. See Goodman, *Merchants of Cool,* Goodman and Dretzin, *Persuaders,* and J. Bryant and S. Thompson, *Fundamentals of Media Effects* (Boston: McGraw-Hill, 2002).

22. Robert E. Lane, *The Loss of Happiness in Market Democracies* (New Haven: Yale University Press, 2001). Twenge, *Generation Me.* Robert D. Putnam, *Bowling Alone: The Collapse and Revival of American Community* (New York: Simon and Schuster, 2001). James Cote, *Arrested Adulthood: The Changing Nature of Maturity and Identity* (New York: New York University Press, 2000).

23. Cote, *Arrested Adulthood.* Berard et al., *Consuming Youth.*

24. For the all-too-common damaging effects of sexual activity and substance use in the lives of emerging adults see Smith et al., *Lost in Transition,* pp. 110-94. For evidence that mainstream middle-class institutions (schools, families) and values (competitiveness, "tough love") push some young people to the breaking point and then abandon these same young people when they turn to drugs and crime, see Elliott Currie, *The Road to Whatever: Middle-Class Culture and the Crisis of Adolescence* (New York: Metropolitan Books, 2004). It must be noted that many of the tragic stories Currie describes also included neglectful, abusive, or addicted parents. Thus immature adults, not just "middle class institutions and values," contribute to the disasters observed in the lives of some young people who seem to have "everything going for them."

25. For descriptions of how family life and the individual life course have changed over time, see Berard et al., *Consuming Youth,* pp. 19-32, and Friedrich L. Schweitzer, *The Postmodern Life Cycle: Challenges for Church and Theology* (St. Louis: Chalice Press, 2004), pp. 4-22.

26. Waters et al., *Coming of Age in America,* pp. 172-83.

27. Newman, *Accordion Family,* pp. 3-5.

28. Cote, *Arrested Adulthood.* Jeffrey Jensen Arnett, *Emerging Adulthood: The Winding Road from the Late Teens through the Twenties* (New York: Oxford University Press, 2004), pp. 3-25, 207-28.

29. For the effects of divorce on children, see Elizabeth Marquardt in "Consultation on the Christian Formation of Youth," unpublished report (Indianapolis: Lilly Endowment, Inc., 2006), p. 60, and Elizabeth Marquardt, *Between Two Worlds: The Inner Lives of Children of Divorce* (New York: Three Rivers Press, 2006). Although the effects of divorce on children have been much researched and debated, it seems clear that divorce *can* be harmful to their psychological and economic well-being. Some evidence suggests that divorce can be harder on teenagers than on younger children. For summaries of this research, see John Santrock, *Adolescence,* 9th edition (Boston: McGraw-Hill, 2003), pp. 170-74, and Jeffrey Arnett, *Adolescence and Emerging Adulthood: A Cultural Approach* (Upper Saddle River, N.J.: Prentice Hall, 2001), pp. 210, 212-15. For the prevalence of phrases like "be yourself" see Twenge, *Generation Me,* p. 50.

30. Schweitzer, *The Postmodern Life Cycle,* pp. 81-96.

31. For the abandonment of teenagers by adults see Chap Clark, *Hurt: Inside the World of Today's Teenagers* (Grand Rapids: Baker, 2004).

32. Christian Smith with Melinda Lundquist Denton, *Soul Searching: The Religious and Spiritual Lives of American Teenagers* (New York: Oxford University Press, 2005), pp. 51, 61-61, 124-27.

33. Smith and Denton, *Soul Searching,* pp. 30-71, 218-58.

34. Smith and Denton, *Soul Searching,* pp. 118-71.

35. Smith and Denton, *Soul Searching,* pp. 118-68.

36. Smith and Denton, *Soul Searching,* pp. 130-31.

37. Smith and Denton, *Soul Searching,* p. 261.

38. Smith and Snell, *Souls in Transition*, pp. 75-87, 280.

39. Smith and Snell, *Souls in Transition*, pp. 103-65.

40. Smith and Snell, *Souls in Transition*, p. 156.

41. Smith and Denton, *Souls in Transition*, pp. 151, 166-67, 259-75.

42. Smith and Snell, *Souls in Transition*, pp. 12, 167-68.

43. Barna Group, "Many Churchgoers and Faith Leaders Struggle to Define Spiritual Maturity," Barna Update, May 11, 2009. Retrieved 6/11/13 from http://www.barna.org/barna -update/article/12-faithspirituality/264-many-churchgoers-and-faith-leaders-struggle-to -define-spiritual-maturity.

44. Barna Group, "Many Churchgoers."

45. Barna Group, "Many Churchgoers."

46. Robert Wuthnow, "Contemporary Spirituality," in *All in Sync: How Music and Art Are Revitalizing American Religion* (Berkeley: University of California Press, 2003), pp. 21-55.

47. Wuthnow, "Contemporary Spirituality," pp. 42, 48.

48. Wuthnow, "Contemporary Spirituality," pp. 32-48.

49. Wuthnow, "Contemporary Spirituality," pp. 32, 39-43.

50. Robert D. Putnam and David E. Campbell, *American Grace: How Religion Divides and Unites Us* (New York: Simon & Schuster, 2010), pp. 168-69. According to Wuthnow, "Contemporary Spirituality," 47 percent of those who said spiritual growth is "extremely important" to them had also shopped for a church at least once. This percentage is identical to the one that Putnam and Campbell found in the general population in 2006.

51. Putnam and Campbell, *American Grace*, p. 62.

52. Richard Cimino and Don Lattin, *Shopping for Faith: American Religion in the New Millennium* (San Francisco: Jossey-Bass, 1998), pp. 55-56, 67-68.

53. Wuthnow, "Contemporary Spirituality," pp. 21-55.

54. Brad J. Waggoner, *The Shape of Faith to Come: Spiritual Formation and the Future of Discipleship* (Nashville: B & H Publishing Group, 2008), pp. 30-49.

55. Waggoner, *Shape of Faith*, pp. 66, 72, 75, 258-59.

56. Waggoner, *Shape of Faith*, pp. 119, 123, 126, 236, 241, 245-46.

57. Waggoner, *Shape of Faith*, pp. 69, 90, 93, 96.

58. Waggoner, *Shape of Faith*, pp. 86, 118, 201.

59. Waggoner, *Shape of Faith*, pp. 187-193, 281-85.

60. Waggoner, *Shape of Faith*, pp. 266-72.

61. Waggoner, *Shape of Faith*, pp. 270-71.

62. Waggoner, *Shape of Faith*, pp. 272, 281-87.

63. For the story of how Evangelical youth ministries promoted romantic spirituality, see Bergler, *Juvenilization*, pp. 157-66, 219-27.

64. Wuthnow, "Contemporary Spirituality," pp. 49-51.

65. Willaim V. D'Antonio, James D. Davidson, Dean R. Hoge, and Katherine Meyer, *American Catholics: Gender, Generation, and Commitment* (New York: Rowman and Littlefield, 2001), p. 43.

66. Putnam and Campbell, *American Grace*, p. 169.

67. Smith and Denton, *Soul Searching*, pp. 194, 208-10.

Notes to Chapter 2

1. Stephen W. Rankin provides excellent critiques of "sound bite" theology about the atonement, the heart, and grace. He convincingly shows how such overly-simplified theology hinders spiritual growth to maturity. Stephen W. Rankin, *Aiming at Maturity: The Goal of the Christian Life* (Eugene, Ore.: Cascade Books, 2011), pp. 66-67, 78-82, 116-17.

2. The phrase "miserable sinner Christianity" is borrowed from Dallas Willard, *Renovation of the Heart* (Colorado Springs: NavPress, 2002), pp. 79-80.

3. Dallas Willard notes that churches so often operate as if they expect no one to change to become more like Christ. He wonders what would happen if we created, announced, and publicized a course on how to forgive our enemies with the expectation that at the end of the course, people would actually be able to do so. See Willard, *Renovation of the Heart,* pp. 82-84, 250-51.

4. Gordon D. Fee, *Paul's Letter to the Philippians* (Grand Rapids: Eerdmans, 1995), pp. 305-61.

5. Rankin, *Aiming at Maturity,* p. 32. Rankin also provides a helpful exegesis of many of the same Scripture passages I discuss in this chapter. See chapter 1 of his book.

6. The phrase "community of disciples on mission" is borrowed from The Sword of the Spirit, an international association of ecumenical covenant communities. See www .swordofthespirit.net.

7. R. T. France, *The Gospel of Matthew* (Grand Rapids: Eerdmans, 2007), pp. 187-90, 228.

8. France, *Matthew,* pp. 228-29.

9. France, *Matthew,* pp. 734-35.

10. Peter H. Davids, *The Epistle of James: A Commentary on the Greek Text* (Grand Rapids: Eerdmans, 1982), pp. 69-70, 137.

11. I. Howard Marshall, *The Epistles of John* (Grand Rapids: Eerdmans, 1978), pp. 124-25.

12. Raymond E. Brown, S.S., *The Epistles of John* (Garden City, N.Y.: Doubleday & Company, 1982), pp. 560-62. See also Marshall, *Epistles of John,* pp. 221-26.

13. Reidar Aasgaard, "Like a Child: Paul's Rhetorical Uses of Childhood," in Marcia J. Bunge, Terence E. Fretheim, and Beverly Roberts Gaventa, eds., *The Child in the Bible* (Grand Rapids: Eerdmans, 2008), pp. 249-77.

14. H. Hubner, "Teleios," in Horst Balz and Gerhard Schneider, eds., *Exegetical Dictionary of the New Testament,* vol. 3 (Grand Rapids: Eerdmans, 1982-1983, reprinted 1994), pp. 342-44.

15. "Perfection" seems to be an unfortunate word choice in the NRSV. "Completeness" or even "maturity" could be used here just as well as "perfection." Even if the author means absolute perfection in 6:1, then given what has just been said in 5:11ff., the sense would be "not only should you get back to being mature *(teleios),* you should keep going beyond that toward perfection *(teleiotes).*" The whole exhortation in 5:11–6:2 makes no sense if the Hebrew Christians are being rebuked for failing to achieve the impossible. In fact, the imperative phrase in Greek that is translated in 6:1 as "let us go on toward perfection" in the NRSV implies the pursuit of something that can be attained. See Gareth Lee Cockerill, *The Epistle to the Hebrews* (Grand Rapids: Eerdmans, 2012), pp. 261-62.

16. Cockerill, *Hebrews,* pp. 254-67.

17. Cockerill, *Hebrews,* pp. 254-67.

18. Some think that *teleios* in Colossians 1:28 and 4:12 refers primarily to what Paul hopes his converts will display at the return of Christ, although they acknowledge that this word

refers also to the ongoing process of sanctification. See, for example, E. K. Simpson and F. F. Bruce, *Commentary on the Epistles to the Ephesians and the Colossians* (Grand Rapids: Eerdmans, 1957), pp. 219-21, and Ben Witherington III, *The Letters to Philemon, the Colossians and the Ephesians: A Socio-Rhetorical Commentary on the Captivity Epistles* (Grand Rapids: Eerdmans, 2007), pp. 147-48, 204-5. But to see "mature" as only or mostly future fails to account for the close connection in the letter between "maturity" and standing firm in the faith, something that both Paul (Colossians 1:28; 2:5) and Epaphras (Colossians 4:12) seemed to think was possible *in this life* for the Colossian believers. For a contrasting view that sees "mature" in Colossians as a reality to be expected in this life, see Michael F. Bird, *Colossians and Philemon: A New Covenant Community* (Eugene, Ore.: Cascade Books, 2009), pp. 68-69.

19. Witherington, *Philemon, Colossians and Ephesians*, pp. 283-93.

20. Commentators are divided on the following questions about Ephesians 4:7-16: (1) To what extent is "maturity" (*teleios* in v. 13) achievable in this life? (2) Is this maturity an individual or corporate reality, or both? All agree that church leaders and members should be working together toward maturity. And all agree that the passage is teaching that Christians should be able to leave behind the doctrinal instability of spiritual "children." Those who take a restricted view of how much maturity is possible in this life do not take into account the cultural background of *teleios* described by Aasgaard, "Like a Child." For a range of opinions on these matters, see Stephen E. Fowl, *Ephesians: A Commentary* (Louisville: Westminster John Knox Press, 2012), pp. 127-44; Margaret Y. MacDonald, *Colossians and Ephesians* (Collegeville, Minn.: Liturgical Press, 2008), pp. 285-95; John Muddiman, *The Epistle to the Ephesians* (London: Continuum, 2001), pp. 202-7; John R. W. Stott, *The Message of Ephesians* (Downers Grove, Ill.: InterVarsity Press, 1979), pp. 169-72; and Witherington, *Philemon, Colossians and Ephesians*, pp. 283-93.

21. Aasgaard, "Like a Child," p. 262.

22. Aasgaard, "Like a Child," pp. 260-61.

23. Keith J. White, "'He Placed a Little Child in the Midst': Jesus, the Kingdom, and Children," in Bunge et al., eds., *The Child in the Bible*, pp. 353-74.

24. William P. Brown, "To Discipline without Destruction: The Multifaceted Profile of the Child in Proverbs," in Bunge et al., eds., *The Child in the Bible*, pp. 63-81.

25. Aasgaard, "Like a Child," pp. 274-76.

26. See, for example, "Holiness, Holy, Saints" in J. D. Douglas, F. F. Bruce, J. I. Packer, N. Hillyer, D. Guthrie, A. R. Millard, D. J. Wiseman, eds., *New Bible Dictionary*, 2nd edition (Wheaton, Ill.: Tyndale House Publishers, 1982), pp. 486-88; and "Holy, Holiness," in Walter Elwell, ed., *Baker Theological Dictionary of the Bible* (Grand Rapids: Baker Books, 1996), pp. 340-44.

27. Cockerill sees a clear connection between the exhortation in Hebrews 5:11–6:2 and the one in Hebrews 12. Cockerill, *Hebrews*, pp. 254-67.

28. Fee, *Philippians*, p. 331.

29. Stott, *Ephesians*, p. 172.

Notes to Chapter 3

1. This description of spiritual disciplines is adapted from John Ortberg, *The Life You've Always Wanted: Spiritual Disciplines for Ordinary People* (Grand Rapids: Zondervan, 2002).

2. Willard uses the analogy of "learning to speak Arabic" to describe the normal way

people change. Dallas Willard, *Renovation of the Heart* (Colorado Springs: NavPress, 2002), pp. 82-84.

3. M. Robert Mulholland Jr., *Invitation to a Journey: A Roadmap for Spiritual Formation* (Downers Grove, Ill.: IVP Books, 1993).

4. For justification of this statement, see Willard, *Renovation of the Heart*, pp. 27-44, 141-56, and Stephen W. Rankin, *Aiming at Maturity* (Eugene, Ore.: Cascade Books, 2011), pp. 33-43.

5. Among the authors who have influenced my thinking, Willard sees the heart as primarily the seat of the will, while Rankin includes will, thought, and emotion (especially "dispositions," which he says have a significant emotional component). Willard, *Renovation of the Heart*, pp. 28-30, 33-35; Rankin, *Aiming at Maturity*, pp. 38-43. Despite their differences regarding the exact "content" of the human heart, they offer remarkably similar advice about how will, thoughts, and emotions must work together in spiritual transformation.

6. In describing the mutual interdependence of thought, feeling, and will I am following Willard, *Renovation of the Heart*, pp. 141-56, and Rankin, *Aiming at Maturity*, pp. 33-54, 107-15. However, their descriptions of this mutual interdependence are not novel. Both authors draw on a long tradition of Christian reflection on these inward dynamics of the human person. For example, Rankin makes use of John Wesley's theology to support this view.

7. Kenda Creasy Dean, "Beyond Truthiness: How the 'Juvenilization Thesis' in Youth Ministry Is Both Wrong and Right," *Immerse*, Fall 2012.

8. My understanding of emotions draws on the cognitive view of emotions as described in the following sources: Willard, *Renovation of the Heart*; Rankin, *Aiming at Maturity*; Matthew A. Elliott, *Faithful Feelings: Rethinking Emotion in the New Testament* (Grand Rapids: Kregel, 2006); and Robert C. Roberts, *Spiritual Emotions: A Psychology of Christian Virtues* (Grand Rapids: Eerdmans, 2007). It is worth noting that the "cognitive theory of emotions" is a contemporary description of a very old way of understanding emotions. Aristotle, Augustine, Aquinas, Jonathan Edwards, John Wesley, and many others over the centuries have understood thoughts and emotions as interdependent rather than as inherent enemies. For supportive quotations from each of these important thinkers, see Elliott, *Faithful Feelings*, and Rankin, *Aiming at Maturity*.

9. Willard, *Renovation of the Heart*, pp. 32-33, 96.

10. For more on the positive role of feelings in fostering better thinking, see Elliott, *Faithful Feelings*, pp. 42-46, and Rankin, *Aiming at Maturity*, pp. 43-47.

11. My description of how emotional patterns are shaped by life orientation is based on Roberts, *Spiritual Emotions*, pp. 11-31, and Willard, *Renovation of the Heart*, pp. 117-39.

12. Willard, *Renovation of the Heart*, pp. 142-49.

13. Willard, *Renovation of the Heart*, Rankin, *Aiming at Maturity*, Elliott, *Faithful Feelings*, and Roberts, *Spiritual Emotions*, all make this point in various ways. That should not be surprising, since Scripture emphasizes the crucial role of the mind in the larger process of spiritual transformation. See Romans 12:1-2, Ephesians 4:17-25, and many other passages in the New Testament.

14. For a more detailed explanation of the New Testament teaching about how Christians can consistently feel love, joy, hope, and other godly emotions, see Elliott, *Faithful Feelings*, pp. 124-92. For a detailed exposition of the New Testament teaching on joy, see W. G. Morrice, *Joy in the New Testament* (Grand Rapids: Eerdmans, 1984). Although Christians do not agree about how much we should emphasize the emotional content of New Testament words like love, joy, peace, or hope, almost all agree that these words have an emotional dimension. And

all agree that Scripture teaches us to fill our minds with God's truth if we want to grow in these virtues and their corresponding emotions.

15. Dallas Willard is especially helpful in his description of how character qualities even come to take up residence in our bodies. He says that a person's character is whatever his or her body is poised to do. And he argues that this embodied character is formed in us over time through the dynamic interplay of thought, feeling, will, and action. See Willard, *Renovation of the Heart,* pp. 159-76.

16. Willard, *Renovation of the Heart,* pp. 90-91. Willard argues that only by training "off the spot" can our hearts be truly transformed.

17. Cloud and Townsend provide excellent guidance regarding how to develop Christian growth groups that help people work through difficult life issues and significant emotional struggles. Henry Cloud and John Townsend, *Making Small Groups Work: What Every Small Group Leader Needs to Know* (Grand Rapids: Zondervan, 2003).

18. Peter Scazzero, *The Emotionally Healthy Church: A Strategy for Discipleship That Actually Changes Lives* (Grand Rapids: Zondervan, 2003), pp. 56-58. Scazzero goes beyond an individual approach to emotional healing and provides resources that pastors can use to build emotionally maturing congregations. Among the many helpful resources he provides are an "Emotional/Spiritual Health Inventory" and an accompanying "Interpretation Guide: Levels of Emotional Maturity" that describes the differences in emotional patterns to be expected among spiritual infants, children, adolescents, and adults. Scazzero is especially good at identifying the kinds of immature emotional patterns that cause people to damage the Christian community. He also offers specific steps that churches and their leaders can take to help people experience healing in those areas of their lives.

Notes to Chapter 4

1. Too many church members support the hiring of a youth minister in hopes of delegating every last bit of work among youth to him or her. The Study of Protestant Youth Ministers in America confirmed that many youth ministers experience stress over the low levels of respect, financial support, administrative help, and volunteer help they receive from their congregations. See Merton Strommen, Karen E. Jones, and Dave Rahn, *Youth Ministry That Transforms: A Comprehensive Analysis of the Hopes, Frustrations, and Effectiveness of Today's Youth Workers* (Grand Rapids: Zondervan/ Youth Specialties, 2001), pp. 41-81. But attempts to integrate youth into the church can also fall victim to adult self-interest. In the 1960s mainline Protestant denominational leaders started talking about making adolescents into "full members of the laity." It sounded good, but in practice led to shutting down denominational youth departments. Not surprisingly, a massive drop in these churches' investments in youth did little to slow the growing exodus of young people from the faith. It is hard to imagine a worse strategy for weathering the youth culture storms of the sixties. See Bergler, *Juvenilization,* pp. 211-15.

2. Christian Smith with Melinda Lundquist Denton, *Soul Searching: The Religious and Spiritual Lives of American Teenagers* (New York: Oxford University Press, 2005), p. 220.

3. Smith and Denton, *Soul Searching,* pp. 218-58.

4. Smith and Denton, *Soul Searching,* p. 111. It is worth noting that by some measures, African American teenagers are more religious than white teenagers. In particular, when it comes to having a spiritually mature understanding of the church and their place in it, African

American Christian teenagers may be doing better as a group than white Christian teenagers. See Brad Christerson, Korie L. Edwards, and Richard Flory, *Growing Up in America: The Power of Race in the Lives of Teens* (New York: Oxford University Press, 2010), pp. 110-44. Using NSYR data, this team discovered that white teenagers are more likely to see the church as existing to serve their needs, whereas African American teenagers are more likely to see the church and its leaders as authorities in their lives.

5. Smith and Denton, *Soul Searching*, p. 111.

6. The church bodies represented in EYM were Assemblies of God, Evangelical Covenant, Evangelical Lutheran Church in America, Presbyterian Church (USA), Roman Catholic, Southern Baptist, and United Methodist.

7. Roland Martinson, Wes Black, and John Roberto, *The Spirit and Culture of Youth Ministry: Leading Congregations Toward Exemplary Youth Ministry* (St. Paul, Minn.: EYM Publishing, 2010), pp. 25-41.

8. Martinson, Black, and Roberto, *Spirit and Culture*, pp. 39-41, 94.

9. Martinson, Black, and Roberto, *Spirit and Culture*, pp. 40-41, 130.

10. Martinson, Black, and Roberto, *Spirit and Culture*, p. 24.

11. Martinson, Black, and Roberto, *Spirit and Culture*, pp. 49-62.

12. Martinson, Black, and Roberto, *Spirit and Culture*, pp. 58-59.

13. Martinson, Black, and Roberto, *Spirit and Culture*, pp. 58-61.

14. Martinson, Black, and Roberto, *Spirit and Culture*, pp. 49-62, 251-57.

15. Martinson, Black, and Roberto, *Spirit and Culture*, pp. 257-59.

16. For a review of this literature, see Brenda Snailum, "Integrating Intergenerational Ministry Strategies into Existing Youth Ministries: What Can a Hybrid Approach Be Expected to Accomplish?" *Journal of Youth Ministry* 11:2 (Spring 2013): 7-28. The consensus to date seems to be that intergenerational ministry and age-specific ministry can each have unique spiritual benefits for adolescents.

17. For a summary of this research, see Holly Catterton Allen and Christine Lawton Ross, *Intergenerational Christian Formation: Bringing the Whole Church Together in Ministry, Community, and Worship* (Downers Grove, Ill.: IVP Academic, 2012), pp. 45-63, 85-97. See also the collection of seven articles in "Special Focus: Intergenerational Ministry," *Christian Education Journal*, Series 3, 9:1 (Spring 2012): 101-93.

18. For a summary of the growing literature on intergenerational spiritual formation and an argument for the importance of revising the church's ministry philosophy to truly support it, see Allen and Ross, *Intergenerational Christian Formation*.

19. Martinson, Black, and Roberto, *Spirit and Culture*, p. 327.

20. Christian Smith with Patricia Snell, *Souls in Transition: The Religious and Spiritual Lives of Emerging Adults* (New York: Oxford University Press, 2009), pp. 212-14, 222-23.

21. The range of percentages results from the fact that NSYR researchers used different measures of strong faith in different parts of their analysis. Smith and Snell, *Souls in Transition*, pp. 166-67, 224-27.

22. Smith and Snell, *Souls in Transition*, pp. 229-31.

23. Smith and Snell, *Souls in Transition*, p. 226.

24. Smith and Snell, *Souls in Transition*, pp. 246-47.

25. Martinson, Black, and Roberto, *Spirit and Culture*, pp. 84-87, 207, 209, 212.

26. Kara E. Powell and Chap Clark, *Sticky Faith: Everyday Ideas to Build Lasting Faith in*

Your Kids (Grand Rapids: Zondervan, 2011), p. 97. *Sticky Faith* is based on a study that followed about 200 Christian teenagers into their first few years of college.

27. Jason Lanker and Klaus Issler, "The Relationships between Natural Mentoring and Spirituality in Christian Adolescents," *Journal of Youth Ministry* 9:1 (Fall 2010): 93-109. See also Powell and Clark, *Sticky Faith.*

28. Strommen, Jones, and Rahn, *Youth Ministry That Transforms,* pp. 136-40, 220.

29. Martinson, Black, and Roberto, *Spirit and Culture,* pp. 91-92.

30. Richard R. Dunn, *Shaping the Spiritual Life of Students: A Guide for Youth Workers, Pastors, Teachers and Campus Ministers* (Downers Grove, Ill.: InterVarsity Press, 2001).

31. Powell and Clark, *Sticky Faith,* p. 99.

32. Martinson, Black, and Roberto, *Spirit and Culture,* p. 133.

33. Smith and Snell, *Souls in Transition,* p. 241.

34. Martinson, Black, and Roberto, *Spirit and Culture,* pp. 124-37.

35. Powell and Clark, *Sticky Faith,* pp. 72, 128.

36. Smith and Snell, *Souls in Transition,* p. 227.

37. Martinson, Black, and Roberto, *Spirit and Culture,* pp. 105, 107.

38. Martinson, Black, and Roberto, *Spirit and Culture,* pp. 175-78. The Sticky Faith study found similar patterns of positive, lasting influence between parents and teenage children. See Powell and Clark, *Sticky Faith.*

39. The Sticky Faith project provides research-based advice to parents and churches about how to help teenagers find a lasting faith. Its books, web site, and curriculum materials can help churches know how to equip parents for more powerful spiritual nurture of their children. See Powell and Clark, *Sticky Faith* and www.stickyfaith.org.

40. Martinson, Black, and Roberto, *Spirit and Culture,* pp. 180-81.

41. Strommen, Jones, and Rahn, *Youth Ministry That Transforms,* pp. 44-53, 76-81, 168-75, 217-19.

42. Smith and Snell, *Souls in Transition,* pp. 251-54.

43. Wesley Black, "Youth Ministry That Lasts: The Faith Journey of Young Adults," *Journal of Youth Ministry* 4:2 (Spring 2006): 19-48.

44. Powell and Clark, *Sticky Faith,* pp. 99, 151-54.

45. Jason Lanker, "Life-Long Guides: The Role and Relationships of Natural Mentors in the Lives of Christian Adolescents," *Journal of Youth Ministry* 11:1 (Fall 2012): 31-43. Powell and Clark, *Sticky Faith,* pp. 99, 151-54.

46. Richard R. Dunn and Jana L. Sundene, *Shaping the Journey of Emerging Adults: Life Giving Rhythms for Spiritual Transformation* (Downers Grove, Ill.: InterVarsity Press, 2012).

47. Anderson and Reese provide helpful guidance about how spiritual mentoring relationships begin and progress. Keith R. Anderson and Randy D. Reese, *Spiritual Mentoring: A Guide for Seeking and Giving Direction* (Downers Grove, Ill.: InterVarsity Press, 1999).

48. Powell and Clark, *Sticky Faith,* pp. 18, 150-51.

49. Rebekah Nathan, *My Freshman Year: What a Professor Learned by Becoming a Student* (Ithaca, N.Y.: Cornell University Press, 2005).

50. Powell and Clark, *Sticky Faith,* pp. 150-72.

51. Smith and Snell, *Souls in Transition,* pp. 15-25, 33-87, 248-51.

52. Mary C. Waters, Patrick J. Carr, Maria J. Kefalas, and Jennifer Holdaway, eds., *Coming of Age in America: The Transition to Adulthood in the Twenty-First Century* (Berkeley: University of California Press, 2011), pp. 28-58.

53. David P. Setran and Chris A. Kiesling, *Spiritual Formation in Emerging Adulthood: A Practical Theology for College and Young Adult Ministry* (Grand Rapids: Baker Academic, 2013).

54. David Kinnaman, *You Lost Me: Why Young Christians Are Leaving Church . . . and Rethinking Faith* (Grand Rapids: Baker Books, 2011), p. 192. For helpful suggestions about how churches can correct these problems, see Setran and Kiesling, *Spiritual Formation in Emerging Adulthood*, pp. 92-93, 95-104.

55. Setran and Kiesling, *Spiritual Formation in Emerging Adulthood*, pp. 29-79.

56. Setran and Kiesling, *Spiritual Formation in Emerging Adulthood*, pp. 98-104.

57. Martinson, Black, and Roberto, *Spirit and Culture*, pp. 119-22, 197-202.

58. Setran and Kiesling stress that one of the best ways churches can serve emerging adults is by providing intergenerational relationships and mentoring that help them exercise godly discernment. Setran and Kiesling, *Spiritual Formation in Emerging Adulthood*, pp. 29-104, 122-37, 205-30.

59. For an exposition of the biblical foundations of intergenerational ministry and a list of relevant Scriptures see Allen and Ross, *Intergenerational Christian Formation*, pp. 77-84, 294-307.

60. Melissa Wiginton in "Consultation on the Christian Formation of Youth," unpublished report (Indianapolis: Lilly Endowment, Inc., 2006), p. 90.

61. Strommen, Jones, and Rahn, *Youth Ministry That Transforms*, pp. 55, 62, 79.

62. Strommen, Jones, and Rahn, *Youth Ministry That Transforms*, pp. 88, 98, 113-14, 174.

63. Strommen, Jones, and Rahn, *Youth Ministry That Transforms*, pp. 261-81.

64. Strommen, Jones, and Rahn, *Youth Ministry That Transforms*, pp. 272-73.

65. Strommen, Jones, and Rahn, *Youth Ministry That Transforms*, pp. 303-37.

66. Strommen, Jones, and Rahn, *Youth Ministry That Transforms*, pp. 327-30.

Notes to Chapter 5

1. Randy Frazee, *The Christian Life Profile Assessment Tool Training Guide* (Grand Rapids: Zondervan, 2005). Randy Frazee, *The Christian Life Profile Assessment Tool Workbook: Discovering the Quality of Your Relationships with God and Others in 30 Key Areas* (Grand Rapids: Zondervan 2005). The blank surveys are found in the workbook.

2. Roland Martinson, Wes Black, and John Roberto, *The Spirit and Culture of Youth Ministry: Leading Congregations Toward Exemplary Youth Ministry* (St. Paul, Minn.: EYM Publishing, 2010), pp. 68-75. The "Faith Assets Assessment" and other tools developed by EYM can also be found at http://www.firstthird.org/eym/tools.aspx?m=3929.

3. Peter Scazzero, *The Emotionally Healthy Church: A Strategy for Discipleship that Actually Changes Lives* (Grand Rapids: Zondervan, 2003), pp. 59-66.

4. For several examples of faith maturity scales, see Kara E. Powell and Chap Clark, *Sticky Faith: Everyday Ideas to Build Lasting Faith in Your Kids* (Grand Rapids: Zondervan, 2011), pp. 196-202. One of the best-known approaches to faith development and faith maturity was created by James Fowler and his disciples and makes use of a structured interview to see which "stage" a person has reached in his or her spiritual development. But although Fowler's theory and interview technique have been widely used in studies of faith development, there has been little empirical research done to validate it. And perhaps because Fowler was trying to develop a universal theory of spiritual development, his approach seems to be compatible

with some versions of Christian theology but primarily shaped by the developmental theory of Erik Erikson. See Stephen Parker, "Research in Fowler's Faith Development Theory: A Review Article," *Review of Religious Research* 51:3 (2010): 233-52.

5. Scott Wilcher, *The Orphaned Generation: The Father's Heart for Connecting Youth and Young Adults to Your Church* (Chesapeake, Va.: The Upstream Project, 2010).

6. For an approach to youth ministry that begins with adults and young people praying and listening to God together, see Mark Yaconelli, *Contemplative Youth Ministry* (Grand Rapids: Zondervan, 2006). For an overview of corporate spiritual disciplines of discernment and suggestions for how to practice them, see Adele Ahlberg Calhoun, *Spiritual Disciplines Handbook: Practices that Transform Us* (Downers Grove, Ill.: InterVarsity Press, 2005). For more information on prayer, hearing God, and knowing God's will, see Dallas Willard, *Hearing God: Developing a Conversational Relationship with God* (Downers Grove, Ill.: InterVarsity Press, 1999), Stephen B. Clark, *Growing in Faith and Knowing God's Will* (East Lansing: Tabor House, n.d.), and Bruce Yocum, *Prophecy: Exercising the Prophetic Gifts of the Spirit in the Church Today* (Ann Arbor: Word of Life, 1976). For an overview of several common ways Christians think about discerning God's will as well as a bibliography on the subject, see Dennis Horton, "Discerning Spiritual Discernment: Assessing Current Approaches for Understanding God's Will," *The Journal of Youth Ministry* 7:2 (Spring 2009): 7-31.

7. Martinson, Black, and Roberto, *Spirit and Culture,* pp. 76-80. See also http://www.firstthird.org/eym/tools.aspx?m=3929.

8. The two songs I quote here are not isolated examples. Between 1997 and 2006, 23 percent of the 60 songs that made it to the top 25 used romantic lyrics. The percentage of top 25 songs with romantic lyrics ranged from 16 percent in August 1997 to 36 percent in February 2006. These statistics were compiled from information tracked by Christian Copyright Licensing International, www.ccli.com (accessed Oct. 2006 through Jan. 2007).

9. For an accessible discussion of how the form of communication used changes the shape of the faith, see Shane Hipps, *The Hidden Power of Electronic Culture: How Media Shapes Faith, the Gospel and Church* (Grand Rapids: Zondervan, 2005). For an overview of the different ways that Christians think about the relationship between theology and cultural context see Stephen B. Bevans, *Models of Contextual Theology* (Maryknoll, N.Y.: Orbis, 2002). I am taking what Bevans calls the "translation" approach, but all approaches to contextualization try to combine fruitful interaction with culture and faithfulness to Christ. And all approaches accept some cultural adaptations and reject others.

10. For more on how youth ministers have tended to take simplistic approaches to culture, see Thomas E. Bergler, *The Juvenilization of American Christianity* (Grand Rapids: Eerdmans, 2012), especially chapters 3, 5, 6, and 7.

11. See Hipps, *Hidden Power.*

12. For information on the role of music in the lives of adolescents see C. Hansen and D. Hansen, "Music and Music Videos," in D. Zillmann and P. Vorderer, eds., *Media Entertainment: The Psychology of Its Appeal* (Mahwah, N.J.: Lawrence Erlbaum Associates, 2000), pp. 175-96; R. Larson, "Secrets in the Bedroom: Adolescents' Private Use of Media," *Journal of Youth and Adolescence* 24:5 (1995): 535-50; D. Roberts and P. Christenson, "Popular Music in Childhood and Adolescence," in D. Singer and J. Singer, eds., *Handbook of Children and the Media* (Thousand Oaks, Calif.: Sage, 2001), pp. 395-413; Kelly Schwartz, "Music Preferences, Personality Style, and Developmental Issues of Adolescents," *The Journal of Youth Ministry* 3:1 (2004): 47-64.

13. For musical "hard wiring" see Terri Bocklund McLean, *New Harmonies: Choosing*

Contemporary Music for Worship (Bethesda, Md.: Alban Institute, 1998), p. 40. For the theory of priming see Jennings Bryant and Susan Thompson, *Fundamentals of Media Effects* (Boston: McGraw-Hill, 2002), pp. 87-99. For evidence of priming effects see Roberts and Christenson, "Popular Music," p. 409; Hansen and Hansen, "Music and Music Videos"; C. Hansen, "Priming Sex-role Stereotypic Event Schemas with Rock Music Videos: Effects on Impression Favorability, Trait Influences, and Recall of a Subsequent Male-Female Interaction," *Basic and Applied Social Psychology* 10:4 (1989): 371-91; and C. Hansen and D. Hansen, "How Rock Music Videos Can Change What Is Seen When Boy Meets Girl: Priming Stereotypic Appraisal of Social Interactions," *Sex Roles* 19:5/6 (1988): 287-316.

14. Hansen and Hansen, "Music and Music Videos"; Roberts and Christenson, "Popular Music," p. 408.

15. Mary Jo Galician, *Sex, Love and Romance in the Mass Media: Analysis and Criticism of Unrealistic Portrayals and Their Influence* (Mahwah, N.J.: Lawrence Erlbaum Associates, 2004).

16. Roberts and Christenson, "Popular Music," p. 410; Hansen and Hansen, "Music and Music Videos"; Jeffrey Arnett, "The Sounds of Sex: Sex in Teens' Music and Music Videos," in J. Brown, J. Steele, and K. Walsh-Childers, eds., *Sexual Teens, Sexual Media: Investigating Media's Influence on Adolescent Sexuality* (Mahwah, N.J.: Lawrence Erlbaum Associates, 2002), pp. 233-64. For the nature of romantic love in adolescence, see Jeffrey Arnett, *Adolescence and Emerging Adulthood: A Cultural Approach* (Upper Saddle River, N.J.: Prentice Hall, 2001), pp. 265-66.

17. H. E. Fisher, "Broken Hearts: The Nature and Risks of Romantic Rejection," in A. C. Crouter and A. Booth, eds., *Romance and Sex in Adolescence and Emerging Adulthood: Risks and Opportunities* (Mahwah, N.J.: Lawrence Erlbaum Associates, 2006), pp. 3-28.

18. Even Larry Lyke, who argues for an essential continuity between the Song of Solomon and the other marriage metaphors found in the Old Testament, argues that the "theology of love" found in the Hebrew Bible primarily teaches that God desires his people and always will, even if they are unfaithful and therefore forsaken at the present time. God is faithful, and the early, golden days of his relationship with his people will be restored. Larry L. Lyke, *I Will Espouse You Forever: The Song of Songs and the Theology of Love in the Hebrew Bible* (Nashville: Abingdon Press, 2007). The focus in these Old Testament writings does not seem to be on God's people trying to stir up feelings of being "in love" with God. Rather, the focus is either on shame and repentance for our unfaithfulness or on comfort that God will restore the "marriage" that we have broken because of his intense and committed love for us.

19. For summaries of the history of interpretation see D. A. Hubbard, "Song of Solomon," in J. D. Douglas, F. F. Bruce, J. I. Packer, N. Hillyer, D. Guthrie, A. R. Millard, D. J. Wiseman, eds., *New Bible Dictionary*, 2nd edition (Downers Grove, Ill.: InterVarsity Press, 1982), pp. 1131-33, and Tremper Longman III, *Song of Songs* (Grand Rapids: Eerdmans, 2001), pp. 20-70. For the interpretation that sees the Song as a satire on the reign of Solomon, see Andrew E. Hill, "Song of Solomon," in Walter A. Elwell, ed., *Evangelical Commentary on the Bible* (Grand Rapids: Baker Books, 1989), pp. 452-62. For an interpretation that tries to combine some of the modern and traditional readings, see Robert W. Jenson, *Song of Songs* (Knoxville, Tenn.: John Knox Press, 1989). For a modern interpretation that sees the Song of Songs as primarily about human erotic love, see Richard S. Hess, *Song of Songs* (Grand Rapids: Baker Academic, 2005), pp. 34-35, 249-51. Hess notes that the book ends on a note of unfulfilled desire. He argues that if the Song of Songs says anything about our desire for God, it is that our human romantic relationships do not satisfy our deepest desires. These desires point to the greater reality of

our eternal communion with God. But if the Song of Songs is teaching about unfulfilled desire for God, then it may be teaching something different than what Americans understand when they hear the phrase "in love with God."

20. Both Jenson and Longman make this very point in their attempts to read the Song as both a human love story and as a source of insights on the relationship between God and his people. Jenson, *Song of Songs*, pp. 4-15; Longman, *Song of Songs*, pp. 67-70.

21. The book of Hebrews especially stresses the superiority of Christ and the access to God he provides. Given the subject matter and audience of Hebrews, it is very telling that the author does not mention or allude to Song of Solomon. J. I. Packer summarizes the traditional view that Christian adoption as sons of God is central to the New Testament and that the New Testament writers meant to contrast this status and access with what was possible under the Old Covenant. See J. I. Packer, *Knowing God* (Downers Grove, Ill.: InterVarsity Press, 1973), pp. 181-208.

22. John Eldredge and Stasi Eldredge, *Captivating: Unveiling the Mystery of a Woman's Soul* (Nashville: Thomas Nelson, 2007); David Hartwell, *Falling in Love with Jesus* (Companion Press, 1996); Dee Brestin and Kathy Troccoli, *Falling in Love with Jesus: Abandoning Yourself to the Greatest Romance of Your life* (Nashville: Thomas Nelson, 2002); Dee Brestin and Kathy Troccoli, *Living in Love with Jesus: Clothed with the Colors of His Love* (Nashville: Thomas Nelson, 2003); Dee Brestin and Kathy Troccoli, *Forever in Love with Jesus* (Nashville: Thomas Nelson, 2004); Jackie Kendall and Debbie Jones, *Lady in Waiting: Developing Your Love Relationships* (Destiny Image Publishers, 2005); Margie Daughtry Wigley, *My Love Song to Jesus* (Xulon Press, 2003). Books written for women are most likely to use the metaphor in their titles, but other genres commonly employ it. General spiritual growth books use it, for example Carole Baergen, *Being with Jesus: Devotions for a Growing Disciple* (Kindred Productions, 2004). Devotional treatments of the Song of Solomon often use the metaphor. See, for example, Nancy Leigh DeMoss, *How to Fall (and Stay) in Love with Jesus* (Life Action Ministries, n.d.), 10-part video series. Worship books also employ the metaphor. See, for example, Jeremy Sinnott, *An Audience of One* (Destiny Image Publishers, 1999). In my experience, young Evangelical males are as likely as females to cling to the idea of "falling in love" as a good way to describe their ideal relationship with Jesus. Their devotion to the metaphor should not be surprising in light of evidence that college males are even more likely than college females to believe some of the myths of romance taught in the mass media; see Galician, *Sex, Love and Romance in the Mass Media*. But in his book *Why Men Hate Going to Church* (Nashville, Tenn.: Thomas Nelson, 2011), David Murrow argues that even the much more common and not necessarily erotic talk of a "relationship with God" or "relationship with Jesus" makes church less welcoming to men. He argues that by casting salvation as a "relationship" with the "perfect man" churches communicate the gospel in terms that resonate more naturally with many women than with many men. He thinks that the men who are the most stereotypically masculine, as American culture defines it, are the ones most likely to find all this "relationship with Jesus" talk to be at best uninteresting and at worst creepy. See also his website, churchformen.com.

23. For an extended discussion of Paul's ministry in Athens and an application of it to youth ministry see Walt Mueller, *Engaging the Soul of Youth Culture: Bridging Teen Worldviews and Christian Truth* (Downers Grove, Ill.: InterVarsity Press, 2006).

24. For more on the need to help young people in particular become theologically "bilingual," see Kenda Creasy Dean, *Almost Christian: What the Faith of Our Teenagers Is Telling the American Church* (New York: Oxford University Press, 2010).

Index

References in **bold** indicate pages with tables or figures

Adolescence, extended: acceptance of, 7-8; factors contributing to, 4-5, 8-12, 14-15; youth ministers in, 108, 109
Adolescent faith, 12-15
Adult faith: challenges to, 11-12; and church shopping, 19-20, 159n.50; effect on youth, 14, 100-101; factors affecting, 23; impact of emotions on, 71-74; of motivated churchgoers, 20-24; thought-will-feeling interaction, 69-71, **70**; understanding of spiritual maturity, 17-19, 22. *See also* Spiritual maturity, developing in congregations; VIM model
Adulthood: instability of, 11-12, 158n.24; markers of, 7, 10-11. *See also* Emerging adulthood
Adult thinking, 45-46
African American churches, 2, 163n.4
Age-specific activities: for emerging adults, 106-7; in youth ministry, 87, 90, 91, 164n.16
Assessing spiritual maturity, 113-18
Assets, congregational, 87-91, 110

Basic truths. *See* Doctrine

Body of Christ. *See* Church, connection to
Bridge builders metaphor, 140-41
Businesses, extended adolescence and, 4, 5, 7-9

Calhoun, Adele Ahlberg, **62-63**, 65
Campbell, David, 157n.15
Catholics, 2, 24
Children. *See* Infant/child-to-adult metaphor
Christian Life Profile Assessment Tool, 115
Church: commitment to youth ministry, 82, 87, 88, 111-12, 163n.1; Congregational Faith Assets, 87-91, 110; unity of, 41, 136; youth ministers' relationship to, 110-11. *See also* Congregational culture; Spiritual maturity, developing in congregations
Church, connection to: and corporate spiritual disciplines, 66; role in spiritual maturity, 40-42, 49, 51-52, 53, 66-67; *vs.* romanticized faith, 134-35
Church attendance, 16, 19, 24, 103
Church shopping, 19-20, 24, 159n.50

Index

Clark, Chap, 104-5. *See also* Sticky Faith study

Cognitive theory of emotions, 162n.8

Cohabitation, acceptance of, 7

College attendance, 104-5

Committed Traditionalists, 16

Complete *(teleios)*, 35-36

Congregational culture: assessing, 116-18; complexity of, 121; effect on youth, 96-97, 116-17; evaluating, 132-35; improving, 135-39; influence of theology on, 112; interpreting, 127-32; metaphors for, 140-42; observing, 125-27

Congregational Faith Assets, 87-91, 110

Contemporary American spirituality, 53, **53**, 72. *See also* Juvenilization of American Christianity

Culture, American, influence of: on adolescent faith, 12-15; on adult faith, 17-24; on emerging adult faith, 15-17; on extended adolescence, 8-10

Devoted youth, 82-84

Discernment, 38, 49, 107, 112

Divorce, 7, 9, 158n.29

Doctrine: articulation of, 13-14, 38, 49, 99; in congregational plan for spiritual growth, 56, 112; perceived as obstacle, 17, 18, 25, 72; selective understanding of, 20-21, 24, 25

Doubts about religious beliefs, 99, 100

Dunn, Richard, 97, 104, 110

Economic changes, 7, 9

Emerging adult faith: age-specific activities, 106-7; challenges, 102, 105-6, 110; developing, 102-8; developing in youth ministers, 108-11; and doubt, 99, 100; factors affecting, 103-5; influence of self-focus on, 15-17; intergenerational activities and relationships, 97, 106-7; measures of, 101-2. *See also* Faith-sustaining factors in teenagers' lives

Emerging adulthood: defined, 5-6; fac-

tors contributing to, 7, 8-10; symptoms of, 6-7, 10, 11-12

Emerging adults: church attendance, 16, 103; rate of return to church, 7, 157n.15; types of, 16; as youth ministers, 108-11

Emotionally Healthy Church, The (Scazzero), 117

Emotions/emotional patterns: cognitive theory of, 162n.8; developing godly emotional patterns, 74-80, **79**, 96, 162n.14, 163n.18; embodiment of, 162n.15; influence on heart, 73-74; interaction with thoughts and will, 69-71, **70**, 72-73, 75, 162nn.5-6; of mature *vs.* immature Christians, 72, 74; as obstacles to spiritual growth, 71-72, 74-75; relation to musical styles, 129-30

Entanglements of the will, 74, 77, 98

Erikson, Erik, 11

Evaluating congregational culture, 132-35

Evangelicals, 2, 21, 125-27

Exemplary Youth Ministry (EYM) Study: Congregational Faith Assets, 87-91, 110; emerging adult youth ministers, 109-10; faith-sustaining factors, 92, 96, 98, 99, 101; intergenerational ministry, 96, 107; observing congregational culture, 125; vital, maturing faith, 85-87, **86**

Faith, basic teachings of, 20-21, 24, 25, 56, 112

Faith-sustaining factors in teenagers' lives: belief system, 99, 100; congregational experience of God, 96-97; cumulative effect of, 93, **95**; effect on emerging adult faith, **94, 95**; emotional patterns, 96; intergenerational worship, 96; parents' faith, 100-101; prayer, 96, 98-99; relationships with adults, 97; religious experiences, 93; Scripture reading, 98-99; in spiritual maturity assessment, 116-17; with VIM model, 96

Index

Falling in love with Jesus. *See* Romantic spirituality
Fee, Gordon, 50
Feelings. *See* Emotions/emotional patterns
Fowler, James, 166n.4
Frazee, Randy, 115
Friendships, spiritual, 21, 97, 104-5

Gardeners metaphor, 140, 141-42
Gospel, transformation and, 27-33

Heart, 69, 73-74, 162n.5
Hebrews, 168n.19
Hess, Richard, 168n.19
Holiness *vs.* maturity, 47-48, **49**
Holy Spirit, gifts of, 41, 44-45, 46
Humility, 46

Identity, search for, 4, 9-10, 11, 25
Infant/child-to-adult metaphor: adult thinking, 45-46; attainability of maturity in, 50; children as examples for adults, 46; parallel terms, 44; present age *vs.* age to come, 45; in process of growth to maturity, 50-52; use with *teleios,* 37-39
Intention, in VIM model, 60-61, 64
Intergenerational activities and relationships: for emerging adults, 106-7; unsuccessful attempts, 163n.1; worship, 96; in youth ministry, 87, 90, 91, 164n.16
Intergenerational spiritual formation, 96
Interpreting congregational culture, 127-32

Jesus: call to transformation, 28-29; Father-child relationship with believers, 132; parable of the rich man, 35; Sermon on the Mount, 34, 35. *See also* Romantic spirituality
Juvenilization in American culture, 2, 4-5, 8-10
Juvenilization of American Christianity: among devoted youth, 84; benefits

and dangers of, 2-3, 24-25; effect on adolescent faith, 12-15; effect on adult faith, 17-24; effect on emerging adult faith, 15-17; and emerging adulthood, 8-12; and extended adolescence, 4-8; factors contributing to, 1-3, 128; and romantic spirituality, 25, 139, 168nn.18-19; symptoms of, 25, **53**, 72

Kiesling, Chris, 105-6, 110

Listening prayer, 124-25
Lived theology, 112
Love: as characteristic of spiritual maturity, 42-43, 45, 46, 49; in emerging adult youth ministers, 110-11; pop culture schemas, 131-32
Lyke, Larry, 168n.18

Mainline Protestants, 2
Marriage, delayed, 7
Mature *(teleios):* vs. natural, 43-44; translation nuances, 33-38, 42, 160n.18, 161n.20
Means, in VIM model, 61-67, **62-63**
Media, 5, 8, 130, 131
Men, romantic spirituality and, 169n.22
Mentoring, 65, 67, 104, 110-11
Merchants of cool, 5
Ministry discernment process: acting on insights, 135-39; cyclical nature of, **124**, 139; evaluation, 132-35; interpretation, 127-32, 167n.9; listening to God, 124-25; observation, 125-27
Miserable sinner gospel, 27, 30, 31
Monitoring congregational spiritual maturity. *See* Ministry discernment process
Moralistic, therapeutic deism, 13-14, 15-16
Mulholland, Robert, 66
Music: interpreting cultural meanings in, 129-35; observing outcomes of, 125-27; promoting spiritual maturity through, 122; and romantic spirituality, 126-27, 129-35, 136-39, 167n.8

Index

National Study of Youth and Religion (NSYR): adolescent faith, 12-15; adult influence, 24; devoted youth, 82-84; emerging adult faith, 15-16, 92; faith-sustaining factors, 92

Natural *vs.* spiritual, 43-44

New self, 42, 49

Observing congregational culture, 125-27

Packer, J. I., 168n.19, 169n.21

Parents, faith of, 14, 24, 100-101, 109

Pastors, understanding of spiritual maturity, 18

Pastor–youth minister relationship, 110

Paul, 30-31, 40-46, 52

Peer mentoring, 110

Perfect *(teleios)*, 33, 34-35, 36-37

Perfection *(teleiotes)*, 38, 160n.15

Planning for spiritual maturity, 118-20

Powell, Kara, 104-5. *See also* Sticky Faith study

Prayer, 96, 98-99, 124-25

Priming, 130

Protestants: adult faith, 19-21; African American churches, 2, 163n.4; Evangelicals, 2, 21, 125-27; growth of conservative *vs.* liberal churches, 2-3; Mainline Protestants, 2; pastors' understanding of spiritual maturity, 18

Psychological adulthood, 11

Puberty, transitions to, 4, 5

Putnam, Robert, 157n.15

Rankin, Stephen, 160n.1, 162n.5

Regulars, 83

Religious devotion, 12-13

Religious experiences, 93

Rich man, parable of, 35

Roman Catholics, 2, 24

Romantic spirituality: in adult faith, 23-24; in Christian books, 169n.22; and connection to church community, 134-35; gendered responses to, 169n.22; and juvenilization, 25, 139, 168nn.18-19; in worship music, 126-27, 129-35, 136-39, 167n.8

Sanctification, 47-48, 160n.18

Scazzero, Peter, 117, 163n.18

Schemas, 130-31

Schools, 5

Scripture reading, 98

Selective Adherents, 16-17

Self-deception, 74

Sermon on the Mount, 34, 35

Service, 21

Setran, David, 105-6, 110

Sex, availability of, 7

Shaping the Journey of Emerging Adults (Dunn), 110

Slow dance worship music, 126-27, 129-35, 136-39, 167n.8

Smith, Christian: adolescent faith, 12-13; emerging adulthood, 5-6; moralistic, therapeutic deism, 13-14, 15-16. *See also* National Study of Youth and Religion

Song of Solomon, 133-34, 168nn.18-19, 169n.21

Sound bite theology, 28, 160n.1

Spiritual disciplines: accessibility of, 68; corporate, 66-67; defined, 61; in emotional pattern transformation, 76, 77-78; function of, 61-64; for specific spiritual maturity elements, **62-63**, 64-66

Spiritual formation, 55

Spiritual Formation in Emerging Adulthood (Setran), 110

Spiritual friendships, 21, 97, 104-5

Spiritual gifts, 41, 44-45, 46

Spiritual growth: biblical process for, 47-48, 50-53; God as source of power for, 52; in motivated believers, 20, 24-25; perceptions of, 18-19, 23-24, 25, 27; relation to spiritual maturity, 27, 48; will/thoughts/feelings interaction, 69-71, **70**, 75

Spiritual immaturity, 43-44, 74, 79.

See also Juvenilization of American
Christianity
Spirituality, contemporary American,
53, **53**, 72
Spiritually Open, 17
Spiritual maturity: aversion to, 1, 28, 33,
72, 77; defined, 54-55; gospel as foundation for, 26-33; lack of understanding about, 17-19, 33, 64; perceived as
unattainable, 28, 31, 38, 55; vs. practice
of spiritual disciplines, 64; relation to
spiritual growth, 27, 48
Spiritual maturity, characteristics of:
adult thinking, 45-46; attainability,
42-43, 45-46, 47-48, 50, 55; conformity with death and resurrection of
Christ, 39-40, 49-50; connection to
body of Christ, 40-42, 49, 53, 66-67;
vs. contemporary American spirituality, 53, **53**; vs. devoted teens, 82-84;
discernment, 38, 49; goal of holiness,
47-48, **49**; godly emotional patterns,
78-79, **79**; humility, 46; knowledge of
foundational teachings, 38, 49; love,
42, 43, 45, 49; new self, 42; perfect/
complete/mature, 33-38, 42, 160n.18,
161n.20; perseverance, 38-39; proper
use of spiritual gifts, 41, 44-45, 46;
spiritual vs. natural, 43-44; stability,
40, 41; wisdom, 43-44; in youth, 85-87,
86t. See also Infant/child-to-adult
metaphor
Spiritual maturity, developing in
congregations: assessing spiritual
maturity, 113-18, 166n.4; developing
healthy emotional patterns, 74-80,
79, 163n.18; emerging adult ministry,
106-8; foundational concepts, 55, 56-
57; metaphors for, 140-42; planning
for maturity, 118-20; spiritual dryness,
96-97; Sunday morning worship,
121-23. See also Ministry discernment
process; VIM model; Youth ministry
Spiritual maturity, developing in emerging adults, 102-8

Spiritual maturity, developing in emerging adult youth ministers, 108-11
Spiritual maturity, developing in youth.
See Youth ministry
Spiritual vs. natural, 43-44
SPYM (Study of Protestant Youth Ministers in America), 97, 101, 109-10, 163n.1
Stability, spiritual, 40, 41
Sticky Faith study: doubt, 100; emerging
adult faith, 103, 104-5; intergenerational worship and relationships,
96-97; resources for parents and
churches, 165n.39
Study of Protestant Youth Ministers
in America (SPYM), 97, 101, 109-10,
163n.1
Suffering and spiritual growth, 22, 23,
38-40, 50, 51-52
Sundene, Jana, 104, 110

Teachability, lack of, 21, 25
Teenagers. See Adolescence, extended;
Adolescent faith; Faith-sustaining
factors in teenagers' lives; Youth
Teleios, 33-38, 42, 160n.18, 161n.20
Teleiotes, 38, 160n.15
Theology, 28, 112, 159n.1
Thoughts: embodiment of, 162n.15; interaction with will and feelings, 69-71,
70, 72-73, 75, 162nn.5-6
3 Bs of religion, 14-15
Transformation, spiritual: as beginning
of spiritual growth, 26-33; effect on
emotional patterns, 78-80, **79**; in
motivated adults, 22

Unity, church, 41, 136

VIM (Vision, Intention, Means) model:
in emotional pattern transformation,
76; implementing in a congregation,
67-69; Intention, 60-61, 64; Means, 61-
67, **62-63**; in mentoring relationships,
110-11; Vision, 58-60, **62-63**, 64, 68; in
youth ministry, 96

Vision statement, in VIM model, 58-60, **62-63**, 64, 68

Vocabulary of faith, 13, 14

Wiginton, Melissa, 108

Wilcher, Scott, 121

Will: embodiment of, 162n.15; entanglements of, 74, 77; interaction with thoughts and feelings, 69-71, **70**, 75, 162nn.5-6

Willard, Dallas: embodied character, 163n.15; emotional patterns, 74, 76, 77; expectation of change, 160n.3; heart-will relationship, 162n.5; thought-feeling interdependence, 72; VIM model, 58, 61

Wisdom, 43-44

Women, romantic spirituality and, 169n.22

Worship: intergenerational, 96; interpreting cultural meanings in, 129-35; observing, 125-27; promoting spiritual maturity through, 121-23; slow dance music, 126-27, 129-35, 136-39, 167n.8

Wuthnow, Robert, 24

Youth: adolescent faith, 12-15; characteristics of spiritual maturity in, 85-87, **86**; devoted, 82-84; effect of congregational maturity on, 96-97; paths to emerging adult faith, **94**, **95**; The Regulars, 83; vital, maturing faith in, 85-87, **86**. *See also* Adolescence, extended; Faith-sustaining factors in teenagers' lives

Youth cultures, 2, 5, 7-8

Youth ministers, 97, 108-11, 163n.1

Youth ministry: age-specific and intergenerational activities, 87, 90, 91, 164n.16; congregational commitment to, 82, 87, 88, 111-12, 163n.1; developing godly emotional patterns, 96; and emerging adulthood, 102-11; setting goals for, 82-87, 99; support for parents' faith, 101, 109; volunteer challenges, 97, 109. *See also* Faith-sustaining factors in teenagers' lives